Mary Turner,

OUR
MARY

THE LIFE OF MARY TURNER
1938-2017

PRESIDENT OF THE GMB
LABOUR MOVEMENT CAMPAIGNER
AND TRADE UNION ACTIVIST

Lawrence and Wishart Limited, Central Books Building
Freshwater Road, Chadwell Heath RM8 1RX

Typesetting: Julie Brown
Cover design: Julie Brown
Cover artwork/photo credit: Andrew Wiard
Printing: Halstan

First published 2019
© John Callow 2019

Published in association with GMB

British Library Cataloguing in Publication Data.
A catalogue record for this book is available from the British Library

ISBN 9781912064236

OUR MARY

THE LIFE OF MARY TURNER
1938-2017

PRESIDENT OF THE GMB
LABOUR MOVEMENT CAMPAIGNER
AND TRADE UNION ACTIVIST

Lawrence & Wishart
www.lwbooks.co.uk

JOHN CALLOW

FOREWORD BY
RT HON JEREMY CORBYN MP

LAWRENCE & WISHART
LONDON 2019

CONTENTS

6

8

32

66

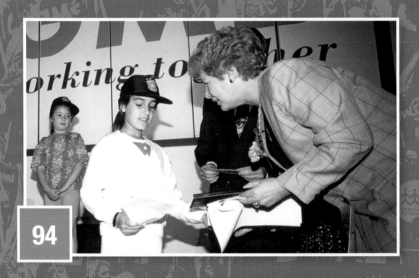

94

122

144

180

Foreword by Rt Hon Jeremy Corbyn MP

I first met Mary Turner in the early 1980s, when I was a local councillor and union organiser, and she was a shop steward for the General and Municipal Workers' Union. A committed socialist and trade unionist, Mary quickly earned a reputation for being both a formidable force and an approachable, compassionate leading figure within the labour movement.

Over the years, Mary and I worked together in North London on many campaigns, most memorably for free school meals, a cause to which Mary was famously dedicated. Wherever we could, we opposed the successive waves of privatisation that were designed to destroy our public services.

Mary knew then that selling off parts of our schools and our hospitals would lead to a worse quality of life for those who depended upon these. Mary believed

◄ Mary Turner and Jeremy Corbyn enjoyed a long and productive history of working together on local issues that affected Londoners. Here, Mary is making the presentation to Jeremy after he addressed the GMB Congress, Bournemouth, 5 June 2016.

that justice and equality for all, not profit for a few, should be the principal aim of our society.

Mary also knew that if you are to make a difference, you have to get stuck in and organise. Change never simply happens by itself, and it is certainly never handed down from those at the top. Real change comes from below – from people coming together and demanding that their voices are heard.

Organising and empowering people was what Mary excelled at. She was moved to action by the inequality she saw in her daily life: children at the schools she worked at growing up in poverty, her fellow dinner ladies and colleagues struggling to make ends meet on low pay.

The Conservative government's most recent attempts to scrap school meals for some 900,000 children shows that we will always have to defend the hard-won achievements of our movement. The Labour Party will fight these attempts to reverse the progress we have made, but it cannot do so without the support of the trade unions and the labour movement as a whole – the greatest democratic force our country has ever known.

Mary was a towering figure in our movement. In her various roles as shop steward, long-standing member of the Labour Party's National Executive, or president of the GMB Union, a position which she held for 20 years, it was clear that she was always driven by her unfaltering belief in the better society that is possible. This book is a brilliant testament to Mary's vision, life and work. ■

HOLDING UP HALF THE SKY

Irish roots

When all else changed, the road remained as a constant. On the eve of Irish independence, the local branch of the Gaelic League had moved to rename all the streets in Thurles, County Tipperary, stripping away the memories of the conquest and the attempts to Anglicise the culture and the language of the busy market town. New names recalling the heroes of the struggles for nationhood (Wolfe Tone, Parnell and O'Donovan Rossa) mingled with those of a romantic, mythic past (Cuchulainn and the Fianna), drawn from the pages of The Tain.[1]

Yet, Derheen Road did not need altering. It was judged to be good as it was: for *Derheen* was a Gaelic word recalling the 'little wood' that had once stretched down from the outskirts of the town to the banks of the River Suir. As such, it was the only indigenous, Gaelic place name in Thurles to have survived unchanged into the twentieth century. It was now a source of quiet pride, and a symbol of continuity with a vision of the past that celebrated a time

> **❝ Women hold up the other half of the sky ❞**
> Thomas Sankara 1949-87

when Ireland, during the early middle ages, had shone as a beacon of learning, law and the arts, to the rest of Western Europe. However, Derheen Road, with its row of narrow, hastily prefabricated two-up, two-down cottages and thin strips of backyard,

◄ 'Mary was always doing something – always doing a job'. At the start of the 1960s, she was working in a café on Priory Road, North London. True to form, Denny had no idea that she was working there until, one day, he walked in to find his wife behind the counter.

◀ The family group, taken in a photographer's studio in Thurles as a keepsake for Francis while he was working away in London. Josephine O'Brien surrounded by her children: from left to right, Mary, Lally, Meg and Jimmy.

came to contrast the high ideals and often mystical impulses of the nation's founders for a new 'Celtic Dawn' with the frequently harsh reality of life in the Free State, during the inter-war period. If Thurles retained its position as an agricultural centre, where farmers brought the produce to market and where freshly-cut tranches of peat from the neighbouring hills were sold in the newly concreted Liberty Square; then it was also a town wreathed by the sickly-sweet smoke of the sugar beet factory, where the Cathedral and the houses of the religious orders (the Franciscans, the Christian Brothers, the Ursulines, and the Sisters of the Presentation) towered high above the secular buildings, businesses and private homes. Farming was in a precarious state in the west of Ireland, with the labourer separated from even the smallest tenant farmer after the passing of the Land Act of 1923, which further stratified society between the propertied 'haves' and the landless 'have nots'. By the 1930s, there was not much work, a good deal of want and, perhaps more significantly, a dearth of opportunity outside of a route into the civil service or the church.

Francis O'Brien, known to his friends and family as 'Fred', worked in one of a number of small bakeries and confectioners that clustered around Liberty Square. He had married Josephine Ryan, 'Jo', and raised a family of three girls and one boy at number 17 Derheen Road. He was a hard worker and a solid member of the Irish bakers' union and Labour Party. A stern and, in some respects, traditional father and head of the household, Fred always wanted to do the best for his family. Jo 'did little bits of jobs' but had the four children to look after. The eldest, Mary Josephine, was born on 15 June 1938, with the others Alice ('Lally'), James ('Jimmy') and Margaret ('Meg') following in quick succession. It was a close and loving family. It needed to be as money and material comforts were always in short supply. Mary would remember fondly the hot rolls that her father brought home from work as a special treat for the children. They all had little jobs to do round the house, with Lally often running to their mother with cries that the other girls were 'ganging up' on her again. Mary was fortunate in that, as the oldest girl, she got the new clothes that would be handed down to her sisters and got to

▲ Francis (Fred) O'Brien was an active member of both the Irish and British Labour parties and a strong trade unionist. He was an enormous influence upon his daughter, exciting and encouraging her interest in politics. In later years, he was always on hand to give Mary advice and support as she rose in the union.

> **A first step in rebellion: Mary informed her father that: 'She wasn't going to the school with the nuns in the big hats anymore!'**

jump into the tin-bath first on Friday wash nights.[2] The kettle was left simmering on the range all night and there was a pot of hot porridge for breakfast before Mary would walk her younger siblings to school in the mornings and then all the way back home again for lunch, before the start of afternoon lessons. The memory of food as a scarcity and the distinction between those at school whose parents could afford school meals for them, and those whose parents could not, was to stay with Mary throughout her life. However, if there was a sting attached to being a poor, bright girl who frequently went without, then Mary never thought fit to refer to it in later life and certainly did not allow her early experiences of want to bother her or to sour her outgoing, thoroughly optimistic view of the world. The curriculum at the Convent of the Presentation was narrow and 'very religious', centring on learning the catechism and breviary, and taught by 'desperate, spiteful' nuns. 'You couldn't even look at the girl next to you, without getting a slap', remembers Meg.[3] Yet, though Mary did not enjoy her experience at the convent, she was quick-witted and did well at her lessons, sailing through

the system without exciting much in the way of either notice or censure.

The Irish diaspora

The family did, however, experience its share of loss and tragedy. A great party had been thrown at the little house at Derheen, when Mary's uncle – Patrick 'Paddy' Ryan – was leaving to enlist in the British Army at the outbreak of the Second World War. In excess of 50,000 Irish citizens decided to forsake the policy of neutrality in order to fight against fascism and many, like Paddy Ryan, were destined never to return home. He was reported to have been captured in the Far East, to have escaped from the Japanese and to have eventually found his way to Australia. But, try as she might, Jo could never track her brother down. The Salvation Army could find no trace of him and even Mary's efforts much later when she visited Australia were all to no avail. Loss was in the air. Jo lost twin boys during a pregnancy, in part through a lack of medical care, and when Meg had fallen ill in infancy with meningitis, her terrified parents had had to cycle with their baby to the nearest hospital, at Cashal some twenty miles away. No public transport was available to them. Even then, punctures on the road meant that the last leg of the journey had to be made by foot.

The impact of the Second World War served to further stratify Irish society and had led to an increase in inequality. The policy of neutrality had served to assist the already wealthy in amassing large private fortunes. It was estimated that, by 1953, 66.7 per cent of the land and capital in Ireland was owned by a mere 10 per cent of the population. Half-a-million Irish women and men left home from the late 1940s to the 1950s in search of work and greater opportunity. Four out of every five Irish children born between 1931 and 1941 emigrated, with 80 per cent settling in the Britain.[4] Emigration to Britain was easy, inexpensive and viable, not least as from 1941 immigration control had been lifted for Irish citizens in order to make good the shortage of manpower for the building and infrastructure projects that were vital to the war effort.

Employment of Irish women living in Britain was concentrated in two areas. Twenty-two per cent worked in the professions, predominantly in teaching, healthcare and nursing, and 40 per cent in the service sector, overwhelmingly in cooking and cleaning jobs. As one academic writer put it, 'millions of [Irish] women intensely engaged in the feeding, cleaning, healing, caring and teaching of Britons and millions of Irish men focused into clearing, constructing and fabricating the economic landscape of contemporary Britain'.[5] It was Mary's aunt, Theresa, who was the first of the family to join the exodus. Mary had always 'just lived up the road' and Jo missed her sister-in-law terribly, while her letters back home helped to persuade Fred that there were better prospects and higher wages to be had in Britain. In 1947, he became part of a pattern of 'chain migration' common to the Irish diaspora whereby one member of an extended family would emigrate and thereafter pull other members after them. Whole swathes of North London (Kilburn, Cricklewood, Camden, and Edgware) were settled by the Irish after the end of the Second World War making them in effect 'Ireland's thirty-third county' and serving to define the culture and outlook of the community.[6] For the best part of eighteen months, Fred shuttled backwards and forth between London and Thurles, taking work as a cleaner and security guard, and spending his holidays with the family. Finally, in 1949, he brought Jo and the children back with him, to settle in Kilburn.

Coming to London Town

The post-war housing shortage made it difficult to find cheap, decent accommodation, while the climate of hostility and racism shown by some landlords towards the new immigrants made the experience unpleasant and hurtful, as well as degrading. At that time, adverts for rooms to rent were tacked to the panels of phone boxes and often read: 'No Cats, No Dogs, No Children, No Irish, No Blacks'. Mary was to remember them well and they served to instil in her an even deeper sense of injustice, and the need to speak-out and fight against it.[7] Adversity made her a natural rebel and gave her an instinctive feel for the underdog. As Kevin Casey, another young Irish immigrant recalled: 'If you didn't stamp your authority … your identity, everywhere you went,

◄ Mary on the portico of the Granville Road flats, in the early 1950s. If living conditions, inside, were cramped, then the street provided personal space and a window upon the world.

they'd walk on you. You had to be strong. Thousands of Irish people will tell you the same thing. You had to be assertive. You had to stand up for yourself'.[8] Mary was certainly able to do that but she also loved the diversity of London, as successive waves of Jewish, Irish, Cypriot, Polish, Afro-Caribbean and Asian immigrants came to settle in the community. She never forgot that she, too, had once been an outsider and, as Jack Dromey says, 'she always gave leadership in opposition to those who sought to divide one community, or one race of people, from another'.[9]

The family occupied four rooms at 47 Granville Road, Kilburn, in what had once been one of a long terrace of substantial town houses. As the area declined over the course of the nineteenth century, they had been broken up into individual, rented flats or had fallen into dereliction. By the time Mary was living in them, they were described as 'age rotted', 'crumbling, broken-down slum dwellings'. Winter was the worst time, with a meagre fire burning in the grate and icicles often hanging both outside and inside of the rattling window frames. The three sisters, Mary, Meg and Lally, shared clothes, a single bedroom

and a double bed between them. If they were lucky, Meg remembers, they would each get 'a penny pocket money, an apple and a packet of broken crisps' as their weekly allowance of treats.[10] With space at a premium, much of the kids' lives were lived out on the streets or playing in the neighbouring park. Though there was a strict curfew of 9pm imposed upon them by their father, Mary became increasingly adept at sneaking unnoticed in and out of the house, making the most of the fact that, as the flat was another two-up, two-down property, with the lower rooms being in a basement that looked up to street level, there were two doors to the home and only one could be effectively watched by Fred at any time. There were other acts of rebellion. Perhaps the most significant was over the choice of schooling. When they were firmly settled and it was time for the family to go out and buy new school uniforms for the children, Mary informed her father that she 'wasn't going to the school with the nuns with the big hats anymore'. A row ensued, but Mary refused to budge and, eventually, got her own way. She duly went off to the Carlton Vale Secondary Modern School, a few minutes' walk away from Kilburn High Street. Lally and Meg rejoiced at her victory, but were crestfallen when they were told in no uncertain terms that *they* were going to the convent.

As not one of the flats at No.47 had a bathroom, and there was neither a communal utility room nor the space to hang out the washing, the public baths at the end of the street became both a necessity for the family and a place to socialise. On the right of the enormous modernist facade built by the council in the 1930s was a wash house, equipped with all manner of tubs, mangles and dryers, and the children would accompany Jo there, on laundry-days, lugging great baskets and bags that contained the family's clothes and linen. While the washing was being done, there was opportunity to pass the time with neighbours and to strike up friendships. Use of the Olympic-sized swimming pool, itself, was too expensive and Mary never did really learn to swim, although in later years she did a pretty good job of floating in various hotel pools or in the sea while on holiday. However, aside from the domestic chores and drudgery, what the

> **Get in a union and be in the midst of it all!**
>
> Fred O'Brien to his daughter, Mary, 1953

Granville Road baths really did offer was the opportunity to get clean, to scrub away the grime of the city and feel good about yourself again. If nothing else, it was important in maintaining self-respect and for maintaining an image with which to face an often hostile and all-too judgmental world. Tales of the 'dirty Irish', who did not even possess the baths to keep the coal in, were popular, racist, stereotypes regularly spread and used against the community.

It cost 2d to use the public bathrooms, for which you had the use of an enclosed cubicle, with a seat, a mirror, and 'a bar of soap and a hard towel'. Time was strictly rationed with a maximum slot of 5 minutes in which to luxuriate under the hot stream of a shower. Often Mary would tuck her feet up onto the seat in an attempt to elude the attentions of the shower room attendant and make it look as if her cubicle was unoccupied. In this way she might eke out more time under the water jets. It was

Mary as a teenager, snapped in the backyard at Granville Road, c.1955-56. ▶

on one of these occasions, when she called out to the girl in the next cubicle to see if she could borrow her soap, that the twelve-year-old Mary struck up a conversation with Barbara Benham. Barbara was two years younger than Mary and went to different school, but her grandmother lived just around the corner from the O'Briens and she frequently stayed over in her house. The two struck up an instant rapport and soon became inseparable. 'She sticks to me like Sellotape', Mary once dead-panned, but the two – though they might disagree and bicker like an old married couple – would stand side-by-side, through thick and thin, for more than six decades of adventurous scrapes, with the odd disaster and a great deal of laughter thrown in along the way. In all that time, they would never have a real

▲ Built in 1937, the Granville Road Baths were an important local amenity, and the first in the borough. As well as showers, there were 24 slipper baths for men and women, and a public laundry with washing machines (located in the brutalist block on the right of the picture). Mary first met Barbara Benham in the baths, at the beginning of a lifetime's friendship.

argument and would never live more than ten minutes away from one another. If money was still often hard to come by, then things were certainly looking up. Fred got a job in the Wrigley's chewing gum factory in Wembley and later at the London Electricity Board factory on the North Circular. Jo managed to find some hours working in childcare when not looking after her own home and family.

Generally speaking, they were good and happy times and the move to London, though in some respects always bitter-sweet, was not regretted. By the mid-1950s, the London Irish, through force, necessity, and sheer tenacity, had forged for themselves a distinct and vibrant culture. Theirs was a largely self-contained society, maintained through mutual support networks that often centred upon the extended family or the Church, and where community was a practical and purposeful reality for the new immigrants, rather than an abstract ideal or a lofty aspiration. Though individual fortunes were being made, particularly in the construction industry, and there were Irish as well as British landlords prepared to exploit the newcomers through rack-renting rooms in

A snapshot of Mary on the seashore on the way to Brighton taken by Denny, 1958 ▶

the capital's slums and tenements, there was also an emphasis upon the collective that expressed itself in every sphere of life: whether at home in the family, through work in the factories or the NHS, in leisure through the dancehalls or through faith primarily rooted in the Catholic Church. Thus, when Mary worshipped, together with the rest of the family, at the Church of the Sacred Heart, it was in a nave crowded to overflowing and in a church that, in order to meet the demands of its parishioners, celebrated no less than twenty-one masses each Sunday.[11] She could hardly fail to appreciate that participation was key and that there seemed to be a marked strength in numbers, and in a belief that was publicly and communally expressed. The same was true out in the world of work. When the whistle blew, 'it felt like the whole of London came out of Smyth's [a local factory which made speedometers and employed a predominantly Irish workforce] on a Friday afternoon. You couldn't walk along the footpaths at a quarter past four, when the factories finished'.[12] It was the collective that mattered and Mary was well aware of it from an early age.

While the O'Brien family were fairly

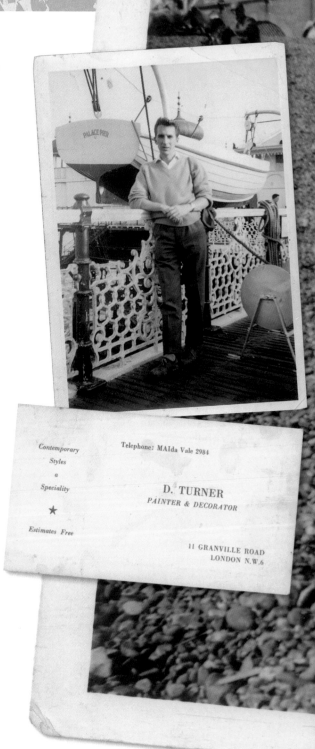

conventional in their religious observance, their expression of trade unionism and their politics was not quite so mainstream. By 1950, just four years after its foundation, the markedly anti-socialist Westminster Association of Trade Unionists could boast some 32,000 members, and was intended, by Cardinal Griffin, to act as a counter-balance to the more radical and secular Connolly Association, which had been leading the way in organising Irish immigrant labour and campaigning for civil rights, higher wages and improved health and safety at work through its journal, *The Irish Democrat*. In affirming his belief in an indigenous, Irish socialism rooted in the lives and works of Connolly and Larkin, Fred O'Brien stood firmly against the prevailing tide of clericalism, 'red baiting' and Cold War paranoia that was making inroads into the consciousness of the London Irish. He imparted both a sense of tolerance towards others and a vision of a

non-dogmatic, and very much down-to-earth brand of socialism to his children. He had seen a contingent of striking Welsh miners arrive in Thurles, in 1926, to raise funds and gather support from the Irish trade unions, by hosting outdoor concerts. His own branch of the Bakers' Union had supported them and found them places to stay in the town. He was a 'very strong union man', says Meg, and 'very strong for the Labour Party'.[13] He was certainly an inspiration to his daughter, advising her that the first thing she should do upon getting a job was to 'get in a union and be there, be in the midst of it all'.[14] Words that she took to heart.

However, the search for work was not quite so straightforward. Mary left school at 15, with a single 'O' Level in mathematics, and headed up to the North East to stay with her aunt Theresa and her family at Whitley Bay. She loved the coast of Northumbria and had spent many happy holidays with her nine cousins,

After his marriage to Mary, Denny set himself up in business as a painter and decorator. His business card marked him out as a skilled craftsman and entrepreneur, but unlike many other self-employed workers he cared for others and retained his Labour politics. ▶

Mary relaxing on a day trip to Brighton, 1958. At that time, she could not have suspected that the resort would provide the setting for many of her later speeches at Labour Party conferences and GMB congresses.

coming to consider it as her second home. Ideally, she wanted to settle there but, try as she might, she couldn't find permanent work. After a period on the dole, with her father's letters suggesting that she move back to join the rest of the family in London becoming more regular and insistent, and with her aunt having a large family of her own to support, Mary finally admitted defeat and took the train back down to St. Pancras. She arrived just in time to reunite the O'Briens for the celebrations of the coronation, in June 1953. If work hadn't been forthcoming in the north-east, the jobs seemed more plentiful in London and Mary was soon hired as a trainee bookkeeper at 'Jackson, The Tailor', a large and prestigious department store on Oxford Street. Immediately, upon signing her contract, she sought out a shop steward and asked to join the union

◄ Mary and Denny's wedding, August Bank Holiday 1958. Mary's parents, Fred and Jo, are on the right of the group. The conservative dress of the older generation is in contrast to the 'Teddy Boy' fashions, of long pseudo-Edwardian frock coats, creeper shoes and quiffed hair, of the bride and groom's young friends.

that was organised there: the Tailor and Garment Workers' (which is now a part of the GMB). A matter of months later, at the age of 17, she also joined the Labour Party though, at this point, her involvement in the union was far greater than her interest in parliamentary politics.

Austerity: 1950s-style

The 1950s were, for the most part, a reactionary period. The Labour government that had created the welfare state had been defeated in the election of 1951. In an act of spite, the new Conservative administration bulldozed most of the Festival of Britain site on the South Bank of the Thames. It had been intended as a showcase for a fresh, modernist re-imagining of the country, where technology and meritocracy would come to the fore in order to benefit everyone, equally. The return of the Conservatives to power seemed to represent a nostalgic attempt to turn the clock back to memories of national power and empire, a vision that would collapse in humiliation as a result of the Suez crisis in 1956. In the meantime, 'austerity' settled like a pall over the land,

with attempts by various fundamentalist groups, not least through the 'Crusades' launched by Billy Graham and other North American evangelists, to target Britain's supposed socialist turn and create a recognisable religious right, capable of uprooting the first signs of a more open and permissive society. As always with attempts to enforce conformity, there will be those who seek to kick and to define themselves against it. If the 1950s saw the importation of the techniques of evangelical Christianity from the USA, then they also saw the more welcome arrival of the first recognisable youth cultures, expressed through music, fashion and the essential creation of 'the teenager', who had different ideas, needs and means of expression to their parents. Mary was alive to it all. She was young and vivacious, with a sense of mischief and of fun that would never leave her. If her Dad disapproved of her short skirts, then an air of subterfuge and a gift for making quick changes out of the 'Sunday best' were essential, after Mass was over, in order to bolt out of the

cellar door to join her sisters, Barbara and their friends on afternoons out that would invariably turn into evenings and nights on the town. In another stab against drabness and convention, Mary dyed her hair, changing from peroxide blonde to black (and back again) as the mood and the prevailing Hollywood fashion took her. She only settled, finally, upon her trademark flaming red hair after Meg, too, had gone blonde and the pair of them had become practically indistinguishable, even to their own friends and family.

Meeting Denny

There was certainly fun to be had at the local cinemas and dance halls which, unlike the Irish pubs, provided a neutral and safe space for both sexes. Mary was popular, quick witted and strikingly attractive. As a consequence she was never without friends and was popular with the boys. Yet, the quality and durability of her relationships set her apart from the run-of-the-mill crowd. From an

▲ Mary with her daughter, Denise, sat out in the sunshine
on the steps of the Granville Road flat, late summer 1962.

early age, she possessed a remarkable capacity for forging deep and lasting friendships and, as events would soon show, for a similarly heartfelt love.

The course of a life often hangs upon the merest threads of chance. And it was chance – or as Mary would have probably preferred, fate – that caused her, at the beginning of the summer of 1958, to bump into Dennis Turner on the corner of Kilburn Park tube station. It is likely that the two had seen each other, before, in the street. After all, their families lived only a few doors away from one another on Granville Road. What mattered on this occasion was that they got talking. Dennis (or Denny as he was always known) was more than a match for Mary: handsome, raven-haired and similarly quick-witted, if in a drier, more understated fashion. He had been planning to emigrate to Australia, working his passage on a merchant navy ship with his cousin. That evening he had been going out to celebrate his last weekend in London. He had two tickets in his pocket for a concert at the State Ballroom in Kilburn and, now, decided to take Mary along. That night changed their lives, and neither ever looked back. Mary

later recalled that he had 'swept her off her feet'. Denny never made the boat for Australia and Mary quickly forgot about Bob, the young fishmonger's lad that she had been seeing up until that point. It was certainly a whirlwind romance. 'I met and married Denny in seven weeks', Mary remembered, but 'my parents weren't happy'.[15] They worried about the suddenness of the match, the youth of the couple and that Denny was a Protestant. None of their objections mattered to Mary and, with some trepidation, Denny visited the O'Briens to ask for their daughter's hand in marriage, as he was in those days legally obliged to do. He later joked that it was the most frightening thing he had ever had to do. Yet, he need not have worried. Mary's parents were duly won round, just as those who had said that the marriage would never last were proved wrong. Not for the first, or the last time, Mary confounded her critics.

Though Denny often, and with good humour, played the foil to Mary, a sort of 'Ricky' to her Lucille Ball, or 'Dagwood' to her 'Blondie' as portrayed in the 1950s sitcoms and comic books, the truth, as she readily acknowledged, was that he

provided the rock of stability, common sense and loving care upon which many of her later achievements were built. Indeed, when she came to be interviewed for the GMB's official history in 2011, Mary was more concerned with seeing that Denny's continual support was acknowledged together with the help she had received from John Cope, as her erstwhile regional Secretary, than with talking about her own career and accomplishments.[16] It was typical of her own generosity of spirit, but it was also true to Denny's own commitment and love that was to span some 57 years of happily married life.

That marriage began with Mary's father digging deep into his pockets, and cashing in a few savings policies, in order to provide for 'a big, white wedding' on the August Bank Holiday, 1958, with four bridesmaids, a large guest list and a sumptuous reception at which, as Meg remembers, 'the beer flowed free'.[17] Denny set himself up in business as a painter and decorator, while Mary thrived on new challenges and experiences at work. She needed to be kept constantly busy, considers Meg: 'She was always doing something, always doing a job'.[18]

Having left Jackson's, she worked in a fish and chip shop and then in a café in Priory Road, Kilburn, before taking a job as a machine setter, composing adverts for a local print shop, whose premises were only a few streets away from home in Granville Street. Remembering her Dad's advice, she again joined the appropriate union, this time NATSOPA, and soon found herself in the thick of things, being elected as the Mother of the Chapel, as shop stewards are known in the print industry. 'I didn't understand what it really meant', Mary laughed, 'until the first strike!'[19]

Whether she knew it or not, Mary was gaining valuable experience all the time. The print unions were traditionally male dominated, and were scarcely for blushing violets. It already spoke volumes that Mary, who was barely in her twenties, was quickly elected to office as a workplace representative and could more than hold her own in that rough-and-tumble world. However, by 1962, she was pregnant with her first child, Denise, and opted to give up work in order to be a full-time mum. She was determined that no child of hers would ever be a 'latch-key' kid. So far, she and Denny had managed to rough

it in their attic room in Granville Road but with a child on the way they needed to find more suitable accommodation if they were to have any measure of a safe and comfortable start to family life. For some time, Mary had been looking for new properties to rent and had gathered up references from her old employers in order to improve her chances of finding somewhere better to live. Indeed she, together with her friends in the GMB, might have been forgiven a wry smile at the note from her former area manager at Jackson's, who described her as not only being an exceptionally 'honest' young woman but as being of decidedly 'sober habits'![20] Despite all of this, nowhere was available that the couple could afford and Christmas 1962-63 was spent in the increasingly gloomy and dilapidated flats where Mary had grown up. A coping stone had already fallen down into the street below from an adjoining roof, the walls were wringing wet with damp, and Mary and Denny's neighbours, Patrick and Joan Reid, spoke of 'the wall bulging out over the stairs and plaster … falling' and flaking off everywhere in the property. The council seemed to have no interest, so the tenants began to organise themselves. It

was at this point that one of those ordinary – yet truly extraordinary – people in the labour movement, whose lives are so often unrecalled and whose achievements are so easily forgotten, came to the fore. Barely fifteen years older than Mary, Laura Godling already looked like an old woman, prematurely aged by a life of poverty and hard graft. A solid trade unionist, she worked as a railway clerk at St Pancras Station. In 1961, she had taken over as secretary of the Granville Road Tenants' Association and set about breathing life and fight into the organisation. She spent much of the following three years attending the monthly council meetings, brandishing a 'Housing SOS!' banner from the public gallery and trying to get the city's housing crisis moved onto the agenda. Mary would often accompany her and was a vocal supporter, both in the council chamber and sat around the table at the regular tenants' meetings. Incrementally and almost without noticing it, she learned how to organise, how to cajole, how to hearten her neighbours – who often believed that nothing useful could be done to improve their position – and how to chair a meeting.

◄ Whatever she did, whether in work or play, Mary chose the collective over the individual. For more than forty years, she and her family and closest friends would holiday at the Butlin's holiday camp at Clacton, on the Essex coast. Mary also had a competitive streak! On 10 July 1964, her son, John, won 1st prize in the 'Bonny Babies' competition and was pictured on the knee of his proud mum.

The fight for decent housing

Matters came to a head on 1 January 1963. There had been a heavy snowfall over the previous days. Drifts had built up on the roof of the tenement and snow had been driven in through the broken slates to lie upon already bowed joists and rotten beams. On New Years' Day, the ceiling above Mary and Denny's room came crashing down onto the cot where their fourteen-month-old baby was sleeping. Miraculously, Denise, although understandably shocked, was completely unhurt, though, as Mary pithily informed a local newspaper reporter, 'the cot was badly battered'.[21] Mary, who was heavily pregnant with her second child, was assured that she would be put at the top of the housing list but nothing happened,

even though a new estate was rising on the corner of the nearby Oxford Road and Kilburn High Road. The Granville Road residents felt that they were again being overlooked. Laura Godling's banner continued to wave and her voice to be heard at council meetings, but no immediate progress seemed to be made. With a gaping hole in the roof patched as best as Denny could, and a damaged cot to show for her efforts, Mary decided to take matters in to her own hands. So, on a January morning, she paid the builders a visit on what was to become the Toll Gate estate. She breezed in, looked over the men's shoulders and told them that she was on the council's waiting list for one of the flats. Could she have the keys, look around and choose the one that she liked? No one thought anything of it and, in all likelihood, the presence of a pleasant and chatty young woman, who possessed a fund of funny stories, made the day's labours speed by more easily. Even when, with Barbara's connivance, Mary's few pieces of furniture and personal possessions began to be moved in bit-by-bit to the ground floor flat at 33 Godwin House, they thought nothing at all of it and

even ventured to help the mother-to-be with the move. As a consequence, she found herself as a squatter – perfectly prepared to claim 'squatters rights', which in the 1960s and early 1970s were fairly permissive – in her first, bright, new home. The council were now faced with a dilemma and, having no great desire to attempt to evict a pregnant wife and mother, whose first child had only narrowly escaped death through its own negligence and failure, capitulated.

Significantly, however, it was not just a personal, private, victory for Mary and her family, but a very public victory for the entire tenants' association at Granville Road. Unlike many other slum clearances in the capital, the existing community was not dispersed. The Reid family, Mary's own parents (who went into a bed-sitter) and Laura Godling all moved together into neighbouring properties on the new estate at the end of April 1963. A gloss was put on the event to save the council's face and for the benefit of the local papers. Mary was said to have been 'on the top' of the waiting list and that it was this that had ensured that she and Denny had become 'the very first' residents to move into

◀ Mary and Denny's rent books as council tenants, 1962-63. Making ends meet was often difficult and Mary would often contrive to be 'out' when the collectors called round.

controlled by the council at 38 shillings a week. 'We have our own front door!' Mary proudly told the reporter.[22]

The tenants' association and a rent strike

So far, so good. The story might have ended there. For, in some respects, Mary and Denny represented exactly the sort of working-class people, bright, creative, hard-working and anxious to better themselves, to whom Margaret Thatcher angled her arguments, her visions of aspiration and loaded offers of private home ownership two decades later. Yet, it did not. Mary and Denny were not to be the sort of people who, after having hauled their way up through their own efforts (it is worth remembering that Denny spent his working life as a small business operator) would pull the ladder up after themselves and leave others to rot. What set them apart from the crowd and made them

the flats. It was a convenient fiction that served everyone well. One young mother, probably Joan Reid, hugged one of her children who had been made ill by the damp of Granville Road and sobbed that it was like 'moving from hell into Paradise'. Mary and Denny took formal possession of the flat, with two bedrooms, a kitchen, lounge, and a centrally heated bathroom. They were duly handed a rent book spelling out for them that the rent was to be remarkable was subtle and nuanced: an attachment to principle, to decency and to a heartfelt socialism that was rooted in practice rather than one that was overly theorised and relied upon posturing and the politics of gesture. Sure enough, they wanted the good things in life. They made no secret of enjoying those that came their way over the years: the holidays, the parties, a new car, the opportunity to travel abroad, or the chance to catch up with good friends over a meal or a bottle in a restaurant. But they wanted everyone to have the same opportunities and experiences. Too often there is a savage strain of puritanism within the labour movement, that likes to wear the hair shirt, to be 'holier than thou' to a point of self-denial and parsimony. Well, there was no one less puritan than Mary Turner, in both her character and temperament. Life was to be enjoyed, to be seized and embraced at every moment and for all that it was worth. Yet, at the same time, however far she would rise in the coming years and no matter whom she got to know from politicians to famous actors and heads of state, she remained essentially unchanged. She would never frame the story of her

◄ Mary with her son, John, in his pushchair outside the Toll Gate estate, North London, 1964.

own life in the terms of her transcending her origins, to climb high and to bask in the achievement of office. Rather, throughout her life, Mary continued to define herself as a working-class woman, of Irish origin, and someone who owned her identity as a dinner lady even when others might use it in order to try to belittle her. She spoke for her friends and her neighbours, and would come to speak for her union members, with such power, courage and conviction because she was one amongst them, who knew, understood and shared their worries, cares and fears, and had known the sting of want and the lash of contempt

of a society shaped and distorted by the cynical, the greedy and the powerful. In this lay her strength and her growing vision.

As a result, Mary was quick to realise that the move to the new estate was not quite the panacea that it had appeared to be for some. Families began to fall behind with their rent and to face the threat of eviction from the bailiffs. Mary's own family was no different. Her daughter, Denise, remembers hiding away from the rent collector with curtains drawn when he made his weekly rounds. 'Mum says weren't not in', she whispered back through the letter box to the collector's enquiries. On other occasions, Mary decided that a charm offensive night work better and began to feed the rent collector whenever he made a call. It served to delay the inevitable: after all, an army of any kind marches upon its stomach. It made the serving of the demands for money more amicable and increasingly almost apologetic, and gave Denny a few more days in which to bring in the work and, more importantly, the necessary pounds and shillings.[23] However, the odd dodge here and there wasn't going to help resolve the situation and there was no point in the neighbours having settled in their new, modish homes only to be swiftly turfed out again and to fall prey to the private rent sharks. Consequently, Mary helped to found the Toll Gate Tenant's Association in 1964. From some, it met with an immediate response of apathy, cynicism and resignation. Some of the former slum residents now considered themselves middle-class and, provided that they could pay their own rents, were not overly bothered when others went to the wall. Others would frequently tell Mary 'It's no use starting anything like that round here, you won't gain anything'. Yet, there were

immediate results. A successful rent strike led by Mary among the majority of the tenants (though the first Denny knew about it was when one of the court summonses that had, hitherto, been hidden away from him by his wife, managed to find its way successfully onto the door mat) meant a far greater sense of community cohesion. One expression of this was to be found in the Christmas party that Mary helped organise for eighty-eight of the local children, complete with food, cake, presents and a visit from Father Christmas himself. The old and the vulnerable were not forgotten either and food parcels were despatched, at the same time, for 52 old age pensioners and widows from across the Toll Gate, Leinster and Stafford estates.[24]

Her campaigning continued mainly against the spread of the high-rise tower blocks which had begun to shoot up against the London skyline, often constructed from shoddy materials, with few local amenities and isolating many elderly or less able-bodied people. Granville Road itself was levelled amid one such development, with a series of new, austere monolithic blocks rising from the hastily remodelled and superficially

landscaped ruins of the terraces. Mary set in motion a series of actions, petitions and demonstrations in order to halt the ghastly redevelopments that failed to consider actual people, or to put them at the centre of planning considerations. 'I love Kilburn', she reflected. 'It always had a great community. People were poor, housing was bad, but there was always a strong community spirit. That's why I opposed the building of the tower blocks. They broke up that community'.[25] On principle, she despised them because she 'hated the way working people weren't thought of as good enough to be worth a house and a garden'.[26] Once again, if it was worth having, then it was worth being shared across society, to be owned and enjoyed by all. No one had a greater entitlement to health, comfort, care or recreation than anyone else.

At the close of the 1960s, with the Wilson government and the stirrings of a more permissive society, these sentiments were mainstream and believed to be both practical and just. The welfare state had been achieved and appeared untouchable. Even the Conservative opposition acknowledged the permanence of the

NHS and undertook not to renege upon its founding principles. Optimism was in the air. It was confidently predicted that the living standards of the majority, and the opportunities that they were afforded, would continue to rise. Certainly for the Turners, things had become, if not easy, then far more comfortable. There were excursions in the car to the seaside, holidays in the Butlin's holiday camps at Brighton and Clacton for New Year and Easter, Friday nights spent by Mary in cavernous bingo halls, and evenings spent playing hands of cards with their friends at a dinner table that caught the sun and looked-out onto rose bushes and a patch of garden. As in her youth, all these activities, hobbies and entertainments were collective as opposed to individual. Mary loved the excitement of bingo and the chance it gave her to unwind, to be herself among friends and to interact with others, whose energies and ideas she embraced. One of her friends went so far as to suggest that she 'lived' for it! In this way, she would never need to employ a focus group in order to tell her about the concerns of her union membership. She knew that instinctively, but it was an instinct grounded upon her weekly experience of the snatches of conversation and concerns voiced by the women whom she lived amongst and enjoyed herself alongside. In this way, she would often be alerted to workplace concerns or might recruit new members to the union from those who sat alongside her and who came to know her as a familiar face at the bingo in Kilburn. In similar fashion, the holidays in Butlin's were very much family orientated, with everyone expected to pitch in together in the camp activities, whether this would result in the sight of Denny whizzing past on roller skates, or Mary and Barbara thinking up ever more extravagant and unlikely fancy dress outfits to wear at the New Year parties and balls. 'Wherever you went', says her daughter, 'Mary would end up on the stage'.[27]

A new job and a new decade

If Mary liked to party hard, then she was also driven to work hard and to take pride in all that she did. By 1968, Barbara Benham had gone back to work, starting a job as a dinner lady at Aylstone School in the borough. Mary, with both of her own children now in full-time education, began to think about returning to the workplace.

A job in the school meals service had much to recommend it, as it brought a much-needed second income into the home and also fitted around the children's own day and needs. Mary could take Denise and John into school in the mornings, work through until the mid-afternoon with the obvious peak at lunchtime, and be free to pick them up from the school gates and cook them their own evening meal. With this in mind, she began to look for local jobs in the winter of 1969-70 and got a job as a dinner lady at the Salusbury Road primary school in Kilburn. Her starting hourly rate in May 1970, as a 'general kitchen assistant', was just over 5 shillings and 8 pence an hour and she was contracted to work a twenty-seven and a half hour week on a permanent contract from Brent borough council. Naturally enough, the first thing she did was to join the union that appeared to be dominant in that sector of government, which traditionally had been the GMWU. Mary paid her 9d a week subscription and never had cause to look back. It was the beginning of a new decade and, for the union that would become the GMB, the start of a whole new era. ∎

Mary takes the platform at Brent Town Hall, Thursday 29 May 1981, to welcome the People's March for Jobs to the borough. Tony Benn and civic leaders, past and present, look on appreciatively.

A HEART FULL OF FIRE

Finding the union and finding a cause, 1970-1981

O n arriving for work at Salusbury Road School, Mary was appalled to find that the dinner ladies, who were mainly young Irish immigrants newly arrived in Britain, had been given no training in the kitchens and that some of them did not even know how to cook. Simply because they were women, it was assumed that they would know what to do. Furthermore, although they spent hours hunched over enormous steel vats or scrubbing out the pots, pans and utensils, exposed to all sorts of chemical cleaning agents in what could often be unbelievably hot conditions, they were not issued with rubber gloves or any form of protective clothing.

In an overwhelmingly female sector of employment, these were often marginal women, vulnerable because they were on part-time contracts and were, more often than not, working in order to supplement the low wages of their husbands and to save their own families from want and real hardship. Worse still was the belief,

reiterated over coming years by Margaret Thatcher and successive Conservative ministers of state, and trickling down to be parroted by countless HR managers in the workplace, that they simply worked for 'pin' or pocket money and, as a consequence, did not really warrant consideration as part of the wider workforce. Mary's response was suitably forthright: 'We do not go to work for pin money. We go to work because we have got to go to work, because successive Governments have not allowed our husbands to earn a decent living wage'.[1] It was every bit as true for her own situation as for all those women that she would come to represent.

Mary immediately made her mark on the workplace and was swiftly elected as the shop steward. She was already quite a seasoned trade unionist and campaigner, and was also that little bit older than the other women, giving her an added authority. If she did not appear as a motherly figure to them, she certainly fulfilled the role of confidant and older sister. The management would make

◀ The Apex banner leads a protest march organised in support of the Grunwick workers through the streets of Willesden, autumn 1976. Tom Durkin, the Secretary of Brent trades council, is at the front, Jack Dromey is at the right of the group.

▲ The first day of mass picketing at Grunwick, 13 June 1977, was also the first day of mass arrests. As in the case of this young couple, the police were none-too gentle with protestors.

cursory visits to the kitchens on a Monday morning but they would, invariably, ignore the dinner ladies. They were beneath them and not considered worth a thought, or a nod, in the greater scheme of things. However, they soon began to take more notice once they learned that Mary had started recruiting the other nine women to the GMWU. She pressed them about providing training, the right clothing for the job and protective gloves. 'Who do you think you are?' snapped one manager. Quick as anything, Mary pointed over to the other dinner ladies. 'I'm their representative!' she said.[2]

The gloves, she explained, were not only to protect the women's hands but also to ensure better hygiene in the kitchen. Management scoffed and bestowed upon Mary the somewhat patronising nickname of 'Marigold'.[3] But that didn't matter, they conceded to the demand. The gloves duly arrived and Mary considered it 'a small win, but still a win and the start of other things'. Once her workmates realised that they could change things, they began to see the value of the union and grew in self-confidence, expecting, and demanding, more for themselves from their employer.

Mary took considerable pride in that. Next to go was a contract that described the dinner ladies as 'servants' rather than as employees. If they conceded upon that, then they would be accepting a subservient role at work and in society based upon perceptions of their gender, skills base and 'worth'. It seemed to hark back to a former age of hierarchies and to the deference shown towards those who possessed power and status. They, just like anyone else, were entitled to dignity and respect at work. So Mary and her colleagues refused to sign the contract and demanded that it be immediately redrafted. Bewildered by the unexpectedly strong and unified response, the management again capitulated and the women were henceforth viewed as an integral part of the council's workforce, alongside other employees in the education service and local government.

Such attitudes were a product, at least in part, of a perception that dinner ladies

Jayaben Desai, on the right of the picture, and her comrades on the picket line at Grunwick, June 1977. The police presence, literally, towers over this heroic group of women. ▶

were fulfilling a relatively unimportant and mundane function within the life of the school that required little or no thought and skill. Nothing could have been further from the truth. Everything that Mary turned her hand to was done with insight, energy, care and pride. She was also naturally inquisitive and eager to learn. Far from the popular caricature of school dinners in the 1970s being boiled within an inch of their lives, invariably stodgy and unimaginative, slopped onto plates through the serving hatches to the cries of 'concrete chips' and 'soggy semolina', Mary determined to make the meals that she served, varied, nutritious and as tasty as possible. She attended a night school course on nutrition and food safety, and harvested more than a hundred suitable recipes from a large variety of cookery books borrowed from the local library. Typed up, referenced and annotated, these contained tips on how best to bone and stuff chickens, and the methods of making jellies and different types of sauces. There were recipes for cheesecake and 'Quick' strawberry ice cream that had Mary's comment beside them: 'Delicious!!' One favourite dish in the school (a version of a Kiev) became known as 'Chicken Mary'.

Leading the fight for part-time workers

The logical extension for Mary was to survey the children, themselves, to see what they really wanted to have served on their plates and to make the corresponding changes to the way that meals were cooked. Salt and sugar were cut down and more wholemeal flour was used in the school kitchens. If these innovations later became the cornerstones of Mary's campaigns for healthy eating at school, pursued with dedication and persistence over almost four decades, then they were grounded in personal experience and the delivery of practical results. It could certainly no longer be said of Mary and her colleagues that they were 'unskilled' workers. Mary fought to gain access to college training for her members, even though they 'were initially terrified of it'.[4] Nominated as a member of the joint works committee, which brought together stewards from across all the relevant unions (predominantly the GMWU, NUPE and the T&G) to negotiate on local agreements for pay and conditions, Mary was also able to gain access to pension rights for her members, where previously

they had been denied to dinner ladies as 'part-time' or casual workers.

Indeed, one of Mary's reasons for joining the GMWU was that it was seen to have 'led the fight for the part-time employees'.[5] In some respects this was surprising as, at that time, the union was regarded as somewhat staid, on the right of the labour movement, often quiescent and highly centralised. Despite some moves to encourage women members and to reinvigorate the post of national women's officer, from the early 1970s onwards, the face of the union was overwhelmingly male and, more often than not, middle-aged or even elderly. Moreover, while its great rival among manual workers, the T&G, had been diffusing its powers in the 1960s and building up its shop stewards' network, the GMWU had attempted to clamp down on the first signs of shop floor militancy at Pilkington's glass in St. Helens and at Ford's cars in Dagenham, with disastrous results.[6] The pages of the union's journal were reasoned and worthy, with a high standard of reporting and solid industrial analysis, but the approach was overwhelmingly 'top down' with members expected to listen to unquestioningly, and learn from the national leadership and full-time officers. As a result, it was felt that few of them actually bothered to read a journal viewed as being dry and academic.[7] When grassroots members appeared within its pages they tended to do so in the context of compensation payments being won or the award of certificates for long service or upon retirement. It was specifically within these areas that the lives and endeavours of the union's membership working in the school meals service were reported during the Wilson, Heath and Callaghan governments. Certainly, the activities of Mary and her Brent dinner ladies carried on firmly under the radar until the dawn of the 1980s.

One person who made sure that he did not escape the union's radar was John Cope, who was rapidly establishing a name for himself, both on the union's London regional council and as a voice for the concerns of the lay membership at annual congresses. After a varied and adventurous career, which had seen him joining the merchant navy at the age of 16 and travelling the world, before working as a waiter in the West End of London and as an electrician at the Elstree film studios,

he went to work for Hoover at its Perivale factory, in north-west London, in 1959. A year later, he was elected as the GMWU shop steward and went on to become the works' convenor. 'They were exciting times from a trade unionist's point of view', he recalled, 'struggling for, and achieving, the 40 hour week', establishing and enrolling some 17,000 union members in the company pension scheme, 'and making progress on equal pay for women'.[8] Possessing a keen intelligence, a quiet authority and a flair for both organisation and negotiation, when John came to speak everyone in London Region, and later in the national union, sat up and listened. He was very much a kindred spirit for Mary, an early mentor who would develop into a lifelong friend and comrade, always on hand with advice and support.

The politics of reaction and recession

In a similar fashion, Edna Rolph had recently taken over as full-time convenor at the Skecco factory in Luton and was beginning to build her own branch into one of the largest in the region. The shop

> 66 'Who do you think you are?', snapped one manager. 'I'm their representative!', Mary replied 99

floor, which manufactured ball bearings, was overwhelmingly male dominated, but in terms of both numbers and culture the union branch was the exception that proved the rule in the GMWU. Since the days of wartime production, it had been run by a succession of strong and capable union women: Connie Hill in the 1940s and 1950s, Mag Yars in the 1950s and 1960s, and Edna Rolph, from the late 1960s until she was made redundant in 1995.[9] In common with the neighbouring struggles of the Hendon and Perivale branches, the biggest battle fought and won at Luton was to secure equal pay for women workers. Unseen and unbidden, the nature of the union was subtly shifting and, in the midst of activity and struggle, lay activists such as Mary Turner, John Cope and Edna Rolph were being drawn together in a common cause.

At that time, Mary's own Hendon branch met in a room above a pub and was very sparsely attended. Tony O'Brien, the branch secretary, was someone whom she liked and very much respected and the two worked closely together throughout the 1970s. However, the political and industrial landscape was altering all around

them, as the impact of the 1973 oil crisis sent-out tremors to the West that were manipulated to the advantage of society's elites. Prices were suddenly ratcheted upwards in relation to wages. The results of the squeeze could be seen everywhere. The optimism of the late 1960s drained away, like the spilled petrol across garage forecourts. The unions, whose membership, power and success had hardly been checked since the Second World War, were about to experience an unpleasant shock. Their first and, in some ways, most ominous defeat occurred within walking distance of the pub where Mary's branch met, at the Grunwick photo processing plant in Chapter Road, Brent.

The unofficial strike at Grunwick had begun on 20 August 1976 with a walk-out by Mrs. Jayaben Desai and four young students who had been employed during their college holidays. Pay and factory conditions, especially during that long hot summer, were poor, the hours were long and the manner in which the brutish management treated its largely female, Gujarati workforce would nowadays be described as 'institutionally racist'. What began as a dispute over overtime and

conditions at work quickly escalated into a struggle for union recognition, as 60 workers joined APEX (now a part of the GMB) immediately and a further 137 walked out before the management could identify and sack all of those who had backed the call for a union. Mass protests in solidarity became widespread after the company failed to heed, far less abide by, the findings of both an ACAS tribunal and a government-backed court of inquiry chaired by Lord Scarman. The largest demonstration of support for the striking women brought some 20,000 people on to the streets of North London on 11 July 1977.[10] Mary was present that day and during the following harsh winter when the camera crews and news reporters had disappeared and the numbers of pickets who stood beside the Gujarati women at the factory gates had dwindled, as the cold bit and numbed. She and the kitchen staff at Salusbury Road regularly took hot food over to Mrs Desai and her comrades.[11]

The dispute was significant on a number of levels. First, it revealed a tendency for heavy-handed and political policing that would grow over the 1980s during the steel and miners' strikes, through to the Wapping dispute and the 'Battle of the Beanfield'. Secondly, it marked a sea change in the way that the organised labour movement thought about racism and immigration. In 1968, London dockers had marched in support of Enoch Powell, now tens of thousands of rank-and-file trade unionists were prepared to stand shoulder-to-shoulder with a group of Asian women and young men. Thirdly, it demonstrated the absolute and ruthless commitment of the new hard right-wing monetarists, from Margaret Thatcher, as leader of the Conservative opposition, to the shadowy National Freedom Association, which provided financial backing to the employers and strike-breakers, to win the dispute by any means that they had to hand. Lastly, it stripped bare trade union self-confidence and the blind reliance of Len Murray and the TUC leadership upon conciliation and legal redress. There were many on the TUC General Council who felt embarrassed by the passion and fighting spirit of the strikers and would have preferred if they, and Mrs Desai, had just quietly gone away. They were unwilling, or simply unable, to understand that Grunwick was far more

than just another run-of-the-mill industrial dispute. Instead, it marked the onset of the rising chill of neo-liberal monetarist ideology that would extend to every nook and cranny of British society after 1979, come close to breaking the unions, raise the spectre of mass unemployment and lead, ultimately, to the withering of the welfare state and the rise of new forms of poverty unthinkable in that summer of 1977. Indeed, Mary's entire political career would be defined by her stand against the assault upon public services and the living standards of working people that followed in its wake.

Hendon branch life

Mary had been witness to the cavalry charges across suburban streets, and the violence meted out by the police snatch squads and the notorious Special Patrol Group, and had been part of a spontaneous mass movement that had united working people irrespective of their race, background or gender – and that had come within an ace of success. If it was an edgy, bitter-sweet experience, then it was also exhilarating. It had demonstrated what

grassroots organisation and direct action could hope to achieve. It was a lesson that was learned and never forgotten.

The embers of the Grunwick dispute were still glowing when Mary and her branch were pitched into the local government dispute of 1978-79. Despite the popular mythology surrounding 'the Winter of Discontent', Mary did not regret the strikes for one moment. To her mind, the unions had delivered the biggest pay rise to date for working women, who had been treated appallingly by management and who had had to endure a pay freeze over the previous three years. However, she insisted upon keeping the school kitchens open so that the children of Brent, many of whose parents were out on strike, did not go hungry. Two hundred dinner ladies, the majority of them NUPE members, were on strike across the borough when a mass meeting was convened at Pound Lane School, Willesden, in order to discuss the allocation of strike pay. The local NUPE officer was, in the words of Barbara Benham, busy 'giving a load of chat' and failing to convince anyone as to either his interest in his members or his commitment

◄ The recession of the early 1980s had its roots in ideology as much as in economics. It ripped apart the nation's manufacturing base and left millions of square feet of factory space lying derelict.

to seeing the strike through. When she got up to ask a relatively straightforward question, Barbara was barked at and told to 'shut up and sit down'.[12] Fuming at the treatment of her old friend, Mary rose from her chair and told the officer in question that it was her money and those of the members that 'helps to pay your wages'. Furthermore, if she didn't get a proper answer on behalf of Barbara, she would leave the meeting and predicted that 'half the room would follow me'. A growl, rather than an answer was all the reply she got

but, as she turned to go, not half, but the whole of the room made to follow her. In a matter of the seconds, the school hall cleared leaving a stunned official alone with his brief case stuffed with notes, to nurse his bad temper. Mary quickly convened another meeting to talk about the benefits of joining the GMWU and what the union had accomplished and meant to her and other part-time workers. Practically all of the women transferred their membership to the GMWU after that, swelling the Hendon branch. Such things were not normally

done and the NUPE official concerned moved charges of membership poaching against Mary. They got no further than the desk of a young NUPE officer, Jeremy Corbyn, who quietly shelved them.

From then on, the Hendon branch began to grow and became a real force to be reckoned with. It was claimed that there was scarcely a town hall in London that Mary and her women had not been ejected from in the late 1970s and early 1980s while singing a rousing chorus of 'Boiled Beef and Carrots'. The increased pressure upon pay, jobs and conditions after the election of the Thatcher government in May 1979 was certainly one factor: there was more to talk and worry about, and to campaign against. However, it went much further than that. 'Women's participation is usually very high', wrote John Cope, and 'one reason for this is that the branch are able to hold meetings in the afternoon when they can bring along their children for whom arrangements are made'.[13] During half-term holidays these numbers swelled further with up to 400 members regularly attending branch meetings. 'It is the policy of Hendon branch', stated John Cope, 'to explain all new legislation where it affects members' interests, rather than allowing them to gather information from press reports. At the end of the meeting members took back forms to their places of employment with the object of recruiting new members'.[14] If this sounds not too far removed from the ethos underpinning the later *GMB@Work* strategy for organising in the workplace, then it shows that the latter's roots were firmly embedded in the practice of the union's north London branches during the late 1970s and early 1980s.

Mary bound her members to her not only through her personal charisma but also by her concern for their welfare. A story taken from much later in her career, but showing how she would have looked after 'her' dinner ladies, will stand for many. As an eighteen-year-old, on her second day

The GMW Journal published in December 1980 left union members in no doubt that they could expect only hard times and thin seasonal fare from Thatcher's new ideologically driven government. ▶

at work, Deborah Warner was introduced to Mary as her supervisor in the school kitchens. She 'sat me down and told me how important it was to be part of a union', remembered Deborah. 'It was there and then I joined … and have remained'. However:

'I was travelling to work at 7 a.m. but having to first drop my son to my mum, [who was] just living across the road from Mary. Mary would often say if she saw me with my son so early that I needed to get a car. Then, on my return to work after having my second child, I called on Mary as there was something I wanted her to explain to me. I was told that my position was

By the time they were pictured here, encouraging support for the 1983 People's March for Jobs, Mary and her branch were the veterans of many campaigns and industrial actions: a strong and incredibly cohesive group of working women. ▶

being covered by one of my staff, yet the difference in pay was so much higher than I was being paid. Mary was having none of that … Mary said 'leave it to me' and … 'we'll see what we can get for you. I want you to get a car and keep your kids safe'. I just thought nothing of it and just gave Mary all the information that she asked for. True to her word, Mary called me at work one day and said: 'Debbie, you should be getting the right pay and I also told them it needed to be backdated' and she told me how much. She said, 'Let me know when you get it and when you do I want you to go and get that car'. I did exactly as she said, and remembered going over to her house to show her the car. Even though it was second-

◀ The first tabloid-sized edition of the union's journal was produced for delegates to the GMW congress in June 1981 and celebrated the People's March for Jobs. Mary and her branch members were featured, prominently, on the cover.

hand, it served the purpose, she said. I felt very safe [after that] for both myself and the kids'.[15]

The branch was to remain her power base, though at times it could seem chaotic. The agenda might be taken in the wrong order, sometimes the correspondence wasn't read or the union's position might get slightly mangled or mixed-up but, as she pointed out to Paul Kenny, where else on a cold November's night, when it was raining heavily outside, would you find a packed branch meeting?[16] Herein lay a real magic.

At the union's 1980 congress held in Bournemouth, her own branch tabled Motion 223 on 'Social benefits'. It urged:

'the EC to press for the increase of the social wage, which has been attacked by successive governments, and believes that it should take the form of providing important services (e.g. School meals) free at the point of use rather than cash handouts which can be withdrawn so easily'.[17]

Mary attended congress as a lay delegate at a time when places in the regional delegations were hard fought for, and spoke for the first time to the representatives of the national union. If she, as 'a first-time delegate, first-time speaker' had any nerves, then she certainly didn't show them and her words didn't fail her. The motion, she explained:

'is a very important issue to me, and also a very important principle. In a socialist society, all important social services should be free at the point of use, available equally to each member of the community and financed by taxation. This is why my branch wants congress to affirm its support for this elementary socialist doctrine: from him according to his abilities; to him according to his needs. We believe that providing services for the community offers an opportunity to maintain full employment'.[18]

The motion, which was carried by the congress delegates and became union policy, brought together a coherent, progressive strategy for an incomes policy with a particular angling of the argument towards marginal and part-time workers, whose voices had not registered especially strongly at previous GMWU congresses. Mary re-iterated her belief that the wave of public sector strikes in 1978-79 had seen 'for the first time in our history the part-time employees [getting] their rights on service supplement plus rates'. These she linked, through the motion, to a discussion of the nature of female employment and in-work poverty, and to the drive to provide 'basic nutritional' school meals for all children. These themes were to become the hallmarks of her career, but it is important to understand that they were there from the very start and that by the time Mary rose to address her first union congress, she had already served a long apprenticeship as a political activist. She had the experience of three completely different trade unions and their industrial cultures, of community campaigning and rent strikes, of protracted national and local pay disputes, and a decade spent as a shop steward in Brent. As a result, while she appeared to have come as a 'bolt from the blue' into the congress hall, she was already a union veteran, used to speaking her mind, commanding attention and getting her own way.

Her background also permitted her to shape a pointed, ideological motion to embrace practical ends and concerns. It was a vision of where progressive politics might have gone, with the greater socialisation and 'levelling up' of working people in Britain had Labour returned to office in the early 1980s. Hindsight should not lead us to dismiss either its appeal or the sense that, in May 1980, it was considered to be within the union's grasp. The battle to be fought, as Mary predicted from the rostrum, was to regain the initiative and enact policies that would restore full employment. The problem was that the Thatcher government, ushered into power in May 1979, breathed a new ideology with a ruthless, populist clarity that brooked no dissent and was prepared to accept mass unemployment and the shredding of the nation's industrial base in order to pursue its dogma of the 'free market'.

The People's March for Jobs 1981

The high interest rates set by the Conservative budgets of 1979-82 had driven firm after firm into bankruptcy. At the same time, government spending cuts, falling disproportionately on the public services, had reduced the demand for consumer goods at home, while the high exchange rate effectively destroyed export markets, further deepening the extent of the recession. Yet, these policies were enacted during a period when Great Britain was virtually self-sufficient in North Sea oil, with almost 90 per cent of the revenues going straight into government coffers through increased taxation. Contrary to media preconceptions and the distorting lens of Thatcherite propaganda, there was an alternative: Britain's industrial base was salvageable and capable not only of recovery, but resurgence. It was perfectly possible, in the early 1980s, to have rebalanced the economy by using the unexpected windfall of North Sea oil revenues in order to cushion British industry by controlling oil prices at the pumps, cutting VAT and National Insurance charges. The Conservatives chose not to.

Their aim was an ideological, almost messianic one: 'rolling back' the state and the total liberation of private corporations from governmental and, by extension, democratic oversight, intervention and control. This meant deregulation, privatisation, massive cutbacks to public spending and the maintenance of a bare minimum safety net for welfare provision. In effect, despite Margaret Thatcher's bellicose jingoism, British government policy would henceforth be shackled to the priorities and preoccupations of global corporations, effectively emasculating itself by undertaking not to offer protection for socially-owned enterprises, national interests or local enterprises. The carrot was the promise of the swift accumulation of vast, almost unimaginable, riches for the few, while the stick was the spectre of rising unemployment for the many. 'Even the worst, least-regulated jobs [should] offer the first rung on the ladder to freedom and prosperity' was the belief set out by Milton Friedman, and eagerly promoted by the new Conservative government.[19] It was a world away from the one-nation Toryism espoused by the Eden and Macmillan administrations. The trade union movement took some time to fully realise that they were dealing with something entirely different and were, after 1979, being made to play by entirely different rules. Almost unnoticed, since the end of the Second World War, the ideology of neo-liberalism or monetarism had been honed at Chicago

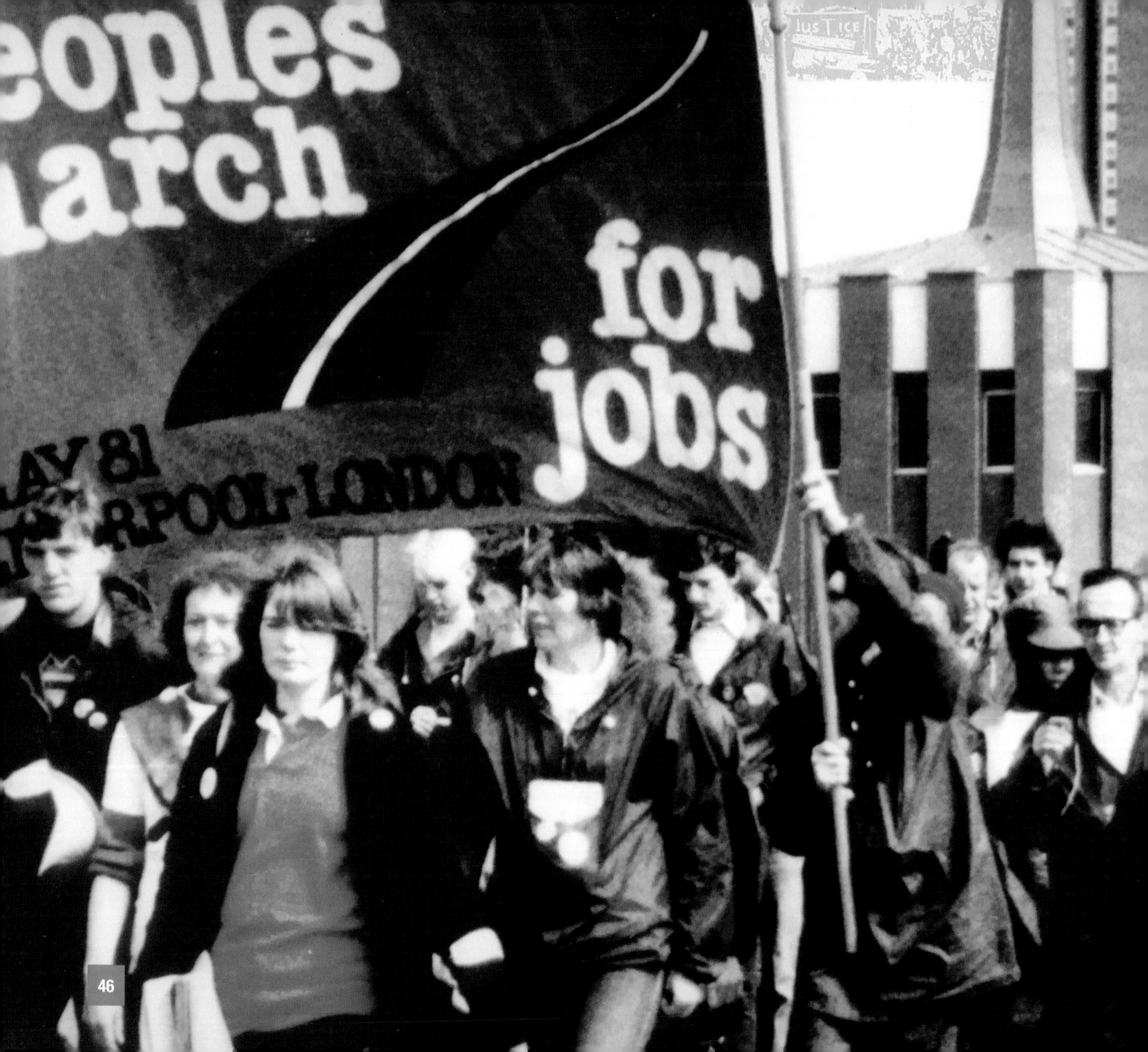
eoples
arch
for
jobs
AY 81
RPOOL LONDON

◄ The North West contingent of the People's March for Jobs set out from Liverpool, in May 1981, in good spirits and with high hopes.

University as a bulwark against the spread of the welfare state and socialism across Europe. Until 1973, it had been an abject and even risible failure in the face of Keynesianism, command economies and Nordic models of socialisation. However, its imposition down the barrel of a gun in Chile, used as a sort of giant test bed, followed by its adoption through the ballot box in Britain in 1979, and then the USA in 1980, had a seismic effect on the global economy and individual governments and societies, an effect still being felt decades later. If a GMB national officer might later sniff that the union did not need to engage with 'ideological politics' or any 'clever stuff', then they might have been in need of Donald Rumsfeld's reminder in 2002 that: 'Ideas have consequences'.[20] Bluff stupidity and political accommodation with the 'free market' were not an answer capable of protecting members' jobs, either then or later.

The bitter medicine of neo-liberalism was

◄ Flyers for the jobs campaigns of the early 1980s show the TUC at its best and most imaginative, with co-ordinated concerts, protests and rallies.

sweetened for a large section of the more mobile, skilled or fortunate members of the working-class by promises of tax reductions and the right to buy their council homes. In this manner, the Thatcherite counter-revolution attempted (and did) bring a large section of the working-class, who had often voted Labour in the past, into the market and to accept a world view that equated a shifting alliance between large corporations and extremely wealthy politicians as 'individual freedom'. Henceforth, their perception of self-interest would permit them to identify with the wealthy against those who argued for redistribution. They now had a stake, however modest, in capitalism and the maintenance of a deeply inequitable system. Incentives to council tenants to buy their homes at knock-down rates enabled those who had savings or avenues of credit to became property owners, while those who could, or would, not were faced with the rapid doubling of their rents and were forced back onto the margins of society. As the council housing stock was not replenished after the sales, a rise in homelessness became the ultimate price of calculated government largesse.

The organised working-class began to be transformed into the disposable poor and the already wealthy became the super-rich, in a system of kleptocracy where wealth and resources were concentrated in the hands of a tiny minority.

Yet, despite the attempts to effectively buy-off a significant portion of Labour's traditional constituency, victory for Thatcherism was far from assured. By 1982, the inflation rate had doubled since the Conservatives came to power, unemployment had spiralled up, and the government's approval ratings had shrunk to just 18 per cent and Thatcher's own to 25 per cent.[21] The impact on the borough of Brent, which had formed part of the vast industrial arc of north London, was particularly savage. It was previously an area where jobs had been easy to come by and where employers had even offered bonuses in order to attract workers. However, amid soaring interest rates, thousands of jobs vanished as companies like Guinness, United Biscuits, Glacier Metals and BICC either shut down their factories or rapidly retrenched. Even Heathrow Airport, a major employer for those living in the borough, cut 17,000 jobs. As John Haylett observed in the pages of the *Morning Star* at the time: '"Empty factory" and "Empty warehouse" signs abound, as industrial estates are rapidly transformed into warehouse estates – scarcely a week passes without further redundancies being announced'.[22] By the early 1980s, London had the greatest concentration of unemployed people anywhere in the developed world, having shed 37 per cent of the manufacturing jobs that it had enjoyed a decade before. Some 32 million square feet of factory space stood empty, while the number of people considered 'long-term' unemployed climbed to 40 per cent.[23] The same picture was repeated across the nation, with former industrial heartlands on Merseyside, Tyneside, in the Black Country and South Yorkshire being the worst hit. Something, to coin a phrase from the depression of the 1930s, had to be done and the unions needed to formulate an appropriate response.

It came, in May 1981, with the 'visionary initiative' of three regional TUC secretaries, Pete Carter in the Midlands, Colin Barnett in the North West, and Jack Dromey in London, to organise a People's

March for Jobs.[24] It immediately evoked memories of the Jarrow Crusade and the hunger marches, half a century before, and fulfilled a similar role in as much as it made a moral case for the right to work, forged a grassroots campaign and rejected passivity and resignation in the face of government policies. Around the nucleus of the regional TUCs, sponsors were quickly gathered, in the form of War on Want, the Indian Workers' Association and the feminist Spare Rib Collective. The Quakers and the Sikh community were particularly supportive, while the bishops of Birmingham, Liverpool, Sheffield and Coventry gave their backing, together with the president of the Methodist conference. From the unions, the AEUW and ASTMS came forward but not, it has to be said, in the first instance, the GMWU. Harold Wilson and Tony Benn were the most prominent politicians to back the march, while a number of academics, clustered around the Communist Party of Great Britain and the New Left, added their voices, together with Brian Clough from the world of sport, and a large number of figures from the arts, popular music and television. The reigning queen of Coronation Street, Pat Phoenix, was one of the many household names who helped publicise the march. A Labour stalwart, she possessed a similar charisma and temperament to Mary and, as the campaign unfolded, they got to know one another, becoming firm friends.

Feeding the marchers

Reaction was not slow in coming. Ray Whitney, the Conservative MP for Wycombe, attacked the involvement of War on Want as 'playing politics' and called upon the Charity Commissioners to investigate a possible breach of the organisation's charitable status. For its own part, War on Want suggested that a far better case for investigation might be the charitable status of Eton College, a bastion of social privilege that was in receipt of tax-payers' money.[25] Whitney's attack fizzled-out as some 200 jobless marchers set out from Liverpool on the road to London. Their numbers swelled to 500 as other regional contingents merged with them en route. Of course, all of these people needed to be accommodated and fed, and, on her own initiative, Mary took up the challenge in Brent. She did not need to pass a resolution, or wait for the approval of a full-time officer in order to act. She just did it, because she knew that it was right. The national union was approached for its support long after the deed had been done.

Having moved to work in the kitchens at Aylstone school, she methodically went through the lists of the council's suppliers for food for the kitchens, contacting each firm in turn to see whether they would be willing to donate to the cause. Results were forthcoming in the form of 500 pints of milk, 200 yoghurts, a ton of potatoes and 'a mile of sausages'.[26] Heinz and United Biscuits, both of which had local factories, were particularly generous, while Mary's pressure on local councillors ensured that Brent Council voted through an extra donation of food to the school meals' service in order to provision the march. As The Guardian was quick to acknowledge, 'many provisions have been given by the public', including a spontaneous gift by a market stallholder in Wembley who rushed over to give the marchers armfuls of fresh fruit.[27] All the Labour councillors in Brent donated a

e's bread for the jobless. . .

'There's bread for the Jobless': Mary together with her branch and helpers of all ages made the headlines as they prepared hundreds of sandwiches with which to feed the young people on the Jobs Express in November 1981.

(centre) with her band of helpers as they prepare to make hundreds of sandwiches for the Jobs Express protesters spending Frida
th Kilburn High School

AY'S reception by Brent trade
for 200 unemployed young people
...ed to Lon' Ex-

dents when local fascists threatened them on
their way back from the disco
He said the Jobs fo...
with ...
centre

A delegation
Bastien

day's attendance allowance of £11 to the hosting of a reception for the march, some donating much more. But by common consent, it was the dinner ladies who were the most selfless and hardworking. Not only did they give up their evenings and weekends to organise, prepare, cook, and serve up the meals to marchers, they also donated a week's wages to the campaign. For part-time, low-paid workers this was an unvarnished and undeniable testimony to their solidarity and socialism.

On 28 May 1981, some 500 tired, footsore and hungry jobs marchers arrived at Preston Manor High School in Wembley, which the council had allowed Mary to open up for them. They filled two large gymnasiums, which had been prepared for the sitting of school exams but then hastily cleared by the dinner ladies to provide accommodation. There were no camp beds, so the marchers put down their sleeping bags on any available bit of floor. The kitchen staff had been cooking all day though the preparations had been going on for several weeks beforehand. A reporter from the *Wembley Observer* noticed: 'Massive cooking pots [that] bubbled with tomato, chicken and vegetable soup. There were sausages, spaghetti, baked beans, ten sacks of chips, bread, apple pies and hot and cold drinks'. There had been some prepared speeches by local politicians and union officers but Mary's welcome was quite different. She kept the message brief, a dig at the Tories, support for Labour, then 'enough of the talking – start eating!' From that moment, recalls Jack Dromey, with 'her flaming red hair, infectious smile and inspirational tone, the marchers absolutely loved her!'[28]

At the Brent town hall reception held that evening, the marchers were welcomed to the borough by the country's first Muslim mayor, Karamat Hussain. They heard Jack Dromey announce to cheers from the hall that the print workers at the Daily Express had demanded space in the paper for a right to reply to a scurrilous article that had attacked the march in the previous Wednesday's edition of the paper.[29] Mary spoke again, as Tony Benn listened attentively on the platform, catching the imagination and putting heart and hope into of all those present. Yet, while she made a dramatic impact that grabbed the attention of the press corps, she had been added to the list of speakers at the last moment and none of the reporters caught her name. She was 'the shop steward for the borough's dinner ladies who had given their free time', and was acknowledged as representing 'some of the ordinary people who contributed so much to the success of the march'.[30] It was, however, an image of Mary in full flight that graced the front page of the next day's *Morning Star*. The reporters might not yet have known her name, but she had made a splash in the national press. It was coverage, and recognition, that many on the TUC General Council would have given their right arms for.

It is doubtful whether Mary got much chance to read the paper or to bask in the glory, as she was up bright and early in the morning, working alongside the rest of the catering staff, cracking a mountain of eggs for the marchers' breakfast before they

set off on the last leg of their journey. After remaining behind to clear up and clean the kitchens, Mary and the dinner ladies followed in their wake to Brockwell Park, where an estimated crowd of 70,000 turned out for the Rock for Jobs rally and free gig. It was an ambitious and imaginative initiative for the labour movement. There had previously been the alternative People's Jubilee at the Alexandra Palace in 1977, and the Rock Against Racism campaigns and concerts, but this was the first time that trade unions had thought about reaching out to youth culture as a new constituency, through music, mass rallies and free concerts. Certainly, the eclectic bill, mixing punk, reggae, and rock music, performed by artists and bands well known in the charts and on the radio, suggested that the cultural reach of the left remained considerable.[31] A local reporter described the scene, where:

'You could pick up a badge proclaiming support for the hunger striker Bobby Sands, or one to say that you don't approve of the royal wedding. The left also provided their own kind of special entertainment. You could throw a wet sponge at a youngster

> 66 *Mary's welcome was quite different.* **She kept the message brief, a dig at the Tories**, *support for Labour, then 'enough of talking – start eating!'* 99

> **" Mary was proud that 'No union worked harder and better... than the GMWU' during the People's March for Jobs and the Jobs Express "**

standing behind a cardboard cut-out of a policeman or take part in a peg-board game to find 'The Red under the bed'. Thousands of people had turned out for the afternoon's entertainment and waded through the paper sellers and leaflet pedlars'.[3]

The crunch came at the meetings held in Parliament between representatives of the marchers and cabinet ministers. Secretary of State for Employment Jim Prior denied governmental responsibility for the rising unemployment figures and ruled out any further aid for either the unemployed or British industry. A *Guardian* journalist noted that:

'The seating in his Commons office placed the deputation so that he was staring directly at gaping holes in the jeans of a marcher known as 'Spike the Punk' – John Best – aged 18, from Manchester. Mr Prior seemed fascinated by the sight of the jeans,

which a protest organiser said "are so old and patched they look as if they came down from the mountain with Moses".'

Culture and generational clashes aside, on a more practical note, Spike asked Jim Prior if he had ever been unemployed. 'No', came the reply. 'No, so you don't understand what it means in loss of dignity?' said Spike.[33] And that was that.

As the banners, including the original banner carried by the Jarrow marchers, that Mary saw fly for one last time at the rally held in Trafalgar Square, were folded away and the marchers began their journeys back home, the majority of labour movement activists came to consider that it marked their greatest propaganda success since Thatcher had come to power. Morale had certainly been raised, but now it was a matter of how best to maintain the momentum. As Colin Barnett, the TUC north-west regional organiser who had led the first contingent of marchers out of Liverpool, put it:

'The test now is whether we can translate the rhetoric into action, whether all the generosity we have encountered among the

working-class can be made into an attitude of militancy, whether we can capture the hearts and minds of more ordinary men and women'.[34]

Already, there were plans afoot for another march on the capital, this time setting out from Scotland and marking what *The Times* saw as 'the first official sign of the left's extension of the People's March into a national revolt against unemployment and the policies of the Thatcher administration'.[35] For their part, communist activists in the trade unions who had played a solid role in organising the march were looking to formalise the protest machinery that had been built up around the People's March for Jobs and to establish 'city committees' focused upon the existing trades councils and unemployed centres in order to co-ordinate the attack upon the government's economic policies. However, when TUC regional secretaries and chairs met at Congress House on 3 June to decide upon a follow-up campaign, they were badly split over tactics and priorities. Indeed, some appeared more concerned with wresting control back to the TUC from the

Labour left and the Communist Party than to escalate the campaign against the Tory government. They feared it might become an independent mass movement. Worse still, some appeared 'embarrassed' by the success of the march.[36] The concern, particularly rooted in the TUC's economic committee upon which David Basnett sat, was that the techniques of protest had become 'the property of the hard-line left'. As a consequence, in order to prevent itself from being outflanked, the TUC rather reluctantly agreed to endorse 'the street theatre strategy' and to back a youth lobby of Parliament, together with industry-based protests against unemployment.

The Jobs Express

The result, in November 1981, was the Jobs Express. In order to highlight the specific problems of youth unemployment, an express train sponsored by the unions was to set off from Newcastle upon Tyne on a week-long tour of Britain's major cities, finishing in London and culminating in a rally and a lobby of Parliament. The idea was that 125 young people – representing trade unionists, the unemployed, ethnic minorities,

trade unionists and Youth Opportunity Programme, or YOP, trainees – would start out from Newcastle and be joined at each station stop by another twenty-five youngsters. Regional co-ordinating committees were set up in each region in the hope that rallies and entertainment could be laid on in each centre to grab headlines and encourage further protests and activity. To accomplish this, the TUC joined forces with the National Union of Students, the British Youth Council, the Afro-Caribbean Organisation and the National Association for Asian Youth.[37] The benefit, from the TUC's perspective, was that it could effectively select a large proportion of the young people who boarded the Express and that there was little prospect of the initiative broadening out into an ungovernable mass movement as its numbers, from the very outset, were finite. However, it did meet a need that had previously gone unheeded by the unions in that it highlighted the difficulties facing school leavers in finding jobs, and the complete inequity and unsuitability of the YOP schemes on offer from the government.

YOP was designed by the Conservatives as a twelve-month training scheme for the young unemployed, offering £23.50 for a week's work, at a rate that was only slightly above that offered by social security. Mary was in no doubt that it was 'slave labour' used 'to line the pockets of the bosses'. Why, after all, she wondered, would an employer give a job to somebody with proper pay and conditions, when they could just as easily recruit subsidised labour through the YOP scheme? Furthermore, she could see the immediate practical implication for her own school meals service where she, as a supervisor, might now be expected to watch over sixty YOP trainees while her own members were dismissed from their jobs.[38] Despite government promises and the hype from careers officers, the YOP jobs invariably tended to be menial with little accent upon actual training. The teenagers who boarded the Jobs Express at Liverpool Lime Street Station were all in YOP jobs and described them as ranging from cleaning, to painting lavatory walls and sweeping up sawdust. It was a case, just as Mary had suggested, of obvious and cynical exploitation that manifested itself, all too often, in little regard for health and safety. In the year 1980-81, according to the government's own statistics, five young people in YOP jobs had died in industrial accidents, while 23 had lost limbs.[39]

Mary, naturally enough, stepped in again with her branch to provide the catering for the teenagers once they arrived in London. In the meantime, things had changed in Hendon. Tony O'Brien had stepped down as branch secretary and Mary had been elected by the members in his place. This served to consolidate her position and provide her with a clear mandate, within the structures of her union, for her campaigns. *The Times* noted that, during this period, Mary could always 'be relied upon to turn up with her redoubtable band of 200 dinner ladies to secondary picket on behalf of steel workers or nurses'.[40] The employers and security services also took notice of the activities of the Brent dinner lady and Paul Foot, the campaigning journalist who devoted his life to uncovering miscarriages of justice, told Mary that she had been placed on a 'blacklist' by the Thatcher government. 'I wore that badge proud', Mary later said.[41]

Three hundred teenagers from the north-west of England duly descended upon Brent, with Mary organising the donations of food and overseeing the serving of hot meals on two evenings, plus cooked breakfasts, 'hundreds of sandwiches' and packed lunches. The Hendon branch, once again, turned out voluntarily and received no payment for giving up their weekend at South Kilburn High School.[42] Mary's own view was that 'No union worked harder and better, and outshone any other union in the TUC than the GMWU'.[43] There were a number of Black youngsters on the Express and, after they had eaten, they went off with their friends for a night out. Some ended up at a disco at the Carlton Centre, while others went to the neighbouring pub. However, the National Front were lying in wait for them on their way back, as part of a planned action of intimidation and violence to wreck the Jobs Express and give the protestors (and particularly the Black kids) a hard kicking. Luckily, the ambush went off half-cocked and a running battle developed with a gang of skinheads, who chased them through the school gates and then tried to rush the door to the hall. As soon as the last of the teenagers from the Jobs Express had bolted through the door to safety, Barbara and Mary wedged it shut and pushed their backs against it to keep it closed, even as the mob bayed outside and attempted to smash their way in. The tussle went on for several minutes but, in the meantime, one of the youngsters had been sent to call the other half of the group back from the pub. Edging unnoticed out of an open window, he returned with the reinforcements, scattering and tumbling the skinheads back into the night, much to the relief of their friends bottled up in the hall and the two flushed dinner ladies who had valiantly defended them.[44]

This time, the scope of the march to Whitehall and the speeches at Trafalgar Square had a wider focus, with the young people discussing issues that affected them over and above the immediate calls for a return to full employment and an end to the hated YOP schemes. Unemployment was linked to wider issues and, explicitly, to the burgeoning peace movement, with the placards and banners now proclaiming not just 'Jobs not YOPs' but also 'Jobs not bombs'. CND had been largely dormant since the late 1960s, but with the deployment of cruise missiles at Greenham Common and NATO's talk of a 'viable' nuclear war and its acknowledgement of plans to launch a pre-emptive nuclear

▲ Mary first came to national attention when she made the front page of the Morning Star on 30 May 1981. As yet, the reporters didn't know her name but they were moved by the force and conviction of her message. The Morning Star provided authoritative coverage of the People's March for Jobs and was the only newspaper praised by Mary when she spoke at her union's congress a month later.

◄ Mary with the Hendon branch and activists from GMB's London Region at the commemoration of the 150th anniversary of the arrest and conviction of the Tolpuddle Martyrs, in July 1984. That year's Tolpuddle Festival marked a particularly poignant moment in the history of the British trade union movement, as those rights which had been fought for and won, were now being challenged and stripped away by the Thatcher government. The miners had gone on strike in March and the workers at GCHQ in Cheltenham had just lost their legal rights to belong to a union.

▲ London comrades: Denny Turner, John Cope, Mary Turner and Paul Kenny at the Tolpuddle Festival, July 1984.

strike if the Warsaw Pact ever breached the Fulda Gap, focused public concerns and sent membership of the organisation soaring, practically overnight. For the young who had filled the Jobs Express, the prospect that every living thing could be wiped out in a matter of minutes and that the release of radiation might burn-off the ozone layer from our little blue planet was of paramount importance.[45] Though they had been told that there was not enough money to provide for job creation schemes and social welfare, there were billions of pounds being earmarked for spending on the development and purchase of new missile systems and the building of a new fleet of Trident submarines capable of delivering multi-headed nuclear warheads. The unthinkable – particularly as set-down in the government's 1980 pamphlet, *Protect and Survive* – had suddenly become thinkable. The peace and unemployed movements were drawn together to argue for a new political and moral economy.[46]

Unfortunately, the limits of moral arguments without the sufficient political force to back them up were made plain when six of the young people were ushered in to meet Margaret Thatcher at the Commons. Michael Carr, a 22 year old from Middlesborough who had spent all his working life on the dole, thought that: 'She took quite a long time to tell us that she didn't have any alternatives in terms of the future. She was sympathetic in a veneered sense, but underneath it was the hard line … We represent unemployed people with no hope. We put forward the depth of feeling and she did not respond'. On his way out of the Commons Office, the Chair of the British Youth Council, John Collins, told a waiting reporter that: 'She gave us a warm smile, but I am afraid she had a very cold heart'.[47] The scene was less measured in a neighbouring committee room where 300 of the 'red-anoraked Jobs Express kids jeered' Michael Alison, the junior Employment Minister.[48]

If the young people who had taken part on the Jobs Express were dispirited, so too was Mary. The campaign had failed to catch fire. Though *City Limits* might have been impressed with the line-up of events organised to welcome the Express into London with bands playing and the new wave of 'alternative' comics performing all across London, and might have praised the TUC's 'unusual imagination in getting the Jobs for Youth Campaign and Jobs Express out of the sidings', but there was little in the way of national news coverage.[49] Despite all of their efforts, it seemed as though the Jobs Express had never happened. 'It did not get a half-minute on the television', was Mary's sad verdict. Worse still, having finished clearing away at South Kilburn High School, she had hurried over to Hyde Park to find that, even with all the bands and different forms of entertainment on offer, the crowds were sparse. 'The youth did not turn out', she told her own union, 'and neither did the people who sit round tables and tell me that they are concerned ... When it comes to actually showing involvement, they could not care less. They have got a job and they are not worried about anyone else'.[50] It was hard to understand why other young people, affected by exactly

the same problems, and the union's core constituency had not come out in solidarity to fight as one. The problem then, as later, was that socialism existed for the people, but, if the people did not appear to want it, there was nothing that could, realistically, be done about it. As the different elements of the labour movement's strength (the steel workers, printers and miners) started to be picked off one-by-one, there was a danger that what was left was a phantom army which could be summoned, but which would not materialise. In this context, direction action and the shop floor would need to be supplemented by parliamentary strength, not because they were necessarily flawed but because, as the 1980s wore on, their efficacy began to significantly reduce.

By 1983 the employment situation in Brent had worsened dramatically. The Hoover factory at Perivale, where John Cope had worked and led the GMWU branch, had closed down and the building, subject to a preservation order, was left as an empty shell. Oxford University Press, where the workforce had donated £100 to the People's March for Jobs in 1981 had relocated and its buildings had been

levelled 'as flat as a cricket pitch'.[51] The whole borough seemed redolent of a ruined economic landscape, with mounting piles of rubble where factories had once been and growing queues in the benefits offices. GKN, another manufacturer, had shut its plant in Brent and moved its production to Europe, while the Swedish owners of the Columbus-Dixon chain had made 500 workers redundant in order to reduce competition with their other European factories. Worse still, Smiths Industries had let it be known that they were looking to close their plant in Kilburn, in the course of the next 6 to 12 months, at the cost of a further 800 jobs. According to the official government statistics – felt at the time to underestimate the scale of the problem – there were 14,703 people unemployed in the borough of Brent, a rise of more than 200 per cent on the number out of work when the Thatcher government came to power in 1979. Of these, there were 2,500 16 to 19-year-olds receiving unemployment benefits and another 400 on the YOP training scheme.

Tom Durkin, the veteran chair of Brent Trades Council, explained that: 'We're not just fighting the scourge of the dole, we're fighting for a different future, for the right to a say in what happens in our lives. We don't want a society where the faceless tycoons of the giant multinational firms, in Britain and abroad, can close a factory in Brent with the stroke of a pen, putting thousands on the dole, with all the worry and breakdowns that can follow'.[52] Personal and industrial devastation was accompanied by a hardening of attitudes. As we have already seen, during the 1978-79 public sector strikes, Mary had argued that the school kitchens should remain open in order to feed the children. In 1982, during the nurses' strike, she changed her mind and made sure that the school meals service was closed in solidarity.

In the run-up to the 1983 general election, there was an attempt to rekindle the spirit of the 1981 jobs march and to generate a mass movement behind a revived version. The gamble was that it might be enough to help push the Labour Party that bit nearer to power, perhaps even over the finishing line and into No.10, even if the spontaneity and optimism of the original march were largely absent.[53] In Brent, at least, momentum was maintained through the establishment of the North West London People's March Reception Committee, which was based around the trades council's nucleus of activists, foremost among whom were Tom Durkin and Mary Turner. To gain advance publicity, they organised a float for the borough's multi-cultural festival that highlighted the campaign and also a motorcade that drove through Brent, Willesden and Kilburn the weekend before the arrival of the march. Mary told the *Morning Star*, the paper that had provided some of the best coverage of the march, that 'These marchers are doing a grand job raising the issue of unemployment. The least we can do is look after them when they come to Brent'.[54] She had been heartened by the large numbers of people, including local shopkeepers, who had been helping out with the campaign and donating foodstuffs, while her fellow dinner ladies right across London were again making financial donations in order to feed the marchers. She promised – and delivered – for the marchers 'a roast dinner with all the trimmings'.

It was much needed. The march was comprised of seven regional columns that converged upon London, passing through 129 towns and cities, and covering roughly twenty-five miles a day.[55] However, some of the worst summer weather in years threatened to wash them out. It was a miserable experience, as a thunderstorm hit the columns north of Leicester, followed by an unremitting deluge of rain that seemed to lash them all the way to the capital. To make matters worse, the marchers suffered from the barks of 'over attentive policemen' anxious to shepherd them along and the abuse of 'motorists angry at the delay'.[56] Onlookers did show great sympathy for the march, but this did not translate into political action. The stewards were bewildered when they tried to strike up conversations with people who felt for the plight of the unemployed but still said that they were going to vote Tory at the impending election. This time, many of the marchers were very young and uninterested in politics. What united them was their shared experience of joblessness. Indeed, twenty-five marchers from the south-western contingent calculated that they had seventy years of unemployment between them. Press coverage, aside from the *Morning Star*, *Socialist Worker* and *News Line*, was patchy at best and

MARCH AGAINST APARTHEID
LONDON SAT.NOV.2

Anti-Apartheid Movement
13 Mandela St, London NW1 01-387 7966

AFRICAN NATIONAL CONGRESS
of South Africa
INVITES YOU TO
A DIWALI DINNER DANCE

at Camden Centre
Bidborough Street
London NW1

on Friday
15th November 1985
7.30pm to midnight

> The African National Congress is the national organisation under whose banner South Africans, of all races, have united in the struggle to overthrow the apartheid regime.
> The aims of the ANC are set out in the Freedom Charter, which was adopted when representatives of all races met at the Congress of the People in Kliptown, Johannesburg, in 1955. The Freedom Charter declares that every South African, man and woman, will have the right to take part in government and to vote; that all national groups will have equal rights and status; that the country's wealth and land will be shared by all its people; that all South Africans will have equal access to work, education, housing and medical care, and the right to security and comfort.
> The apartheid regime has continued to unleash and intensify its reign of terror through legal and administrative channels, the army, the police, social and economic pressures, torture, hunger, disease — these are all manifestations of the state's violence.
> The ANC seeks support from all who are committed to a just society — governments, organisations and individuals who are opposed to apartheid, oppression and exploitation.

FOR FURTHER DETAILS/TICKETS CONTACT:
T. Vassen (679-3106) or A. Jassat (837-2012)

TICKETS £7 SINGLE
BAR AVAILABLE

▲ The unions were one of the few sections of British society that consistently opposed apartheid and offered support to the work of the ANC. Mary campaigned for the release of Nelson Mandela from imprisonment on Robben Island and met him, years later, when he was President of a democratic South Africa. However, during the 1980s campaigns to free him and demonstrations in support of anti-racism and majority rule (as advertised in the pages of the GMB journal) were neither easy nor popular.

the response from many of the cities did not come close to matching that of the 1981 march. As Patrick Wintour reported in *The Guardian*, 'Where in 1981 the union movement still had a faith in its ability to beat Thatcherism, now the mood is one of fatalism and powerlessness. Rumours circulated on the march last week that the TUC hierarchy would call off the march because of the election'.[57] In Leicester, itself, union members in factories which had gone on strike in a show of solidarity with the marchers in 1981, were now reported to be either 'too scared' to repeat their actions, or had similarly joined the queues of the jobless. It was, perhaps, a case of the TUC attempting to play the same trick again, in a changed political and industrial landscape, and with diminishing returns.

From Mary's own perspective, the timing of the march was far from ideal. She was out every night campaigning for the Labour Party, preparing to go away to her own union's congress as a delegate, and then arranging for the food and supplies to be delivered for the marchers, as well as juggling the day job in the school kitchens and her family life. Yet, she was delighted to be amongst the marchers once again and the feeling, summoned up by some of the youngest, that the past month had been the most important and empowering experience of their lives, seemed to make it all worthwhile. She served up the roast dinners before tearing across the city to catch a train to Scarborough for congress. The union had just been renamed as the GMB, recognising its merger with the boilermakers, but celebrations and considerations of past histories were muted. Everyone was living in the present, waiting upon the result of an election upon which their futures hinged.

Begging to disagree. Len Murray dismisses Mary's suggestions during the traditional Sunday march through Tolpuddle, July 1984. Murray was a supremely cautious general secretary of the TUC, believing in social partnership and refraining from giving the striking miners his full support. Mary's appetite for direct action and grassroots activism was anathema to his approach. He had announced his early retirement two months before Tolpuddle and, in February 1985, as the Miners' Strike was entering its final weeks, he was ennobled as Lord Murray of Epping Forrest. ▶

From the congress podium, Mary reminded delegates of 'those people who are walking for the 4 million unemployed' and thanked the marchers for a 'job well done' before pressing home the message that without the election of a Labour government debates over the framing of legislation were, largely, pointless. Congress had to be curtailed in order that delegates could hurry home in order to continue to campaign for Labour in the last 48 hours before the election but it still devoted an enormous amount of time and painstaking effort to discussing a joint TUC-Labour Party report on working time regulations. Against the flow of platitudes and rather deferential speeches from both the floor and platform, she reminded union members of the missed opportunities under the Wilson and Callaghan governments when 'we could have done something about' the requirements for overtime but 'we did not'. As a result, 'the social evil' of overtime had been allowed to spread unchecked, while the Tory government's 'idea of a shorter working week is unemployment'. Everything hinged upon the election of a Labour government and not the passing of hopeful motions that could never hope to be realised while Thatcher was in Downing Street. 'If we do not get a Labour government on Thursday', she told delegates, 'we will not need this' debate. Moreover, the impact of another five years of Tory rule would cut a swathe through the GMB's already decimated membership so that next year 'we will all be down the road' at a job centre 'and will need a school hall to hold our congress'.[58]

Yet, Mary chose to join this blunt message with a rather more subtle one. Passing almost unnoticed at the time but later coming to fruition with union policy and the return of Labour to office in the 1990s, she added that 'while we say we must legislate, we must also remember that we must work for a decent living wage for every manual worker, whoever it may be'.[59]

Chances lost: the 1983 general election

The election result was crushing. The Labour Party lost 3 million votes and fifty-one seats, giving the Conservatives a landslide victory with a majority of 140 seats in Parliament, and only narrowly averting eclipse at the hands of the new SDP/Liberal alliance which polled only 2.2 per cent less of the popular vote. There was no disguising the devastation brought about by the defeat. 'We lost very badly', wrote GMB general secretary, David Basnett, in the union's journal. 'We must face the fact that the Tories are not going to alter their economic policies … It means the use of unemployment to undermine the ability of unions to defend their members'.[60] One report delivered to the boilermakers' section was even more starkly worded, recording that 'we had a most lousy result' and that the people had 'rejected us'. Despite the fact that the recession that the experts had promised would 'bottom-out' had 'instead … grown deeper leaving more misery to our membership', the public and, by extension, significant numbers of GMB members, had remained apathetic to the

messages of the Labour Party and the union.[61] The Conservatives had certainly been helped by the right-to-buy policy for council houses and promise of tax cuts, but the combination of a military victory in the Falklands war of April – June 1982 and the defection of a significant portion of the right-wing of the Labour Party to the media friendly SDP, proved decisive. The outpouring of patriotism, amid the return of the naval 'task force' and triumphalist victory parades, had created a feel-good factor that took the sting, for the moment, at least, out of the unemployment figures, while the creation of the SDP as a vehicle for former Labour MPs who opposed nuclear disarmament, disliked socialism and welcomed NATO, served to split the Labour vote. Mary had been scathing about the rank treachery of 'the gang of four' former Labour MPs and ex-cabinet ministers at congress, mocking Roy Jenkins' famous love of claret and his closeness to the establishment, while rebranding the SDP (probably with Jenkins, Shirley Williams and David Owen firmly in mind) as 'Simple, Dimple and Pimple'. However, she was not blind to Labour's own faults. It had run a shambolic election campaign, its resources and funding were in tatters, and instead of fighting the Conservatives they had been disunited, spending too much time fighting and squabbling themselves in the House of Commons. It was no wonder then, 'that the youth were disillusioned' and had not turned out to vote.[62]

Further hard lessons were to come. One last attempt to sustain the unemployed workers movement with the creation of Campaign '84 fizzled out. That was not only the result of general apathy but also because of the unions' own changing priorities and the necessities of engaging with the harsh realities of the government's new employment policies and practices. While the unions remained concerned about the Manpower Services Commission's special programmes and their effects upon regular jobs, the T&G and NUPE had enjoyed some success in recruiting young members from the YOP and WEEP schemes, and used the argument that through their participation in such hated government schemes they could then negotiate for better wages and conditions for the young trainees.[63] The TUC, itself, was a major partner in

the Manpower Services Commission which administered YOP. Unsurprisingly many teenagers involved in the schemes in 1981-83, felt that trade union rhetoric at times rang 'a bit hollow'.[64] Mary's own branch tabled a motion to the GMB congress in 1982 condemning 'the TUC's total involvement in the YOP proposals which is contrary to our own union principles'.[65] 'We are not here', she reminded the delegates at Eastbourne, 'to implement the Tory policy or manifesto; we are here to implement trade union rights, and that is the right pay for the job'.[66] Unwilling to jettison the idea of partnership, lose its own chance of recruitment, or cause waves within the leadership of the TUC, the CEC opposed the motion and it was defeated on the floor of congress. Mary sensed that a moment had been lost and that the future for many would be bleak. 'We had the greatest opportunity when unemployment went over 3 million to fight and get real jobs, not YOP schemes', but instead the movement had squandered its chances, settled for grubby compromises and been let down by some of its senior MPs.[67]

Up to this point, the linking theme of Mary's career had been London and the distinct political culture fostered by Brent trades council and, by extension, the Greater London Council or GLC. Many of the causes that became mainstream within the labour movement and wider society (anti-apartheid, gay and lesbian rights, support for a negotiated settlement to the troubles in the North of Ireland, CND, and support for ethnic minorities) were first charted by the GLC, and other Labour metropolitan councils, in the early and mid 1980s.[68] At the time, they were treated with scorn and contempt, not least by the tabloid press, and dismissed as simply the products of 'the looney left'. They were certainly objectionable to the hard right of the Tory party, with one of Thatcher's hardest lieutenants, Norman Tebbit, declaring, in March 1984, that 'The GLC is typical of this new, modern, divisive version of socialism. It must be defeated. So we shall abolish the GLC'.[69] It mattered little that the removal of the unitary authority for the capital seemed to fly in the face of reason, practice and economic common sense. After all, the GLC represented a population larger than many small countries and had begun to carry out strategic planning through heavily-subsidised public transport and the establishment of a Greater London Enterprise Board (GLEB) designed to protect jobs and create opportunities for skills and real, meaningful employment in the capital.

It is not enough to say what you are against, you also have to say what you stand for. Mary fully understood and supported the GLEB as a means to create jobs, fight unemployment and demonstrate to the rest of the nation that there really was a viable economic alternative to Thatcherism. Of course, the existence of a 'good example' was another reason why the Conservatives wanted to move swiftly to crush representative local government in the cities. In its first year, GLEB had created or saved more than 2,000 jobs and pioneered new co-operative schemes and forms of 'social ownership' in partnership with the unions. These helped the disabled into work, encouraged women to develop 'non-traditional skills' (such as in the building or engineering industries), created new apprenticeships and sought ways to provide support for, and prevent discrimination against, members of the BAME community in the search for meaningful employment, and had actively set about promoting the benefits of trade union membership to those individuals and wider ethnic minority communities.[70]

The problem, in part, was that the GLC and metropolitan authorities in Liverpool and Sheffield, when creatively servicing and manoeuvring with the local government grants' system, had staked everything on the unpopularity of the Thatcher government and the belief that they would be able to outlast it, weathering any storms until the return of Labour to power. In 1981, this had looked like a fairly reasonable gambit but the election defeat of 1983 profoundly changed the entire political landscape. Henceforth, the Conservatives could pretty much do as they liked and the slashing of public services was at the very top of their list. The Rates Act of 1984 capped the spending of councils and, in the words of Professor J. A. G. Griffith, was 'little removed from a proposal to replace elected councils by administrative units'.[71] It was a move from which local government and representative grassroots democracy has yet to recover. Westminster could now instruct a local council as to the maximum amount it could set, and collect, in rates and, should the council refuse, send in commissioners to take over the running of town halls and services, replacing elected councillors with the secretary of state's appointees. It was scarcely surprising that, with the notable exceptions of Liverpool and Lambeth, local authorities paused for thought and tended to comply.

The destruction of the GLC

At the same time, the government pushed through its plans to abolish the GLC and the other metropolitan councils, all of which were under Labour control. By way of contrast, the county councils, largely Conservative controlled, were left alone. The attacks centred upon the alleged over-spends of the cities, when in actual fact local government spending was falling in real terms. They also targeted support for equalities policies that, at the time, Norman Tebbit described as 'the encouragement and funding of every minority cult and creation which the mind can imagine'.[72] Mary and her branch threw all of their energies into the 'Save the GLC' campaign, lobbying, marching and gathering petitions. The Tories came perilously close to losing the abolition debate in the House of Lords. Labour, meanwhile, won a last local government election in the capital by a very convincing margin.[73] In some respects, Mary was not a natural supporter of County Hall, the seat of the GLC. The overwhelmingly young and college-educated staff who had come to prominence around Ken Livingstone in 1981 were in many respects the first of those in public office forged by the experiences and politics of the student uprisings of 1968, and their attempts to foster a new political culture in London with its respect for minorities, differences, and those who sought sexual as well as political liberation, stemmed directly from Marcuse and the New Left.[74] Mary's life experiences were very different, but she respected the fight that the GLC was putting up against the Conservatives, fully approved of its backing for a peace process in Ireland, went on trade union CND marches, and, recalling her own background, supported the

development of equalities policies.

There was a last swansong for the GLC before its abolition at the stroke of midnight 31 March-1 April 1986, as a fireworks display lit up County Hall and the South Bank. Earlier in the day, the Hendon branch had been out in force at a demonstration to support the GLC. It had meant an early start, with Mary sailing out of the house with a wave and her habitual farewell to Denny that, 'if we're not home, the rent is in the cupboard and come down the police station to bail us out!' The regular coach with Peter, the regular driver, had been booked and duly dropped the women off along the Embankment. By the time it came to leaving, Mary and Barbara had become separated, in the crowds, from the others and had ended up carrying the vast London region banner, with its tassels, harnesses and long poles, and the coach was nowhere to be found. Undeterred, they spent the next couple of hours getting on and off a succession of crowded London buses, causing their own form of gleeful mayhem with their attempts to manoeuvre the banner and, in so doing, knocking off all manner of hats, scattering luggage, skewering evening papers and,

more than once, getting the poles wedged in the stairwell. They returned home in triumphant high spirits, with the banner still intact, only to find their husbands frantic with worry. When they had not returned with the others on the coach, they had thought that they must have been arrested on the demonstration, and had begun to ring round every police station in London but with no obvious success. It was all very much in keeping with Mary's 'work hard, play hard' philosophy and her gift for getting herself into and out of scrapes based upon misunderstandings and mix-ups. Looking back on those days, Mary would smile that it was always 'fun, as well as damn hard work'. Life around her was never dull and in this way, as in so much else, she transcended expectations to make her own career in the union and in politics every bit as lively and creative as was her own personality. Though the strains of *Nimrod* might have sounded plaintive, and the GLC flag had been rung down for the last time, amid all the fireworks, Mary was in no doubt that fresh battles – ones that were there to be won – lay ahead, both for herself and the GMB. ∎

The school kitchens were always open for all who needed to be fed. Mary, on the left, with her dinner ladies including Barbara Benham, 3rd from the right, and Denny, at the back, helping out.

BREAKING THE MOULD

Election to the union's governing body, 1983

It is perhaps hard to appreciate today, with the fundamental changes that have been made to the GMB over the last fourteen years, just how different, difficult and challenging were Mary's voice and message to a union that had traditionally disliked confrontation, carefully measured every pronouncement, and been used to having the ear of ministers.[1] Cloaked in a veneer of respectability, the young women it employed to type away at the union's Ruxley Towers centre were, more often than not, members of the Young Conservatives and came from well-heeled families, while, with notable exceptions, some officers considered themselves a breed apart and felt they had joined the professional middle-class, putting aside the aspirations of the shop floor for days spent out on the golf course. This was perhaps not surprising as the union had been in quiet, institutionalised decay for a long time.

Will Thorne's original, militant, and activist based union had been thoroughly overhauled, with the eclipse of London Region in 1910-12, and remoulded by J. R. Clynes and Margaret Bondfield after their own image into an organisation that believed in attracting members through the wide range and quality of the benefits it offered, and which stood as the unquestioning auxiliary of the Parliamentary Labour Party. Outclassed by the T&G, which had stolen much of its fire and thunder during the immediate post-war years, it was only after the retirement of Lord Cooper in 1973 that the union started to reappraise its role and wrestle with questions of its identity. Did it, for instance, wish to remain a blue-collar, general union, or did it want to attract members from the new white-collar electronic industries and the managerial grades?[2] By its own public admission in 1970, it appeared to resemble 'a sleeping giant'.[3] The changes wrought by the entry of greater numbers of women into the workplace and the shift in societal

Neasden Hospital: one of Mary's many problems

...ntral Executive Council member... outside Neasden Hospital, in North ...trade union...

▲ In January 1986, a West German camera crew filmed Mary over the course of a week for a documentary on the 'life of a woman trade unionist'. The film showed her working and branch life, and clashes with management, and (in the cutting pictured) Mary gave an interview about the fight to save Neasden Hospital. Mary told the reporter that: 'Despite admitting [that] the transfer to another hospital could kill up to 30 [elderly] patients, NHS managers have set their sights on the £10 million which the sale of the hospital could raise'.

attitudes that had taken place as the result of the second wave of feminism did, however, begin to make themselves apparent. With women comprising a third of its membership by the early 1970s, these changes and workplace realities demanded some kind of a response.

The appointment in 1971 of Pat Turner, an academic who had previously sat on the Commission of Industrial Relations, as Director of the Women's Department,

was visible acknowledgement of this re-prioritisation in order to retain and attract women to the union. However, it was far from plain sailing. Articles entitled 'Trade unions – Still for men only?', and 'Do men at TU meetings still sneer at women?', and in the case of Marian Veitch, the former women's officer, possibly the least generous obituary ever written for a former employee, published in the union's own journal, probably did not help the cause.[4] An account of a course held for women shop stewards at Skegness made it sound little short of horrific and would, today, have probably resulted in a number of grievance complaints, while Olga Mean opposed the creation of a women's section within the union, and Paula Shaw concluded, rather bleakly, that, at the dawn of the 1970s, a woman would have 'to take the only road open to her with her limited qualifications and education (both practically dormant after the kitchen sink years) and join the race for jobs on the factory floor'.[5]

As a consequence, Mary, with her husky, Cockney accent and flamboyant, larger-than-life personality, appeared as something quite different and challenging to the union norm. She was working-class through-and-through, was backed by her branch and increasingly by her region, and was both intelligent and articulate. Yet, she had no interest in a 'career' in trade unionism as a paid officer, had never attended the series of seemingly interminable weekend schools run by the women's department, and was independent (in terms of both her own personality and her economic position, as a waged woman) of the GMB's formal power structures. Consequently, she couldn't be easily co-opted or side lined. Furthermore, the national union, while it was still unsure about her, certainly needed her presence, as it could not entirely divorce itself from its stated aims. Since the early 1970s, the union had said that it had wanted more lay member involvement and more women in its councils. Now that that had happened, the union was not entirely sure that it had ended up with the 'right' sort of woman. But it was a case of being careful for what you wished for.

What it could not ignore was Mary's phenomenal energy and commitment. She served on three joint negotiating committees in Brent representing local authority workers, and was elected chair of the Brent joint committee in 1982. She was a school governor, a member of Brent Trades Council and a branch delegate to the Brent East Constituency Labour Party. Through the 1981 People's March for Jobs, Mary had delivered practical action for the union and, as the result of her appearance on a Labour Party election broadcast that had been screened on the eve of the local government elections in May 1982, she had already established something of a national profile and an appeal that transcended the borders of the borough of Brent. The cameras had followed her through her daily work routine in the school kitchens, scrubbing pans and serving food to the children, before delivering a clear and concise message that the policies of the Conservative government were slashing public services and putting the health of the nation's children at risk. It was only because of a Labour-controlled authority, she told the viewers, that 'parents at work in Brent know that their children are getting a hot meal at lunch time'.[6]

On the frontline of public services
At the same time, Mary had got to know Mikki Doyle, one of the founders of the Women in the Media Group and the pioneering Women's Editor of the *Morning Star*. She contributed a column on the fight to preserve the school meals service to the paper's 'Women's Page'. It was the only time that Mary went into print at any length and the article served to draw together the various strands of the campaign to maintain a healthy diet for the nation's children and to confirm her own role as an expert voice from the frontline of public services. If the growing amount of media coverage she received was not exactly against the advice of the nation union, then, as Larry Whitty recalls, head office 'had to be brought to support it'.[7] The GMWU was the dominant union in local government until the late 1960s but NUPE had made great gains, pushing its way into London, and was organising in those areas where the GMWU had been complacent, or failed to organise. This constant range war between the two unions was a hallmark of the period and gave an added edge to Mary's success in pulling over membership from rival branches from 1978

onwards. In contrast to the private sector section, the GMWU's public services sector, with its well-established shop stewards and branch secretaries, many of whom had been in place for twenty or more years, had quite a staid structure. Mary was certainly impatient with Charlie Donnet, her national officer, and would often tease and cajole him at congress. Clever, bureaucratic, a little introverted and very cautious, Charlie was from the right-wing of the labour movement. He 'didn't move fast and didn't like people who kicked over the traces'.[8] To say that he and Mary were chalk and cheese was something of an understatement.

His joint pay negotiations with management at one end of Belgrave Square and the unions at the other were regularly enlivened and disrupted by Mary's demonstrations and pickets. During lunch breaks great platters laden with sandwiches and finger foods would shuttle back and forth between the two venues, and Mary's women would frequently help themselves as the harassed caterers attempted to thread their way through the press of the crowd. On one memorable occasion, on a particularly grim and cold

day, Mary and Barbara asked to use the toilets in the building where the two sides met. On their way out, they heard voices booming out from one of the committee rooms and stopped to listen when it was Charlie Donnet speaking. Wanting to know what was going on, they pressed closer and closer to the door, with Mary clambering up on Barbara's shoulders in order to listen through a vent high above. All of a sudden, they overbalanced, tumbled forward and hurtled through the door which obligingly swung open to send the pair sprawling at the feet of a surprised Charlie Donnet and the employers' delegation. Anyone else might have been embarrassed by the fall but Mary thought it was a hoot and never tired of telling the story. As a consequence of the protests and the continual disruption of their meetings, both sides decided to reconvene for a 'secret' meeting at Weston-super-Mare. Word of this leaked out via LBC Radio and Mary, as a devotee of late night local radio phone-ins, heard of it and set about organising a demonstration in the seaside resort. 'There weren't many of us', Mary recalled, 'but we annoyed the employers and they feared us'. Concern

was such that, in expectation of flying pickets and a mass demonstration, Avon and Somerset police cancelled all annual leave and intercepted the coach carrying Mary and her branch at the county border. Expecting a ruse, the inspector demanded 'where are the rest of the coaches?' He was furious when he was told that they were only ones coming. He stomped-off, instructing a particularly gauche young policeman to 'stick like glue' to Mary and Barbara and never let them out of his sight. The result was that the pair delighted in taking the unfortunate lad on a 'mystery tour' of every sex shop, dodgy bookshop and lingerie department that they could find in the town. His cheeks flushed redder and redder, as Mary played the minx and asked his opinion of a succession of risqué outfits and products. 'Do you think my husband will like this?' she called out from a changing room, to his obvious embarrassment and discomfort. Finally taking pity on him, Mary and Barbara headed to join the rest of the branch at a pub on the seafront for lunch. After a few minutes, they noticed a woman looking distinctly out-of-place, in a large hat and expensive suit, sipping nervously from a glass of advocaat in the privacy of the side bar. From her furtive glances, they decided that she was probably the wife of one of the employers. Eluding their new policeman friend for a moment, they sidled over and struck up a conversation. Soon they were getting on like a house on fire and Mary offered to refill her glass. 'Oh, yes, that would be lovely'. As Barbara headed towards the bar, Mary *sotto voce* suggested that she slip a slug of vodka into the fresh drink and, in this way, the afternoon passed in a pleasant and convivial manner. All of a sudden, the woman – whose hat had slipped down over her eyes – pulled herself together, announced that she 'wasn't having any of this' and shot off out of the bar. No one thought anymore about it until the pay talks had broken up and Charlie Donnet came 'dancing over to the women, with a cry of "We won!"' Apparently, the chair of the talks had been suddenly called away from the meeting and returned, looking somewhat chastened, to change his vote in favour of the workers. Knowing glances were exchanged, and the women believed ever afterwards that it was the perhaps

not-so-quiet advice of the chair's wife, rather than the negotiating brilliance of the GMWU, that had won the day.[9]

Aside from the excursion to Weston-super-Mare, Mary had rarely campaigned outside of Brent. However, a particularly brutal dispute at the Chix factory in Slough, centring upon the mistreatment of a predominantly Asian workforce, brought her out in support of Paul Kenny, a newly appointed London Region officer, who had been 'thrown in at the deep end'. Paul was immediately impressed with the fact 'that she had an energy that other people didn't seem to have: a spirit of fire and a sense of hope that infected people with enthusiasm'. It was the first time he had encountered someone in the GMWU with feelings, and who asked 'not why, but why not?'[10]

> **There weren't many of us, but we annoyed the employers and they feared us**

Mary at a joint Labour Movement and CND rally in 1986, with Jack Jones, the legendary leader of the T&G, and Bruce Kent, who served as General Secretary and then as Chair of the Campaign for Nuclear Disarmament. With the Cold War threatening to go hot, and US missiles on British soil, the Peace Movement experienced rapid growth during the 1980s. ▶

Transforming London region

As yet, London Region, led by Harry Robertson, a hard-nosed Scot who was described as being 'old school' and 'not likely to shake the world up', had largely gone unnoticed and unremarked. With its membership heartlands located north of the River Trent, and the Lancashire and North regions seen as predominant in the union's affairs, the GMWU had been perceived during the 1960s-70s as being a 'northern' union. A sustained period of membership growth over the 1970s came to a crashing halt in 1979-81 with the recession that cut vast swathes through the membership and provided a near-fatal shock to the system. In the winter of 1981, David Basnett had told his union members that: 'As a result of economic recession, closures and redundancies in some of our most solidly organised factories in the private sector and the effects of public expenditure cuts and staff cut-backs in local government and the health service, we have lost about 100,000 members'.[11] The closure of gas showrooms, the mothballing of shipyards, and the retreat of the glass industry from St Helens, spelled the end of many existing industrial cultures

within the union and forced amalgamation with the Boilermakers' Society, to create GMBATU, swiftly renamed as the less cumbersome GMB, on 1 December 1982.[12]

At the same time as the union's membership was undergoing traumatic upheaval, the way in which the union was governed also began to shift, though at first this was a subtle, incremental process. The union's internal democracy had been unchanged since the days of J. R. Clynes, with powerful regional secretaries appointing officers directly, deciding upon branch organisation and structure, and controlling the union's finances. This had led to a top-down approach within the union. A series of grey and authoritarian general secretaries, running from Charles Dukes through to Tom Williamson and Lord Cooper, saw an incredible degree of centralised power and control in the hands of the general and regional secretaries. Full-time branch secretaries were entirely dependent upon the favour of their regional secretary, who could either add to or subtract hundreds of members from their lists at the stroke of a pen. Mary knew this all-too well. Her old friend Tony O'Brien had challenged the status quo on both the

regional council and the executive, and been destroyed by David Basnett as a result. It was hardly surprising that others took this warning to heart or that regional councils had come to mirror the attitudes and priorities of their regional secretary very closely. As 'rubber stamps', they were rarely open to anything approaching meaningful debate and were largely concerned with procedure. However, through successive motions brought to congress by John Cope's Perivale branch, the case for a greater measure of lay member democracy was gradually established. The largest upheaval occurred in 1976 when the old General Council and National Executive, the chief products of J. R. Clynes, were abolished and replaced by a Central Executive Council or CEC.

Without these changes, it is hard to see how Mary Turner could have risen through the union or, indeed, how the GMB could have hoped to have rejuvenated itself. Henceforth, congress would be the supreme governing body of the union with the CEC standing in its stead as the union's 'parliament' in between congresses. In 1983, the CEC comprised an elected chair (almost invariably the union's president), the ten regional secretaries, and two members from each region, elected by the regional councils.[13] It was, therefore, entirely possible to effect change from within provided that you could win a sufficient majority on the councils. The trouble was how to make that initial breakthrough.

Recruiting, organising & campaigning

John Cope had taken the reins as recruitment co-ordinator in the London region and had immediately set about holding a series of organising conferences aimed at lay activists. He was amazed by the popular appetite for a new approach to building the union from the grassroots, with eighty members applying for just thirty places, and concluded that: 'It has been a real boost that large numbers of lay activists are so keen to be involved in recruitment methods'.[14] Yet, John was well aware that for these changes to be successful he needed to build a team around him. He possessed an incredible gift for spotting raw talent within the union and for giving people a chance. In the first instance, there were Paul Kenny and Mary Turner; later there would be Gary Doolan, Sharon Holder and John McLean. A later general secretary would owe his initial advancement in the union to his notice, when a young Tim Roache was taken out of the post room in London Region and sent off to the Nottingham office to gain experience and become an officer. Beginnings, however, are difficult times and often turn upon the workings of simple chance or accident. By then, Mary had become a very popular figure within the London region, and in an overwhelmingly male dominated environment. Not for the first time, people underestimated her. She could smile, the eyes would twinkle and there would always be a ready quip but there was a core of steel folded into her being, and an unbreakable, instinctive sense of what was 'right' within the labour movement – and what was most certainly not. She was always well informed and a meticulous operator in terms of recruitment and the ability to organise and hearten her members. She could hold her own and hold court in a bar, the inevitable cigarette in hand. But while stories of her partying are legendary in the union, the alcohol never affected her or her judgment. The gaze was always clear, registering who was there and who was not, taking in all that was said, gaining insights, and forming ideas. Just as importantly, she would always be up bright and early the next morning, never the worse for wear, and ready for the business at hand. She possessed a formidable will and, just as importantly, a formidable constitution.

For John Cope and Paul Kenny, the first task was to capitalise upon Mary's personal following and ensure that she was elected to the regional council. Despite Harry Robertson's entrenched opposition, they felt reasonably confident of the votes, and the soundings that they had taken, when they walked into the meeting held at Caxton Hall, in North London. However, the agenda had been altered. The first item that came up for consideration and vote was not, as they had expected, the nominations for the regional council, but those for the national executive. Before anyone could think or catch breath, a voice from the floor nominated Mary for one of the two positions on the CEC and the hands duly shot up. Mary won by popular acclaim. When the vote for the regional

council finally took place, she won that by a landslide as well. On the way out, across the little courtyard, John Cope called out to Harry Robertson asking if he'd had a good day. The regional secretary had a face like thunder and barked a gruff and dismissive response back. 'Oh well', said John, unable to resist the opportunity, 'It happens. But just one last thing … you were very lucky that your job wasn't up for election today or Mary would have had that too!'[15]

In this way, in time for the union's congress in 1983, Mary became the only woman on the CEC, which consisted of 34 seats. There had only been two women on the executive before her: Laura Kirkton, from Liverpool Region, and Peggy Topping, from Scotland. Neither had lasted long and it was confidently predicted that Mary would not last more than a single, two-year, term of office. She had replaced Len Henstock and it was widely held that she 'had taken a man's place'. Moreover, her withering attack on the rank treachery of the SDP leaders at congress had greatly displeased David Basnett, who had known Jenkins and Williams well, and disliked her far from diplomatic language. The GMB had not tended to rock the boat, or talk the language

of class politics. As a result, it was put about that Mary was not expected to 'go the distance'. She was a seven-day wonder who would burn brightly before fizzling out and being quietly forgotten. One officer drew her aside and let it be known that she should make the most of her triumph while she could because she would not be there in two years' time. It was a brash and bullying attempt to put a shot across her bows and to undermine her confidence. Years later, she would recall the sting of the comments when she was talking to the present author, but there was distinct pride in her voice and a fierce gleam in her eyes when she recalled that she did not allow them to throw her off course, for even a moment. 'I stayed, and they went', she said.

The union's leadership was certainly less than appreciative of her attempts to stir things up and reports of her speeches and activities in the union's journal were, initially, condescending. She was 'the cook who came in from the cold', and 'a singular individual if ever there was one'. She and Barbara did not carry, but rather 'struggled' with the union banner at an anti-cuts demonstration in Cardiff. There were sniffs at 'her inimitable style and particular forte

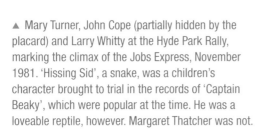

▲ Mary Turner, John Cope (partially hidden by the placard) and Larry Whitty at the Hyde Park Rally, marking the climax of the Jobs Express, November 1981. 'Hissing Sid', a snake, was a children's character brought to trial in the records of 'Captain Beaky', which were popular at the time. He was a loveable reptile, however. Margaret Thatcher was not.

of bashing the Tories', as though these were negative traits, and when Mary was out campaigning she was described as having 'one of many problems'.[16] However, as Mary made plain before the GMB's 1984 congress 'it was on my ability' that she had been elected to the CEC.[17] Though she did not believe in a rigid system of quotas – indeed, the introduction, in 1987, of 10 reserved seats for women on the CEC might have been viewed as an attempt to swamp Mary and drown out her distinctive voice – she felt that 'after getting on the executive I was amazed at the feeling amongst the women who tried to get

▲ Mary carrying the London Region banner at a march against unemployment in Cardiff, July 1981, with Barbara Benham walking beside her. The coach to get them to Wales left central London at 5am and Mary and Barbara had had to delicately prise the banner from underneath the bed where Denny was still sleeping, blissfully unaware. He had always maintained that Mary could do anything she liked for the Labour Movement, 'so long as that banner didn't come in the house!' Mary figured that what he didn't know wouldn't hurt him.

through the system'.[18] 'Women', she told the still overwhelmingly male delegates, 'are a very important part of this union. They, too, stand on the picket lines, answer the calls of demonstrations. The union's fight is their fight whether they be male or female. Take a look at the miners' wives, [who] … stood for the miners themselves, who are

facing poverty, harassment, intimidation and even prison in support of their husbands and their union'.[19] 'The fact of the matter is', Mary continued:

'that there have been very few recent appointments of female officers in the last three years. Female officers are less

◄ Mary delivering a speech on unemployment at the Labour Party Conference, September 1985. Earlier, she had told her own union: 'I stand here as a woman and do not apologise to anybody for it. I do not apologise for being a trade unionist or a member of the Labour Party, and when my region elected me I always stood for and said it was on my ability'.

it did to get the somewhat phoney equality on pay'.[20]

It was a matter of everyone being treated equally. Mary, as she often did at the TUC or Labour Party NEC, used a specific instance to broaden out the argument to encompass issues that affected her own members. Thus, the development of women union officers was a necessary part of a wider struggle to secure meaningful legislation that would ensure that manual workers, the low paid and part-time workers, who were often women, had the same rights and conditions of employment as the managers. 'After all, what difference in worth is there if you are a dinner lady or a dustman to if you are a council officer? Yet the law does not see it like that. When we lost the cleaning contract in Brent the women didn't get redundancy money because they were part-time'.[21] It was this link of understanding, attitude and impulse between Mary and those that she represented that enabled her to survive on the CEC for more than just that first term. She understood them because she was

than 3 per cent of this union, and they are declining ... Given the appallingly low number of female officers, we must take additional steps to encourage female activists, many of whom are very, very capable of becoming officials in our union, to actually apply for jobs, and to look at providing a special training for female activists ... let us hope that it is not going to take as long to get true equality of opportunity and representation as

one of them. As a member of the executive, she began to visit the region's branches, invariably driven by the indefatigable John Cope. She travelled throughout East Anglia, where few CEC members or regional officers had either visited, or particularly bothered with, before. Word of her travels reached Harry Robertson's ears and she was summoned to give an account of herself and forbidden to enter onto 'anyone else's patches'. Mary simply refused to acknowledge the injunction: she was their representative on the union's governing body and she would visit any branch that invited her within her own region, as she was accountable to them and not to the regional secretary. Not for the first, or last time, Robertson was incandescent, but Mary won the argument. She continued to go to branch meetings and, of course, made use of them to campaign and to consolidate alliances. In a similar fashion, there were attempts to set up Edna Rolph as a possible rival. However, neither woman was prepared to be played in such a way and they made a common cause that benefitted them both. At the same time, the retirement of Harry Robertson in 1986, and the appointment of John Cope in his stead, suddenly made everything seem possible.[22] 'John Cope was the first, real breakthrough', Mary once told me, full of pride in his achievements, 'that changed everything!' At the same time, she, too, was breaking the mould and, after being triumphantly returned to the CEC in 1985, was now there to stay. In the words of Paul Kenny, 'Mary didn't so much break through a glass ceiling but six feet of concrete roof that was reinforced with iron bars'.[23]

The battle for school meals, 1979-95

While Mary could be found successfully campaigning for the retention of the GMB political fund in the summer of 1985, and leading a mass picket by NUPE, COHSE and GMB members in order to save the north London Neasden Hospital from closure in February 1986, she continued to work as a dinner lady and to be defined in terms of her growing expertise in making the case for the school meals service.[24]

The provision of free school meals had been established at the beginning of the twentieth century in order to tackle malnutrition among the urban poor. Yet it

was based upon permissive rather than compulsive legislation and was not an act of altruism on the part of the ruling classes. Rather, it was the result of the poor performance of the British army during the Boer War which had seen undersized, undernourished and generally unfit Tommies sicken under the heat of South African skies and be thoroughly outclassed on the battlefield by the Boer guerrillas, who were farmers rather than regular soldiers. With the introduction of compulsory education, through the election of a Liberal government with support from the fledgling parliamentary Labour Party, it was recognised that hungry children could simply not be expected to learn in the classroom. In 1906, the Education (Provision of Meals) Act allowed Local Education Authorities, or LEAs, to make financial contributions from the public purse to school canteens and, in certain cases, to provide the poorest children with free meals.[25] School milk was introduced in 1924 by the first Labour government and, by that decade, more than a million children were being provided with meals. However, it was the effect of wartime, rationing and the passing of the 1944

Education Act that made school meals compulsory. Minimum nutritional standards were enacted by law in order to ensure that the diets of children at school were balanced and healthy. In 1947, Clement Attlee's Labour government undertook to meet the full cost of school meals in all state schools and aimed to provide a free midday meal for every child, as a universal right.[26] Although the level of provision would vary between councils, this principle (that guaranteed food standards and provided either free or heavily subsidised meals for every child) continued to govern the provision of school meals until the 1970s.

The first change came in 1974, when Margaret Thatcher, as Secretary of State for Education, put an end to free school milk and, in so doing, became the 'milk snatcher' to a generation of British children. However, worse was to come with the passing of the 1980 Education Act, the brainchild of Keith Joseph, Thatcher's chief monetarist ideologue in her cabinet. This abolished the national nutritional standards and price controls. Local authorities were able, and sometimes even tacitly encouraged, to abandon the service completely save for a minimum safety net to protect the most vulnerable and disadvantaged. Local authorities were now only legally obliged to provide free school meals for children on supplementary benefit or income support. This had the effect of stigmatising the provision. Mary wrote at the time that 'labelling "free dinner

> **" Mary didn't so much break through a glass ceiling as six feet of concrete roof that was reinforced with iron bars "**

kids" as surely as evacuees had labels tied on them' was a divisive and humiliating measure, and made the managers in her school end the practice of making those children with free meal tickets line-up separately to their friends. It was also noted that Mary routinely fed children from other schools who turned up at her kitchens.

By April 1981, approximately a third of all local authorities were only providing this minimum safety net. Price rises led to a dramatic fall in take-up. In real terms, about 20 per cent of the nation's children lost access to free, nutritional school meals within the twelve-month window from October 1979 to October 1980. In local authorities which raised prices to 55p or more, numbers halved. Where the price was raised to 45p, the numbers dropped by almost a third. Some local authorities (initially, those under Conservative control) used the falling numbers to justify abolishing the school meals service almost in its entirety and for making the staff redundant.[27] Further cuts came by stealth. Clause 59 of the Social Security Bill in 1986 went largely unnoticed by all save the GMB at the time. The final legislation ended the ability of local authorities to subsidise the meals service in Special Schools, further disadvantaging those children with special needs or disabilities. It also spelled the ending of free school meals for families on Supplementary Benefit.[28] As a result of this, and further changes in benefit laws, some 400,000 children from low income families lost their right to free school meals by 1988.[29]

This was not simply the by-product of fiscal retrenchment, brought about by the recession. Instead, it was driven by ideology, a particular view of human nature, and the desire to 'free' the market from any control by the state. Thus, Edwina Currie, a junior minister with a particular flair for self-publicity, was to reject any responsibility of government for social policy. She claimed that food poverty existed only as the result of irresponsible spending choices of parents and the general fecklessness of the poor. She didn't 'think the problem has anything to do with poverty. We have problems ... we can tackle by impressing on people the need to look after themselves better'.[30] Where recognition and discussion of food poverty did take place in the 1980s and early 1990s, it was almost invariably stimulated by the activities of Mary Turner and the GMB. As with the GLEB, Mary had seen a viable alternative to the Tory cutbacks.

She had been sent by the union to attend the Public Services International conference held in Finland, in 1981. When she first received the invitation, she could hardly believe it and quipped that she had thought that it had been devised by Charlie Donnet as a means of getting rid of her after the hard time she had given him

◀ John Cope addressing delegates from London Region branches, c.1984-85, at a day school. Extremely bright, unflappable and unfailingly cheerful, John was Mary's political mentor and comrade over almost five decades. Under his regional secretaryship, London Region grew in strength and influence, moving to the left and acting as a powerhouse of talent in the union.

at congress. However, what she found in Helsinki and Tampere was eye-opening. 'In Finland', she said,

'every child has a free school meal by right, whether they be rich or poor. There is no classification of unemployment or employment; they get their meal. It is carefully balanced in nutrition. Not like our EEC and our Common Market, they do not build up piles of milk, fish and meat to go rotten. When they over produce there, it is distributed into the hospitals and into the schools to keep the costs down and feed their old, sick and needy. I feel that before the next Labour Government comes in, they should now set up a working party to look at these Scandinavian countries and see how they feed their young, their old and their sick, and we should implement it in this country by right'.[31]

This Nordic model of socialisation would remain Mary's lifelong ideal and her

inspiration for the way that the school meals service could, and should, function in Britain. It was also a case of the union providing opportunities for its members to grow into their roles, experience new things and develop their professional knowledge. In a similar fashion, she went to Canada in 1982, in order to attend the congress of the Canadian public services union, the NUPGE. She struck a strong bond with the union's general secretary, John Fryer, who was another firm socialist, and made use of her time there to visit schools and their kitchens. In this way, she was learning all the time.

The savage reality, however, was that the school meals service was being squeezed in Britain at both ends. Education budgets tended to be prioritised towards teachers and classrooms. If it was a case of councils having to lay off teachers and stop buying books and equipment, or to sack the dinner ladies, cheapen the food, or close the kitchens, then the teachers and the classroom resources would win every time. Conservative policies were so pernicious, and so successful, because in this way they set one group of workers against another, and prioritised one set of social provisions over another. After 1986, there was little many rate-capped councils could do about it. Many councillors, including Labour ones, could often not see that they were being played off, one against the other. The continual harping of government about the 'necessity' of 'competition' – a sort of dog-eat-dog ruthlessness that has slid, like an ear worm, into popular parlance and even been accepted by some bureaucratised trade unionists into their jargon – made matters worse, using the argument that the introduction of private companies into the sector would encourage savings and better value for money for the taxpayer, as well as greater choice and variety and the availability of more 'attractive' services for children. In reality, the effect of the introduction of Compulsory Competitive Tendering, or CCT, of public services was to establish cost as the determining factor. As a result, what the government referred to as 'best value' meant processed foods, frozen pizzas, packet mixes for desserts and sauces, pre-prepared vegetables. It was a race to establish the lowest common denominator and for the private consortia

to rake-in the highest margin of profit from the public purse. Food standards were lowered and portions became smaller. Cash-strapped LEAs felt they had no choice and, in any case, the consideration of the lowest cost was written into the legislation enabling CCT as part of a local authority's 'due diligence'. If an education committee rejected the lowest tender, on grounds of nutritional quality or in order to protect jobs and conditions, they could be held personally liable to challenge from the private companies.

As Mary pointed out to the TUC, the CCT schemes quickly resulted in six companies acquiring more than two thirds of the entire catering trade. 'When the government forced local authorities to introduce compulsory, competitive tendering,' she said,

'*safety meant nothing; all it is is profits before people*'. *Local authorities have been the greatest believers in health, hygiene and training. With the introduction of compulsory, competitive tendering those standards have declined, and are declining every day with the introduction of cook-chill. Cook-chill can kill, [and] will kill*'.[32]

The reheating of pre-cooked food and meat products was far more likely to lead to food poisoning and, in the context of the meals on wheels service for the elderly, was a real threat. Cost pressures meant that foods high in preservatives, fats and additives, which were cheap and readily available, would become the order of the day. The emphasis on freedom of 'choice' was also detrimental to nutrition. What child would opt for a salad, a pasta dish or a juice, when chips, sweets, sugary cakes and fizzy drinks were on offer? The kitchens were stripped out with the equipment sold on by the new private companies, and regeneration ovens, which simply reheated stacks of aluminium foil containers, were introduced. All of this was much quicker, simpler, and required a less-skilled workforce. As Jeanette Orrery was told by management, 'you don't need much in the way of a brain to scissor open a packet, do you?'[33] Consequently, pay, conditions of service, and hours were all cut as the service was deskilled and demoralised. The poorly-paid became even poorer, and more marginal to a society that talked glibly about 'professionalism' but which, through burgeoning business studies courses and HR departments, sought to institutionalise, legitimate and codify methods of exploitation and a system built upon inequality. As Mary never tired of saying, the Conservatives and their willing henchmen among the managerial classes would 'steal the eyeballs out of your sockets, and then come back to steal your eyelashes'.

The trouble was that the vision of 'choice', growing consumerism and the appeal to the basic human instinct of greed, which suggested to the individual that they might be the ones to succeed by being the first to scramble over the backs of their fellows, was incredibly potent. Raw cutthroat instinct was dressed up as 'entrepreneurship', popular culture was tamed by 'the Pepsi generation' and by a series of bland, reactionary pop hits such as Huey Lewis's 'It's Hip to be Square' and Madonna's 'Material Girl' which provided a comfortable soundtrack to Reagan's America and Thatcher's Britain. It was the age of Gordon Gekko, stripped of all irony, and served up to the public in the form of Lord Hanson. It was there in the sneer of Alan Sugar and in the rictus of Richard Branson. The power-

suit dominated the catwalk and projected both an outward vision of the identification with corporate values and an immediate expression of the widening gulf between the skilled and the unskilled. As Margaret Thatcher memorably summed it up, with a vivid and savage brilliance, the definition of failure was anyone 'who still used public transport after the age of 30'.

Against her, the left, after the militancy of the early 1980s, had few answers and was becoming far from fashionable. It seemed to offer complaint, while Thatcherism offered 'aspiration'. The dinner ladies, with their overalls and marigold gloves, seemed to be the least fashionable of all, deemed hardly worthy of notice.[34] If Mary had had to endure the dismissive comments of her own union colleagues that she was 'just a dinner lady', then this was amplified a thousand-fold for her sisters in stripped-out school kitchens up and down the land, when faced with managements about to privatise their services and tear up their contracts of employment. Worse still, the impact of the recession meant that although women were no longer laid off faster than men, as had happened during previous slumps, they were far more

vulnerable to casualisation and de-skilling, with the result that the move towards achieving equality in employment between men and women was lost.[35] As Mary told workers in Brent: 'Women workers have been the top of the hit list: school meals ladies, home helps and cleaners, the people who have given the most and earned the least'.[36]

It was with all this in mind that Mary had gone into print, in July 1982, with her article in the *Morning Star's* 'Woman Wise' column on the school meals service. It was intended to breathe heart and a sense of militancy into her membership. 'Government', she wrote,

'is treating the women workers like something the cat brought in, and it thinks that they can be swept away just as easily … As an active member of the GMWU, I know that this union has done more for the rights of women workers than any other union, and it would be proud of the turnout of about 600 [at a meeting on school meals that she had recently called in Brent]. I say to women meals workers all over the country: Don't shrug your shoulders and say "Well, what can we do?" Join the union

and organise yourselves. You have not asked for confrontation, and you have been loyal to your contracts. But stand up for what is yours by right, legally negotiated ... Show them that you are not as weak as the government thinks. Fight to save the meals service – and your jobs!' [37]

As she knew full well, public services had been left reeling. In 1982, Devon County Council was one of the first battlegrounds for the school meals service with some 1,800 dinner ladies targeted as being 'the weakest group' in local government.[38] Five dinner ladies, members of GMWU and NUPE, laid down a challenge in the courts to the decision to terminate their contracts in September that year, with new contracts that would enforce a £3 per month deduction for their own meals and withdraw their holiday retainer payment, under the fiction of continuous employment.[39] Their tenacity paid off in terms of their individual settlements. But Mary, who had hoped that a general fight could have been made in Devon, was dismayed by the lack of spirit shown by the majority of their colleagues. Indeed, it is likely that the failure of the

In May 1986, 25 sacked Glasgow printworkers marched to join the pickets outside the gates of Rupert Murdoch's News International plant at Wapping. They were fed at Aylstone School by Mary's branch, with John Cope lending a hand. ▼

GENERAL & MUNICIPAL WORKERS' UNION

SAVE Brent

Brent was one of the metropolitan boroughs ravaged by Tory cuts to expenditure, and rate caps, in the 1980s. This badge was one of many produced by Mary's trades council in order to rally support for the work of local government and public services. ▶

unions to draw 'a line in the stand' in Devon had pushed Mary to set pen to paper in the first case. Believing that nothing could be done, the overwhelming majority of members had simply taken what the employer had offered them 'as alternative jobs were few and far between'.[40] Hard on the heels of Devon, Merton, a Conservative controlled borough in South London, scrapped its school meals service in March 1983, save for the statutory requirement for the poor and the disabled, with 350 redundancies announced among GMB members. 'Unaffected of course', noted the union's journal, 'are [the] boys and girls in private education – many belonging to Tory members of Merton Council. These children will continue to enjoy a cooked, midday meal'.[41] The catering service that covered further education colleges was another prime target for cutbacks, with Kilburn Polytechnic and Willesden College of Technology threatened with losing their canteen staff.[42] For the moment, the change from kitchens serving meals prepared on site to snack bars dispensing junk food was seen by the union as a compromise that avoided outright closure.

In Brent, the first group of workers to be privatised were the school cleaners. They received a letter sent from the council by recorded delivery, on a Saturday morning, instructing them that their hours were to be halved, their pay to be cut, and their holidays, pensions and sick benefits to be drastically reduced. 'To this day', Mary told me with a catch in her voice, 'I will never forgive or forget'. She had 'watched the faces' of those women and the memory of their heartbreak remained with her. She chose to return to the theme at a later TUC Congress, furious that many of the delegates had begun to scurry out of the hall when a debate was called on part-time workers, as though it was none of their concern. 'Part time workers in this country are increasing', she told the TUC,

'We lost the cleaning service in the education department of my borough. We lost it because we would not accept that the part-time, low-paid women workers should take a cut in a wage that was already low … there is no way that I or my union will be blackmailed with a "how low can you go" policy'.[43]

Ironically, the congress chair, Alec Smith moved to shut-down the debate and was dismissive of Mary, saying that he didn't see where the points fitted within the context of the motions under discussion. He, too, was a member of the GMB.[44] Yet it was the membership of his own union that was suffering. What had been a stable workforce in the 1970s became increasingly precarious in the 1980s-90s. In December 1991, the GMB followed the case of Lorraine Scott, a union member and single parent who was trying to make ends meet by working two jobs: as a dinner lady in a Dundee secondary school and as a cleaner at a nearby primary school. For this she took home less than £100 for a 40-hour week, making attempts to juggle home and family life and to pay the bills extremely difficult, and that for back-breaking work and very long days. The article had appeared in the union's magazine as part of the GMB's push for a national minimum wage, which had been prefigured by Mary's contribution to the debate on incomes policies back in 1980, and which would become a part of Labour Party policy in time for the 1997 general election.[45] In the meantime, Mary was clear that it was people like Lorraine Scott who suffered the worst from the cutbacks and the drive towards the privatisation of public services. 'The people who pay the price', she said,

'have been women who are already among the lowest paid in local government. School meals workers are incredibly dedicated. Most are parents themselves, so they're not going to let a child go without a meal, even though they're getting kicked in the teeth by the private companies ... The women keep working because they need the job ... some of these women have two or three jobs, doing cleaning shifts before and after their meals work. We have very short breaks, which we're often not able to take, we get insulted by some of the children and the noise levels are incredible. Teachers have to deal with thirty or so children in a hall. We're used as a cheap nursery provision at lunchtime. We're expected to get the children through in half an hour, there's never enough crockery, so we're constantly washing up and getting ready for the next group. Many of the facilities date back to the 1950s, because schools are just not interested in providing good equipment, they want the space for classes'.[46]

It was an unenviable position and one that was destined to become a whole lot harder. Brent Council was the largest employer in the borough with some 13,000 staff, and its education department, covering 101 schools and 34,000 pupils, was the largest service provider that it controlled. In the 1980s, its non-teaching staff included everyone from administrators and drivers in home-to-school transport to caretakers, cleaners, midday supervisors and the school meals service.[47] A high proportion of school children were dependent upon receiving free school meals, with at least 20 per cent coming from families with low or no income earners and receiving DHSS benefits.[48] Women in Brent were found to be disproportionately represented in low-paid, part-time work but now constituted a larger proportion of the unionised workforce, rising from 25 per cent in 1971 to 31 per cent of all trade union members in the borough.[49] Rate capping had already hit services hard and the Conservative and SDP/Liberal alliance council that had come to power had initially tried to make the shortfall by dipping into its reserves, but soon moved to cut an extra £100,000

a year in expenditure. In the first instance, this was to be found through increasing the charges at OAPs luncheon clubs, at the day nurseries, and for the meals on wheels services.[50] As with school meals, nutritional standards for the elderly were downgraded and up to two weeks' worth of ready meals were now delivered to the homes of vulnerable OAPs, to be reheated as and when required. This certainly saved on ingredients, cooks and transportation costs but it also removed daily contact with the elderly and further isolated many OAPs within their own homes. As Mary made plain in relation to the threat that hung over the meals on wheels service, 'the GMB doesn't just care about one group of people, it cares for all ... as long as you have the principle of caring that's all that matters'.[51] On the other hand, 'The Tories don't use meals on wheels, they don't use school meals and they don't use the NHS. What we want is a healthy eating programme and legislation to maintain standards'.[52]

These standards for healthy eating and the welfare of old and young, alike, were of central importance to Mary. Rather than being just a matter of diet

Mary addressing a joint GMB – NUPE rally for school meals' workers at Hillingdon Civic Centre, 26 June 1989.

or child development, she saw school meals as being part of a holistic approach to education that sought to encourage parental involvement, and to act as a democratising and liberating process. It was a world away from the obsession with testing, metrics, and the profit motive, which was increasingly accompanying the move to turn schools into businesses. In opposition to this drift, Mary helped to pioneer schemes across the borough that sought to teach those young people excluded from mainstream schools the catering and hotel skills that would equip them with a better chance of getting a job. A series of Cash Cafeterias was established in order to remove the shame and humiliation occasioned by free meal tickets. The first of these had opened at the Queen's Park Community School in Brondesbury. It served healthier food options such as salads, jacket potatoes and orange juice. There were no colas or sugary drinks and chips were only sold in small portions. A metal-work class at the school were asked to produce hundreds of shiny metal discs that looked like coins and could be used by free-lunch pupils so that they couldn't be identified in the

lunch queues. 'Years later, when we were fighting privatisation, adults who had been children, and now had children of their own, turned up at council meetings to support us', Mary recalled, 'it was lovely, really lovely'.[53] Having seen children start to arrive in the playground as early as 7a.m., she also saw to it that the schools began to establish breakfast clubs across the borough.

As a consequence, long before Jamie Oliver grabbed the media spotlight for his campaign on school meals, a healthy eating programme had been pioneered in Brent that was available to all. This was consolidated in 1992, when Mary and the GMB moved to endorse a campaign launched under the umbrella of the Food Commission, which pushed for the introduction of a 10-point School Meals Charter. The campaign had two main aims: first, to set nutritional standards for the meals that were being served in order to improve children's diets, and secondly, to stem the decline in central government funding which had led many education authorities to raise prices or close kitchens completely. As had been the case prior to the 1980 Education Act, the food experts agreed with the GMB that the single most beneficial change would be compulsory, nationally-agreed nutritional standards which would apply to local authorities and contractors.[54] In 1996, Mary, having recently been elected to the NEC of the Labour Party, pushed for school meals to be treated as another part of the curriculum, just as she had experienced it in Finland, where every child received a free school meal and was educated in the preparation and serving of food. 'It wouldn't take much money to do it properly', Mary said, 'just a bit of thought. At the moment children have no idea about nutrition. I know young girls who don't even know what a Brussels sprout looks like'.[55] There were also very good, practical, pedagogical reasons for this move. Children who did not eat properly at midday were more likely to be disruptive in class or to have problems concentrating in the afternoon, while truancy was found to have risen when children left school at lunchtime in order to buy sweets, fizzy drinks and snacks.

Mary was never in any doubt as to the importance of the school meals service

> *When I worked in the kitchen, the bosses were always scared of her going in there, **"Don't bring Mary Turner down!"**, they'd say, and rush to sort out the problem*
>
> Maria Sulis

and was incredibly proud of its role. 'For a great number of children', she said, a cooked school meal was

'the only balanced meal of the day. At the schools I worked in, they used to have everything cooked on site, there was balanced nutrition and lots of choice. In the cash cafeterias the cheaper food was the healthy food, baked potatoes, quiche, [and] vegetarian meals. But there are children on the borderline who don't qualify for free school meals and they suffered when prices went up. If a meal is £1.30 a day, it becomes expensive for families on low incomes. So packed lunches get brought in and the quality of those depends very much on the parents. If parents don't have much money, they may try, but the children end up going to school with just a couple of slices of bread and jam, or chocolate.

I heard of one seven-year-old child sent to school with a can of beer, because that's all there was in the fridge'.[56]

Mary's constant campaigning led to many local authorities thinking twice about cutbacks or it caused them to retain, or re-introduce, their free school meals. As Maria Sulis, who had known her since joining the GMB in 1994, says, Mary 'was always there with the union for advice. You just had to ring her and she'd be there for you. She'd always get back to you quickly, sharply and in complete confidence'. Moreover, 'when I worked in the kitchen, the bosses were always scared of her going in there. "Don't bring Mary Turner down!" they'd say and rush to sort out the problem'.[57] For a time, in the 1980s, Mary was able to hold the line in Brent and received considerable support from Jeremy Corbyn, who had been newly elected as MP for Islington North.

The unions are a key pillar of civic society. Their members are people who care about – and for – others. Mary Turner and Barbara Benham raised money over a number of years for the Guide Dogs for the Blind, and this dog, 'Maba', was named in their honour, taking the first two letters of their names and putting them together. ▶

However, attempts to unite all the workers involved in education in shared actions and solidarity produced only patchy and very mixed results. A one-day strike in the borough saw many members of the NUT join the cleaners and dinner ladies with the majority of Brent's middle and high schools closing, but the strike was far from solid in the primary schools, with only a third shutting. The trouble was that the restriction of trade union freedoms, through legislation that outlawed secondary picketing and sympathetic action, encouraged sectoral differences and excused a failure to act across grades, across the divide between blue and white-collar, and between the different unions themselves. It was a divide and conquer strategy. Resistance to it was not helped by the changes within the Labour Party that saw the rise of Neil Kinnock's strategy of 'new realism', which in many respects prefigured New Labour and its accommodation with the free market. Thus, in 1988, Mary found herself leading a campaign against the ruling

▲ The meeting of the political and industrial wings of the Labour Movement. Neil and Glenys Kinnock are welcomed by the GMB leadership, John Edmonds, Dick Pickering and Mary Turner, c.1989.

Labour council when it tried to further cut the school meals service. 'I fought it as vigorously as I fought the Tory Council', she told Kamala Hayman, 'It doesn't matter who is in power, if they are damaging the service I will fight them'.[58] There would be no betrayals, no double standards based upon 'double think' and no sell-out of her membership.

Matters would come to a head with the decision of the Conservative majority after the elections in 1990 to privatise the borough's school meals service. After much hard work, Mary and her colleagues won the tender for the provision of school meals, beating-off rival bids from two other companies and an international consortium. Within days, this decision was overturned by the education committee, when it met in September 1994, and awarded, instead, to the second-placed commercial interest. The dinner ladies were understandably devastated but, rather than accepting the decision as final, they launched a public campaign that saw practically every shop in the borough, and, of course, Mary's own bingo hall, raising petitions against the rolling programme of privatisation and the cuts in provision. The winning bid, by a Scottish company known as CCG, envisaged just 17 of the 60 menu choices on offer to be made on site in schools, with the rest brought in frozen, and simply reheated in the ovens.[59] There were public meetings and rallies, and Mary, Barbara and the women made sure that they packed the town hall and chief executive's office every time the council sat or the education committee had a decision to make, making their point and disrupting the business as best they could. By February 1995, Mary had gathered 8,000 signatures against the planned rises in charges for school meals in the borough. The Conservative mayor, Councillor David Games, refused to allow it to be presented or discussed 'on procedural grounds', when the council met. Outside on the street 'a rain-swept but vocal' protest by GMB and Unison members greeted the arrival of the councillors. It had been hoped that some of the Conservative group would break ranks over the issue, but when it became clear that they would not, the protestors in the public gallery became increasingly angry and vocal. 'They were well under the whip', said Mary afterwards,

'They should be looking at the needs of all, not just their own'.[60] As the local paper reported, time and time again the mayor used his casting vote to break the deadlock, between the tied votes of 33 Conservative councillors against 28 Labour and 5 Liberal Democrats. The school meals service, £2 million allocated for urgent school repairs, a plan to save Carlton Vale Infant's School, and attempts to make home help for the elderly free again, all fell by the wayside that night.

No new contracts had been offered to the existing workforce in advance of the takeover, and no proper contract had been drawn up with CCG before the council vote, although CCG had promised to recognise the GMB. In this climate of uncertainty, Mary told reporters that 'The way staff have been treated is a disgrace. Some of these cooks are among the worst paid employees in the borough. They will not forget this. We are taking legal advice on a High Court judicial review'.[61] As she took their case to arbitration and through a series of employment tribunals, Mary began to feel that she 'saw far more of the chief executive of Brent than I ever did when I was still at work'. She vowed to overturn

the Conservative majority at the next local election and, in fact, a dozen Tories did fall giving control back to the Labour group, but the damage had been done. 'It was all a sad reflection on the society that we have gone back to', she said, 'where public service sector workers are attacked and worker is set against worker'. It was perhaps to be expected, but the manila envelopes that dropped on to the doormats of Mary and Barbara's homes, at the beginning of 1996, were to confirm that they were going to be made redundant. It was end of era in Brent but not to the women's commitment to the health of the borough's children. Neither would allow the plight of the low paid, women workers, and children whose diets and life chances were being sacrificed on the altars of greed, economic dogma and political expediency, to be forgotten by the GMB. Furthermore, just at the time that Mary's career in the school meals service was coming to an end, her role within the union and the Labour Party was beginning to expand and would, within the space of a year, enable her to make the case for healthy school meals, provided as a universal right, to a New Labour government. ∎

THE PRESIDENT OF THE UNION

The rise of Labour women, 1986-1996

Lisa, Mary's granddaughter, would come over after school, Mary and Barbara would head off to the vast bingo hall in Cricklewood, and Mick Ryan would arrive 'regardless of the weather' and sit down for the evening with his best friend, Denny, to watch the latest TV cop show, *The Sweeney* remaining their firm favourite, as they reminisced and caught up on the week that had been. Lisa, young and inquisitive, loved every moment of it. 'I would sit in the hallway finishing-off my homework', she recalls,

'while answering the phone to everyone who called for Nan and taking the messages, as though I was Nan's secretary, which I really enjoyed. It was whilst taking these messages that I began to understand what a trade union was and what the Labour Party was all about ... The GMB was everywhere in the house but understanding the Labour Party was hard for me. I looked up to my Nan, I was interested in what she believed in, I asked questions about why she was so passionate about the things that she fought for and she always enjoyed answering them.

Then one day, Nan told me that she was taking me to central London for a Labour Party meeting. It was then that I happened to meet Neil Kinnock. Nan and Neil sat, for what felt like ages, talking about this and that, and how they would be going forward with this policy and that policy. Before you knew it, a couple of weeks later, Nan had me out campaigning, and knocking on doors and asking people to vote Labour.

From that day forward, I knew what the Labour Party was all about, because I listened to Nan telling others from morning to night for weeks on end. It was on one of these door-knocking rounds that I had my first encounter with someone who, let's

◄ Mary had a rare gift with people, regardless of their background or whether they were old or young. This enabled her to make the presidency of the GMB her own. Here she welcomes youngsters to the union's congress in Blackpool, in June 1994, and listens to what they have to say.

just say, was not a big fan of Labour. He was rude and aggressive. He opened the door, saw the cloud of red rosettes, saw red himself, and made his disgust known. After this little outburst, he went to shut the door in my Nan's face, but what he didn't see was that I was stood just beside her, holding my clipboard, thinking that I was her little secretary and organiser. He never got to slam that door, as I put my foot in the way and jammed it open.

I felt upset with the way he was towards my Nan, so I politely told him so and explained why my Nan was doing what she was doing to make the world a better place and for people to have a better life. My Nan's face was a picture of shock that, at a young age, I had listened to what she believed in, I understood part of the Labour Party's values and I was willing to have my say.

Once I had had my say, he did apologise, through gritted teeth, but insisted we closed the gate on the way out. If it had been down to me, I wouldn't have closed that gate. But Nan insisted we did because that was who she was. Regardless of who upset or attacked her because of what she believed in, she was this normal, caring, considerate person, with this energy about her that no one else had'.[1]

That energy was a prerequisite, in combining family life with a taxing day job, running the branch, attending the regional committee and the CEC, as well as taking a growing role in the Labour Party, at both a local and national level. There was always something to be done, whether it was finding 400 turkeys to be sent to the families of striking miners in Kent over the Christmas of 1984-85 (and forgetting to buy one to take home to her own family in the process), fighting to save Neasden hospital from closure, or together with Barbara Benham and Noreen O'Callaghan turning out to feed twenty-five sacked Glasgow print workers, who had marched all the way down from Scotland to join the Wapping pickets in May 1986, with 'Turkey, two veg and roast potatoes followed by apple pie and cream – washed down with lemonade and something a little stronger'. The principle was always the same. 'The union is well known locally', Mary told reporters, 'and we've always been willing to help brothers and sisters in times of struggle. We know what it's like! Murdoch's attack on print workers must be beaten back. If he gets away with it, just think what other employers will be encouraged to do to less organised workers'.[2] The next day, those same print workers would be charged by police horses outside 'fortress Wapping', Rupert Murdoch's *News International* plant that was the centre of his attempts to break the print unions, one of which Mary had once belonged to.

The politics of gender, the union and the Borough of Brent

On every occasion, the Hendon branch had responded magnificently. As Tom Durkin, the veteran chair of the local trades' council remarked during the miners' strike: 'No words of praise are too much for the tens of thousands who have supported the miners in Brent, all those who have collected cash, food and clothes, handed out leaflets. Stuck up posters, organised meetings and social

events, picketed Neasden Power station for months … It was a mighty effort to have raised over £125,000 in Brent by Christmas and to have regularly sent van loads of food and clothes to Kent and other coal fields'.[3] However, it did not take the sting out of the defeat, or the sense that it had been helped by the complicity of some of grandees of the trade union movement. 'No wonder they give peerages to [Len] Murray, [Frank] Chapple, [Joe] Gormley and their ilk. It is for services rendered in holding back and dividing our unions from acting together to smash anti-union laws, against mass unemployment, and rate capping cuts … and [for] cuts in the colossal arms bill'.[4] As Mary told the GMB congress in June 1987, after another convincing Conservative victory at the polls, 'Today Margaret Thatcher is going to take our jobs – your jobs, my jobs. She may take our jobs; she may take our hospitals; she may take our homes, but she will never take our Socialism!'[5]

Yet, the problem remained of how to achieve the return of a Labour government. Socialism can only thrive in an atmosphere of optimism and after industrial defeat from the steel strikes, to the miners, to the printers and political defeat at three consecutive general elections, it seemed that the post-war settlement, based on Keynesianism and consensus, was well and truly broken. There would be no way back to the world that had existed before 1979 and, as horizons narrowed, there was less space for idealism or even for hope. Yet, at the same time, if traditional industrial politics were fracturing and the power of the unions was on the wane, then the impact of the second wave of feminism was slowly impressing itself upon the Labour Party and its structures. Before the 1983 general election, there were only eleven women Labour MPs out of 269. As Harriet Harman wrote, 'Though we women worked hard as grass-roots members of the party, the decision-making was done by men, whether in Parliament, in the National Executive Committee, in the local councils or in the constituency committees … it was anathema to us that we, as women, would remain "outsiders" and should forever be petitioning men rather than making the decisions ourselves'.[6] Women's sections were established in some CLPs, mirroring the contemporaneous call for Black sections within the party. But calls for a women's section on the NEC were opposed and the 1984 Labour women's conference was closed down after an attempt to storm the platform in protest at a failure to provide crèche facilities, and embarrassment at the party's almost exclusively male leadership. Within the women's conference, there was a political, cultural and, to an extent, social divide between those Labour women who came to socialism through feminism and those women trade union delegates who approached feminism through their socialism. The former tended to be from more middle-class backgrounds, the latter tended to be working-class. Differences were also expressed through dress and demeanour, with the trade union delegations always being smartly turned out and giving short shrift to one of their sisters from a CLP who brought the ballot round the conference floor dressed in a boiler suit while absent-mindedly munching on an apple. Bridging this divide was a new wave of women trade unionists who would come to include Margaret Prosser from the T&G, Anne Gibson of MSF, Maureen Rooney and Cath Speight from the AEEU, and, of course, Mary

Turner. Anni Marjoram, Ken Livingstone's policy advisor on women during his time as mayor of London, considers that this grouping captured the zeitgeist and 'had a huge impact for women in both the unions and in the Labour Party, far more than the minority of university educated [women] officers'.[7] It was a long, hard battle. Attempts to ensure that there was at least one woman on every shortlist were the subject of cynicism and obstruction and were referred back to the NEC for consideration. At the same time, the party's leadership refused to back plans to create a women's minister with full cabinet status. At the 1986 Labour women's conference, jeers and howls of disapproval greeted the announcement that there would only be support for a token, non-cabinet post. Mary considered that her own GMB delegation felt 'totally alienated by the labour movement … from the bottom to the top'.[8] 'Discrimination', she said, 'was so prevalent that it was difficult to believe women had had the vote for over 50 years. Yet women were at the forefront of most industrial struggles'.[9] Once again, she and her colleagues used the point to make a wider argument that

women were increasingly consigned to the economic margins in Britain, with few statutory rights, much lower pay and little in the way of redress against unfair dismissal. In the short term, this did much to focus Mary's attention in the GMB upon marginal workers within the public services section, to urge the union 'to get rid of what we had in the past, that narrow craft text' and to start looking at the 'four and a half million part-time workers in this country, 14% of the workforce' who might, reasonably, have expected full-time jobs before the Tories had come to power.[10] It also emboldened her to argue for female representation in areas of the union, such as the engineering section, where, traditionally, women had not hitherto been a major presence or force. In the long term, Mary and her allies across the unions did much to reorganise the Labour women's conference, to lobby (male) general secretaries and (largely male) executives in the unions, behind the scenes. They were instrumental in winning the battle for all-women shortlists in the constituencies' selection of parliamentary candidates. This passed, almost unnoticed, in 1992, amid the conference furore over OMOV, thanks

in no small measure to this grouping and to Maureen Rooney's ability to peel the votes of the engineers away from the electricians section (which had formerly been the EETPU), who were implacably opposed to the measure.[11]

For her part, Mary was fortunate to have the ear of John Edmonds, as the general secretary of the union, who always treated her 'like an equal'.[12] Mary had been with him, in the Pembroke hotel in Blackpool, when he heard the result of the 1985 ballot electing him to succeed David Basnett. Having been seen as the most progressive of the candidates and with the support of the broad left within the union, he was certainly serious about modernising attitudes within the union towards race, gender and sexuality.[13] The move towards a reserved seat for one woman from every region in the GMB was a move in this direction. However, as we have seen, Mary was also clear in emphasising that all she had achieved was through her own hard work and merits rather than solely on account of being a woman.[14] This said, the 'time [had] now come for positive action' in order to tackle the problem of women's under-representation and for the GMB 'to stop putting off until tomorrow what we can do today'.[15] In this way, the GMB and the Labour Party began to move, however haltingly, in step.

Mary had never been in any doubt that the Labour Party was there for her, as the 'people's party'.[16] 'As a union', she told the GMB, 'we are in a position to encourage our members, and particularly our active members, to become involved in the activities of the Labour Party, which should be a natural extension of our trade union interests'. However, it was not just a case of women per se being under represented on its bodies but, in particular, both female and male manual workers. As early as June 1981, she had been warning of this as 'a weakness we should be concerned about'. Labour simply did not look like the people whose interests it existed to represent, and this was a tendency that worsened over the 1990s as the party increasingly adopted parliamentary candidates from the professions rather than the public services or shop floor. Mary stood twice, herself, in selections for the Brent East constituency. Always keen to expand her horizons and to look for new challenges, Mary had applied for other jobs outside the school

meals service in book-keeping and wages departments in local firms, had offered her and Denny's services for various voluntary projects, and had even looked, in the mid-1970s, to the Gulbenkian Foundation (a charity bequeathed by the estate of a Portuguese philanthropist, to promote the arts and sciences) for grant-aided work,

to promote their borough.[17] A step into parliamentary politics, particularly as the representative for Brent, seemed like a logical next step and presented itself when, in 1989, the Labour leadership attempted to have Ken Livingstone deselected from his Brent East seat.

It was part of a wider struggle over the

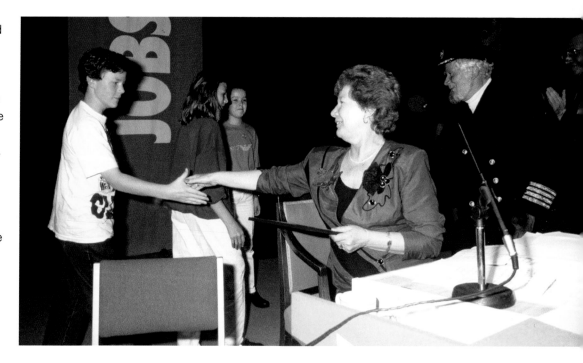

A point of order! Mary makes her views known at the GMB's Rules Revisions' Congress in June 1993, when the annual hosting of congress and with it lay member democracy came under threat. ▼

direction of Labour, after three savage election defeats, and an attempt, by Neil Kinnock, assisted by Peter Mandelson, to knock out a would-be challenger to his throne as leader of the party. Livingstone had made no secret of his belief that Kinnock, having lost once at the polls, 'stood absolutely no chance of winning' against Thatcher.[18] The two men loathed one another on a personal level, but there was an added ideological dimension. Having come from the left of the party, Kinnock was moving rapidly to the right. In the summer of 1989, the NEC signalled a policy shift that acknowledged the industrial defeats of the earlier years of the decade and the fundamental shift of the British economy from industry and towards services. Were Labour elected, the anti-union laws would remain, as would nuclear weapons, and Labour also moved away from its commitment to bring back into public ownership the privatised utilities

◀ The fight for jobs was still at the forefront of the GMB's campaigns when Mary, as vice-president, gave out awards for a children's competition at the union's 1993 congress, in Portsmouth, with a little help from 'Captain Birdseye'.

and industries such as British Gas, British Telecom, British Airways, British Petroleum and British Steel. At the same time, the publication of the Brent MP's book, *Livingstone's Labour: A programme for the nineties*, looked like – and was – an alternative manifesto for the party and a bid for the leadership. The next general election was expected to fall in 1991-92 and, in his mid-forties, Livingstone might well have expected to pick-up the mantle if Kinnock fell to another defeat at the hands of the Conservatives. As a consequence, a pre-emptive strike was launched in Brent, where Livingstone had just lost control of his constituency's apparatus to what, at the time, were described as an alliance of 'soft left' and 'non-aligned' members in the CLP. In the first of many ironies surrounding the selection battle, Livingstone made it known that he had no problem with the 'de-selection of MPs' and that he believed that they should face regular challenges, particularly over such issues as defence and Ireland. 'If they don't want me', he told *The Guardian*, members had 'the right to remove me'.[19]

Demographic changes had turned the

constituency into a marginal seat and internal dissention over the council's willingness to make 'emergency' cut-backs and impose a hike in council house rent, had split the Labour group and brought their feuding out into the public domain. As far as Livingstone was concerned, more could have been done to tackle the council's waste of resources through inefficiency but, in likening its chief officers to members of Pol Pot's genocidal regime in Cambodia (which had infamously ordered engineers to make water run uphill), his gift for fashioning the headline-grabbing quote backfired and alienated many of his natural allies. Mary, after some prevarication, chose to stand against him in the re-selection process, having become critical of the lack of time he spent on the affairs of his own constituency.[20] She was considered the 'credible' challenger by the press and had incredibly strong roots in the community as the local and, in many respects, the natural candidate. However, the field against Livingstone was split two ways by the decision of the former MP, Michael Barnes, to also stand. A second irony was that all three hailed from the left of the party and, in the terminology

of the Blair years, would have been firmly considered to have been within the ranks of 'the awkward squad'. The final twist lay in the fact that the party's recent change of rule (pushed through by Kinnock and Mandelson) excluded the block votes of unions in the CLPs and sought to empower individual members. This helped Livingstone's grassroots organisation and wiped-out Mary's hold on the union votes. Without this procedural move, he might well have been in some considerable trouble. This said, it was still the splitting of the opposition vote that proved decisive, and Livingstone achieved a comfortable victory with 64 per cent of the vote from 600 individual party members, in a secret ballot.[21]

Mary's disappointment was palpable but even in defeat she had a rare and remarkable gift in politics for being able to refrain from the personal and not to make enemies. She had fought Ken Livingstone as she had thought it best for the people of Brent, and out of a sense of unwavering loyalty to the Labour leadership, but when it was all done and dusted, there were no recriminations or bitter grudges. Indeed, Livingstone was quick to acknowledge

her 'traditional Labour values', strong local backing and personal charisma. In later years, Mary would campaign for his re-admission to the Labour Party, chair the special NEC sub-committee that ruled in his favour, and 'hugged and kissed' him when his membership and Labour candidature as mayor of London were confirmed.[22] In some respects this was all the more remarkable, and selfless, as his readmission had followed a recent jockeying for power in the borough that had set the seal upon her second attempt to become the MP for Brent East. Livingstone had decided not to stand again and the party leadership, scared that they might lose a valuable seat, had agreed to refrain from imposing its own external candidate. Paul Daisley, the leader of the council, was a convinced Blairite but, surprisingly, had thrown his weight behind Livingstone on a number of important local issues and had been vocal, early on, in his calls for his return to the Labour fold. As a consequence, he was acceptable to the eyes of both Livingstone and the Blairite party apparatus, and was able to see off Mary's challenge in the 2000 selection contest. She again came in as the runner-up but, this time, in a field of six prospective candidates. It was, considers Malcolm Sage, 'the Labour Party's loss but the GMB's terrific gain'.[23]

Campaigning for the union, for the young, and fighting racism

It was very much the case of one door closing and another one opening. All the while, the London region of the GMB had been growing in terms of its strength and influence under John Cope's careful stewardship. It was also gaining some good friends and valuable allies. One of these was Dick Pickering from the powerful Lancashire region, who would distinguish himself as a very able chair of GMB congresses in the 1980s and 1990s. Described by John Edmonds as having 'a big frame and an insistent manner' commanding attention, he had begun his career, in 1967, as a bin man working for Manchester City Council.[24] He quickly became a shop steward for the refuse collectors, then branch secretary, and member of Lancashire's regional council, and, in 1976, was elected to the union's executive. In 1983, he embarked upon

his first spell as chair of the GMB, as the office of union president was then known. Having initially worried that Mary might contest the election, he was relieved to discover that her focus remained firmly fixed upon gaining the presidency of the public services section of the union, which she did in 1993, rather than the national office.[25] This laid the foundations for a firm friendship and a very effective working relationship that deepened upon Mary's election, at congress in 1988, as the union's vice-chair. This was the first time in the union's ninety-four-year history that a woman had held the position and further evidence, if any was needed, that Mary was punching her way further through the GMB's 'concrete ceiling'.

Mary would often deputise for the President, chairing sessions of congress for the first time and welcoming all kinds of guests to the hall. These ranged from the light-hearted, with the actor playing 'Captain Birds Eye' making an appearance to emphasise the company's commitment to children's healthy eating, to the deeply moving. Thus, in 1995, a campaign to halt child slavery supported by GMB donations and political lobbying was underscored by

a speech by young Tamoor Hussein who, though often under the threat of violence, had helped organise other children to free themselves from bonded labour in cramped and dangerous carpet factories in Pakistan.[26] Two years later, there were tears at congress when a group of these children, freed from slavery and given access to schooling, were introduced to the delegates by Mary and took to the platform to give their thanks and sing a message of hope for 'living for others who are weaker'.[27]

She could also be found alongside John Cope, watching the games and presenting the prizes at an international football festival for youngsters, sponsored by the GMB, that was held at Northwick Park in London. Teams from the USA, Poland, still labouring behind 'the Iron Curtain', and Denmark, competed against home-grown sides. Girls' teams also participated at a time when it was still far from the norm.[28] In similar fashion, the GMB also sponsored the Co-op Young People's Film and Video Festival at London's South Bank in October 1994, and Mary acted as the guest of honour, handing out the awards to children from Blacko School in Colne and students from Sheffield College on the completion of

a short course in animation and film. As so much else collapsed amid the retrenchment of national and local governments, the union began to take on an increasingly important role as one of the few props of civic society left standing. While Margaret Thatcher had infamously claimed that 'there was no such thing as society', Mary and the GMB were there to show that, indeed, there was and that it was something that everyone should participate in and be proud of. Thus, when she presented NVQ certificates to young people training at the Kilburn Skills Centre, together with the local MP Paul Boateng, in June 1992, she was quick to stress the integral role played by unions in education, training and the securing of meaningful employment.[29] The GMB was not just there in the bad times but for the good ones, too, when there was much to be enjoyed, commended and celebrated. That did not mean that Mary's often ceremonial duties got in the way of putting a more serious messages across. At the start of 1991, amid cutting winds and freezing weather, Mary spoke to some 400 school pupils at Morpeth School in Bethnal Green. She was supposed to be talking to them about careers advice but

the subject quickly broadened and turned to a discussion of the need to protect their rights at work and the threat posed by hard right-wing and neo-nazi groups who were seeking to exploit local tensions between the Somali, Bangladeshi, Greek and Irish communities.[30] It might be delivered with a smile but, make no mistake, Mary always carried with her a strong and unvarnished message that was no respecter of person or position. All were to be treated equally, regardless of who might be upset: if it was right, then in Mary's book, that was simply that, and there were few things more certain than the need to stand against the discrimination, hatred and abandonment of reason displayed by racism.

By the late 1980s, London Region was certainly no respecter of rank. Under John Cope, it had moved firmly to the left and its annual congress motions certainly shook things up and gave the union's national leadership more than the odd headache.[31] In 1985, congress delegates had overturned

Mary drew her strength from the union's members at congress. This strip of photos shows her through a week of triumphs and tribulations at the GMB's 1991 congress held in Bournemouth. ▶

the recommendation of the CEC and had voted to affiliate to CND for the first time, while by 1987 the debate on nuclear power was conducted against the background of the Chernobyl disaster in the USSR.[32] These themes resurfaced, powerfully, in 1990, when London Region tabled a motion urging that an incoming Labour government should reduce military expenditure in line with the average level of other west European countries. This would have, effectively, spelled the end of the Trident programme and a budgetary saving of around £6 billion that could have been put to better use in providing work and welfare.

Dick Pickering had, in the meantime, resigned from his position as chair after a row about the increase in the union's membership fees and a parallel readjustment in the ways in which shop stewards could collect and benefit from them. Surprising some, he had stood again for office in 1987 but had been defeated by Olga Mean, who represented health service workers in the northern region. Hindsight is a wonderful thing, but if you stripped it away, for the moment, to reveal the way that the union considered and projected its leading women activists and officers in the late 1980s and early 1990s, then Mary would appear as only one of the major lay members (alongside Olga Mean and her great rival, Vi Baldwin), while from the sheer number of column inches devoted to her progress in the pages of the union's own journal and the *Daily Mirror*, one would have had to guess that Donna Covey was tipped for the top among the GMB's office corps.[33] Mary lacked the levers of power among the CLPs, as shown by her defeat in Brent East, which Olga Mean possessed across great swathes of the north-east; she never wrote for journals or gave interviews for academic studies, as Pat Turner had once done, and was far less media friendly than Donna Covey. As a result, during that particular period, it is Covey who appears as the outward-facing image of women in the union, while it is Olga Mean – or Pat Turner, for the previous decade – who, to date, appears where any academic study, or Labour Party memoir, touches upon the legacy of GMB women.[34]

The GMB had been a dominant union in the north-east, with large numbers of members clustered in local government, the NHS, energy, and what was left of the shipbuilding industry. A number of parliamentary seats had traditionally been seen as within the union's gift, with Giles Radice being parachuted in to Chester-le-Street in 1973 and Peter Mandelson being backed by all nine GMB branches through Olga Mean's local influence, and that of Tom Burlinson, as regional secretary and close friend of Neil Kinnock, to take the nomination for Hartlepool in 1992. At the time, the union was believed to have been 'flattered' that this 'very talented' figure at the heart of the party machine was in need of its help and patronage.[35] In this manner, the seeds of New Labour were sown among the former coalfields, pit towns and shipbuilding areas of County Durham, Cleveland and Tyneside, with Alan Milburn in Darlington, Peter Mandelson in Hartlepool, Stephen Byers in North Tyneside and, most famously, Tony Blair in Sedgefield. By and large, it was the wielding of the unions' block votes that had entrenched them in these solid Labour, working-class strongholds, doubtless in the belief that favours would be recalled at a later date and that proximity to power would inevitably bring results and influence. The trouble with playing at 'high' artful politics, as opposed to building from the grassroots, is that the elites do it so much better, have been doing it longer, and have far greater, and more tempting resources to use by means of patronage. Playing a 'Game of Thrones' style strategy when it came to Labour Party politics, continually moving the chess pieces, jumping from one short-term expedient to another, and seeking to plot as opposed to work your way to power, will only get you so far, especially as people tend to have long memories. The unions should have known better than to believe that the momentary advantage gained would not have political ramifications that would last for years and be capable of mutating the base materials of politics, and of the labour movement, into a fool's gold.

The power of a union activist to hold sway over the party was, of course, rooted in their ability to maintain their powerbase within their own union. The problems that Olga Mean had at the GMB's Congress in 1990, began, but did not end, with London's motion on the scaling-back of the defence industry. From the chair, she had announced that the motion was now opposed by the executive and judged

it to have been defeated on a show of hands in the hall. However, craning their heads around, many of the delegates did not read the situation like that and called for a card vote. No, came the ruling from the chair: that was that, the motion had fallen and congress should move on to the next business. There was a commotion, angry voices, appeals and raised order papers. The London delegation got up and went to walk out en masse. The platform was in danger of losing control of the hall, something unheard of for a union as normally respectful, respectable and thoroughly reasonable as the GMB. John Edmonds had the presence of mind to intervene, urging the London delegation to return to the hall and prevailing upon Olga Mean to accede to the calls for a fresh vote. A second, card vote was duly called and registered 232 votes for the London motion and only ninety-four for the opposing CEC position. It was a humiliating and, largely, pointless defeat for the union's leadership and one that served to effectively hole Olga's authority as congress chair below the waterline.[36] Her term of office was over and the election for chair of the GMB was to be decided by congress vote with Dick

Pickering challenging and keen to win back his old position. The vote did, indeed, return him with 228 votes from the delegates unseating Olga Mean, as the incumbent, who only polled 178. In the election for vice-chair, Mary was also challenged. However, she convincingly won the vote, polling 246 votes ahead of Geoff Wheatley, the Birmingham and West Midlands regional secretary, and with Gordon Lewis, of South West Region, trailing in third place with only 18 votes.[37] If anything, the experience had taught Mary how a congress should not be handled and it was a relief to many to see Dick Pickering's steadying hand back upon the helm in subsequent years. As Mary readily acknowledged, she learned a great deal from him and they had a good time on the platform, at the TUC and at the Labour Party conference.

These were hard and uncertain times for the labour movement. The understandable fear engendered by yet another, and this time surprise, defeat at the polls in 1992, followed two years later by the tragic and unexpectedly early death of John Smith, left the unions circumspect, self-conscious and desperate for Labour to regain office. A whole political generation had come

Mary presents awards to the winners of a film festival organised by the GMB in association with the Co-op and London's South Bank Centre, October 1994. ▶

and gone, since 1979, and the union had changed, too, gasping and grasping for survival. Initially, this had been pursued through a merger strategy, which, in 1989, brought in APEX, representing pay, clerical and computer staff with 75,000 members, the Tailor & Garment Workers with 73,000 members in 1991, and FTAT with 31,000 members in 1993. These were all unions that had been experiencing falling membership, whose size would not threaten to swamp the GMB. They had been brought to the merger table in order guarantee the survival of their industrial identity through economies of scope and scale. The amalgamations helped maintain the GMB as a sustainable, independent organisation, masking its own core membership decline, but generating hopes that fresh recruitment drives would be more effective in the wake of these mergers, rejuvenating the constituent arms of the new super union. Though there was some evidence to support this in the success of increased recruitment in Remploy in the 1990s, it was not repeated across the merger partners. The initial transfer membership figures did not always accurately reflect the true number of fee-

paying members. Changes in industry employment patterns and the rise of globalised, cheap imports from developing nations cut further swathes out of the British textile and furniture industries. Ironically, while both the Tailor & Garment Workers and FTAT enjoyed a considerable measure of autonomy within the GMB, the arrival of FTAT into the GMB 'family' of unions coincided with the eclipse of the APEX Partnership. In 1994, this saw the GMB overhaul its organisation and opt for an industrially based structure. Critics noted that the mergers also offered a means of implementing thoroughgoing organisational change without raising too many hackles in congress, but while wresting some power back from the regional secretaries to head office.[38]

However, a failed attempt at amalgamation with the rival blue-collar union, the T&G, in 1993-94, coupled with the failure of the existing merger partners to deliver all that had been hoped for, effectively grounded any strategy of growth through amalgamation. In its place, the union adopted an approach based on organic growth. Ten per cent of budgets were allocated to an ambitious

recruitment strategy that failed to live up to high expectations and was, in turn, swiftly abandoned.[39] A major problem for the GMB, given the cuts to public services and the growth of 'flexible', part-time or short-term contracts, was one of membership retention. There was an annual turnover of roughly 15 per cent throughout the decade. But while new members tended to be in the lower, or part-time, subscription categories, the departing membership through retirement or further lay-offs tended to come from the 'Grade I' or high-paying rates of fees.[40] With the union dependent upon subscriptions, these patterns of loss and change hit its income and started to drive the union into deficit. The difficulty was that while members, when surveyed, stressed the benefits of regional structures, the human face that they presented and the effectiveness of their services, the duplication of functions that it entailed also ran up costs that the union was increasingly struggling to meet at the national level.

A whole range of other initiatives was tried. These included the adoption of the 'Working Together' logo (as a 'friendly', rather than combative, image for the GMB), the signing of no-strike deals, the willingness to embark on joint ventures with employers in bidding for newly privatised services, the use of charity sponsorship in order to try and tempt young workers to join, and attempts to recruit the self-employed, together with the promotion of individual rights of workers where collective bargaining was now largely absent. Industrial quiescence found its mirror in the retreat from political radicalism. Tom Burlinson considered that 'People these days don't expect unions to be highly political like they have been in the past. They want unions to care for them and that is why GMB has an advantage – we are not seen as a hard-headed organisation but have consensus and mediation built in'. The union would have 'to move with the times'. Describing himself as 'new trade union Labour', it was Burlinson, by then deputy general secretary, who made the case for scrapping Clause Four to the GMB's congress in 1995. It caused some outcry in the hall. Jacqueline O' Neill, from London Region, asked why the commitment to public ownership had been 'dumped' in exchange 'for a few vague words'. Denise Elliott, from South Western, pointed out that the issue had not even been discussed at the previous year's congress, yet 'this year we are told we should not argue because it is an accomplished fact'.[41]

Yet, Clause Four stood as a 'straw man' to be knocked-down, a high-profile signal to middle England and the CBI that New Labour would not challenge global capital or seek to undo the basis of the Thatcherite counter-revolution. At the time, many in the unions considered that the debate was purely academic, while John Prescott played the boor and mocked Sidney and Beatrice Webb (the far from militant Fabians who had written the clause in 1917) as being 'middle-class intellectuals' and, therefore, irrelevant to the labour movement. It would not be the first, or the last time, that the unions would willingly confuse philistinism with the 'authentic' voice of the people, in order to overturn genuine progressive policy commitments. However, words do have power. That is why the rich have their children educated in the classics, philosophy and political theory at the public schools, while removing these same subjects from the state schools. The replacement of the pledge to work towards 'the common ownership of the means of production, distribution and exchange', with a nebulous aspiration 'to create for all of us the means to realise our true potential', was a recognition of neo-liberalism and the rejection of socialism, or even social democracy, as the guiding imperative behind the Labour Party.[42] Tony Blair understood it, the CBI understood it, the Murdoch press understood it: too often the general council of the TUC preferred not to. Yet, from it, all else under New Labour flowed.

The GMB, caught in the cross-currents, was desperate not to do anything which might jeopardise the return of Labour to power. It was not an overly ideological union with recognisable left and right factions in the manner of the T&G, Unison or the AEEU. Rather it possessed regional powerbases that had markedly different outlooks, priorities and political complexions. In this way, it was particularly susceptible to the argument that power could be won through 'triangulation', identifying two previously conflicting views such as those of capital and labour and placing itself in the middle, in the attempt to gain the support of both.[43] This was

pushed home to the union when Tony Blair addressed the GMB congress in 1995. He certainly offered a package that was likely to appeal to trade unionists, including halting the review of the check-off system every three years, the introduction of a minimum wage, the granting of a legal right to join a trade union, the signing of the European Social Chapter and the promise of better protection for part-time workers. However, he also repeated that there would be no repeal of the Conservative employment laws requiring ballots before taking action and the outlawing of mass picketing. Job 'flexibility', he told the union, was here to stay and furthermore (in an Orwellian piece of doublethink): 'Security today is adaptability. It is about equipping people so they have the skills and the opportunity to move from one job to another, to work part-time or full-time and to cope with change'.[44] This was a vision forcefully seconded from the platform by John Edmonds who announced that there would

'be no attempt by the GMB to put the clock back to the Seventies under a Labour government … We should admit that

the old ways did not serve us well. The [Callaghan] government tried to use the trade unions to keep down wages and the trade unions pretended that cosying up to the government would produce special favours'.

Furthermore, he concluded that he had no problem with Blair's pledge that the unions would be treated with 'fairness not favours'.[45] Well, no one could say that the union had not been told. Indeed, one of the remarkable things about Blair's relationship with the unions was the way in which he was prepared to be upfront with them about their loss of influence and to make it crystal clear just how little they might obtain from him.[46] There was no subterfuge on this. No meant 'No' and, for the most part, the TUC accepted It.

Nature, however, abhors a vacuum and if some in the unions were falling over themselves to shed the ideological baggage of their past and to come to an accommodation with capital and the CBI, then the Conservative Party thought about moving to occupy the vacant space. It had tried to break the link between the political and industrial wings of the labour

Mary was always on hand to provide the rallying call for the Labour Party. 'Why on earth', she asked in 1996, 'do they think trade unionists will vote for' the Conservatives?

movement through the introduction of ballots and of opt-outs from the unions' political funds. These moves were robustly defeated in the GMB, not least through Mary's energetic campaigning.[47] However, the Conservatives understood that a union, in its most basic form, is simply a tool for wage bargaining and the securing of better working conditions. It did not necessarily have to espouse socialist politics, or indeed any explicit form of politics at all. The continual watering down of the labour movement's message and the tendency to take the allegiance of its natural supporters for granted, permitted the Conservative Party to start a campaign to encourage their own partisans to join unions with a view to seizing control of moribund branch structures. Of course, when the challenge came, the modernisers within the TUC were nowhere in sight, as they possessed few or no answers. Instead, it fell to Mary speaking at the Labour Party Conference, in 1996, to sound the rallying call. 'Why on earth do they think trade unionists will vote for them?', she asked.

'Should anyone forget, this is the government which denied trade union rights at GCHQ. They make it easier to sack people like the printers at Wapping, the Liverpool dockers, workers at Magnet [kitchens]. In local government and hospitals, workers have been sacked for profits. Labour is the party for trade unionists because it is our party.'

'I bet', she concluded, 'that the Tories don't have a dinner lady on their platform next week' at their own conference.[48]

By this time, she had been elected as the lay president of the GMB's public services section and had taken one of the union's two seats, alongside Dick Pickering, on the NEC of the Labour Party. She was certainly thrilled with the new position that allowed her an opportunity to influence and shape policy. 'It gives a voice to working people, especially working women', she told Kamala Hayman, and the local paper thought that her presence was sure to guarantee them precisely that within Tony Blair's New Labour.[49] The trouble was that the NEC, itself, had been comprehensively overhauled, with the abolition of the women's section, the creation of guaranteed places for cabinet ministers and a decrease in the number of trade union representatives from 17 out of a total of 30, to 12 out of 32, so removing their majority in its counsels.[50] Its powers were also reduced. A new National Policy Forum was created as 'the buffer' between the shadow cabinet and the NEC. The unions had a mere 30 seats, many of the members were appointees handpicked by the leadership, and debates were tightly controlled. The forum was increasingly used for the formulation of party policy while the NEC was downgraded to the status of a largely administrative body and met less regularly.[51] A withering critique of the effectiveness of the trade union representatives on the NEC appeared in *The Guardian* in March 2001. It suggested that while they 'were the only people at the national executive meetings with a real chance to challenge New Labour's agenda' on privatisation and the low level of the minimum wage, the great majority did not 'utter so much as a whisper' of complaint. Indeed, the 'bargain with Millbank seemed to be that, provided Blair, Prescott and others argued the government's case in a language of social justice, they would not press union policies at the NEC'.[52] The honourable exceptions to this, it was noted, were Mary on the issue of public services, the Communication Workers

> **Mary was 'a critical Labour loyalist – exactly what the trade union movement should be in the corridors of power'**

Union's Derek Hodgson over plans to privatise the Post Office, and Diana Holland of the T&G on employment rights and gender issues.[53] As Lewis Minkin makes clear in his definitive history of the Labour Party's administrative apparatus during the Blair years, Mary 'often spoke out' and was particularly 'forceful over the proposed closure of Remploy'.[54]

Tony Robinson's spirited memoir from a slightly later period captures something of the atmosphere: 'Its moral compass and its dynamism, came from a group of women steeped in 1970s feminism, who'd climbed as far up the ladder of the labour movement as it was permitted for anyone to climb who didn't wear a suit and tie, and a little further still'.[55] If he noted that the majority were 'utterly focused on protecting and enhancing Tony [Blair]'s position', then he would make sure to introduce Mary at a G20 protest as 'the scourge of the Labour Party NEC'. She

certainly brought something different to the table, considers Jack Dromey, 'an authenticity' that was rooted in the realities of work. 'She always brought to the corridors of power the voice at the sharp end', making frequent reference to her members and to her community at a time when those voices were often stilled, or muzzled. She was there to tell the party and government about the concerns of working people. She was 'never backward in coming forward' and was certainly never there to be simple voting fodder for the leadership, to put a hand up at the right moment. As a result, she soon gained the reputation for being 'awkward', being unafraid to challenge, but she was, in fact, 'a critical Labour loyalist – exactly what the voice of the trade union movement should be in the corridors of power'.[56]

An early clash that would have later repercussions came in November 1996, when the party leadership moved to impose

a candidate of its own choosing upon Wirral South. The constituency, though on Merseyside, was affluent and a traditional Tory bastion, held with a 7,800 majority at the previous election. However, the death of the sitting Conservative MP, Barry Porter, prompted a by-election that New Labour felt it could not afford to lose.[57] The Conservative government, beset by scandals and riven by disputes over Europe, seemed to be lurching from one crisis to another. A general election was expected within a year and, having won every single by-election since 1988, Labour had no wish to break its run of success and gift a morale-boosting victory to the Conservatives, even in one their safe seats. As a consequence, Blair and his advisors were keen to impose a candidate who would appeal to well-to-do, former Tory voters. They chose Ben Chapman, a former career diplomat who had served as director for trade and industry in the Government Office North West. He had only been a member of the Labour Party for six months and *The Guardian* reported that one Labour official had thought that his time in the civil service might even have excluded him from membership.[58] With the constituency party effectively side-lined in the process, the NEC were pushed to approve his candidature amid dire, but as it turned out, false, warnings that the Conservatives were planning to call a snap poll. Mary Turner led the protests, backed by Diane Abbott and Dennis Skinner, emphasising that their objections should be noted in the minutes of the NEC.[59] However, the argument for tactical realpolitik won round the rest of the meeting. They seemed to be vindicated, for the moment at least, when Chapman won a sensational victory in the by-election in February 1997, with a 17 per cent swing to Labour that grabbed the headlines and boded well for the coming general election.

Sadly, before that election was called, the GMB was rocked by tragedy. Dick Pickering had been chairing a GMB pension committee meeting, on 9 October 1996, and went straight from it to a meeting of the Economic and Social Committee of the EU Parliament that was held in Brussels the next day. He was taken ill at the meeting, collapsed and died shortly afterwards. Not only did fate rob him of the opportunity to see the return of the Labour government that he had worked so hard to secure, but he had also been chosen as the next

president of the TUC. Writing in *The Guardian*, Keith Harper paid tribute to 'One of the most capable, unselfish servants of the movement' who had 'died with his boots on, working for his members'.[60] There was no better epitaph for a trade unionist. Mary was devastated. As she told the Commercial Services Conference, held at Scarborough in January 1997, it had been Dick Pickering's 'greatest hope to see the return of a Labour government fighting for justice and committed to decent employment laws'; the task of GMB members was now to get out, campaign and make every vote count in order to make that hope a reality.[61]

She had heard the news of his death late on the night of 10 October while driving back from a meeting with John Cope and Penny Robinson. Before anything else was said, another woman in the car, who happened to be an officer much favoured by the leadership, thought to send a warning shot across Mary's bows: 'And don't you think for a moment that you'll be standing for president!' John Cope cast a quick look back in the driver's mirror and chuckled. He knew full well that from the moment Mary was told that she *shouldn't* or *couldn't* do

something, then that was exactly the first thing that she would go and do.[62]

Sure enough, Mary's mother Jo was there, watching from the public gallery, when Mary was elected as president of the GMB and welcomed the delegates to congress, in June 1997, little more than a month after the Labour victory in the general election. Optimism was in the air: 'We've won!' Mary exclaimed. 'For 18 years we have waited for it to happen – and when it came, it was a landslide'. Labour was committed to getting people back to work, cutting unemployment and helping the young into employment. A Low Pay Commission was to be established, tax credits provided in order to lift families out of poverty, and – particularly close to Mary's heart – there were pledges 'to attack the underlying causes of ill health' through the eradication of food poverty.[63] It was certainly a moment of great personal and political pride in a job well done. But Mary was not one to rest on her own or anyone else's laurels. She put the political at the forefront of her first speech to Congress as GMB President: 'Today we meet united, determined and prepared for the opportunities that a new Labour government offers', she declared. A good start had already been made with the restoration of trade union rights for workers at GCHQ and the introduction of a national minimum wage. But there was a note of caution to be had, too. 'We have survived the Tories who were determined to break trade unions above anything else', she said, 'but we cannot be complacent. No one should believe this election will solve our problems. Let us savour the moment, but then get recruiting and go to work!'[64]

Keeping the Red Flag flying, 1997-2003

The cottage had long since folded back into the landscape of County Meath. The thatched roof had fallen-in, the walls had collapsed after almost a century of wind and rain, and the stones had long since been reused for neighbouring walls, cowsheds and farm buildings. Two rough slabs remained stubbornly in place, as the only reminder that the family home of Jim Connell, author of Labour's anthem, *The Red Flag*, had ever stood there. For a time, it had seemed that Connell, himself, might have been condemned to a similar obscurity. Ably assisted

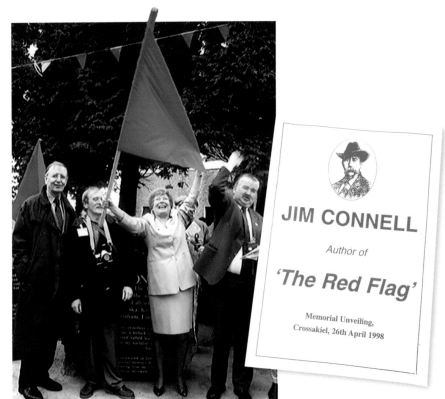

JIM CONNELL

Author of

'The Red Flag'

Memorial Unveiling,
Crossakiel, 26th April 1998

◄ Mary flies the Red Flag, alongside Tommy Grimes, at the unveiling of the monument to Jim Connell, Crossakiel, Ireland, Sunday 26 April 1998.

by Connell's own flamboyant lifestyle, legend took over from fact. His career as poacher, trade unionist, self-taught communist lawyer, author and writer of verse cut across too many academic specialities and could not easily, or safely, be comprehended, sanitised and defined. Yet, he represented the bridge between

agrarian unrest and industrial trade unionism; between the Irish Republican Brotherhood and internationalist socialism; and between political activism and the arts. His daughter, Norah, recalled that 'During every election, our house was not only a centre of activity for the district but attracted socialists from all over London.

As a child, I collected money for the miners at every strike and lined up on the Embankment with sash and banners for May Day and Labour processions as a matter of course. Keir Hardie, Tom Mann, Pete Curran and many other pioneer socialists came to our house and over a roaring fire sat up talking half the night with Jim Connell'.[65] His memory was rescued from obscurity through the life-long work of the late Andrew Boyd. His importance grew in proportion to the struggles waged by New Labour to have *The Red Flag* replaced as the closing anthem at party conferences, and the extent to which he was acknowledged as a link between Irish and British workers.[66]

The Troubles had cast a bloodied pall over the 1970s and 1980s. For a time, any reasoned discussion about securing a negotiated peace in the north of Ireland was submerged by furious denunciations from the tabloid press that dialogue equated to treachery and support for terrorism.[67] Throughout the Troubles, the Irish trade unions had played a selfless, and largely unsung, role in maintaining the fabric of civil society and in forwarding the civil rights movement.[68] Mary was

incredibly proud of her Irish birth and heritage, maintaining an Irish passport and making sure that she was always at the Irish nights at Labour conferences and TUC congresses. She had been outspoken in her condemnation of the policy of strip-searching in the Six Counties and had been horrified by the callousness of the Thatcher government's treatment of the Maze hunger strikers in general and of Bobby Sands, MP, in particular. Then, there was that matter of Mary being on a government 'black list' for her activities during the People's March for Jobs, a burgeoning security services file and her Irish citizenship. Taken together, these appeared to make her a terrorist sympathiser in the eyes of the not overly-bright Special Branch officers. Consequently, in the wake of the Brighton bomb when the Provisional IRA very nearly succeeded in wiping-out Thatcher and her cabinet, the hotels in the town used by TUC congress delegates were raided, at dawn, for suspects. Mary had still been up in the bar when an apologetic hotel manager asked her to come through to reception, where the officers were waiting to take her in for

questioning. It was so bizarre that Mary thought it all a practical joke, proffering her slim wrists for the handcuffs, and winking at one bashful constable, but then, when it became apparent that all this was in deadly earnest, telling them in a more barbed fashion that if they insisted upon strip-searching her, as women were in the Six Counties, then they had better make sure that it was 'the handsome' officer who was chosen for the task. Within hours, a barrage of furious phone calls from the GMB's legal team to Brighton police station secured her prompt release, an apology of sorts, and an end to matters.[69] It was indicative of the attitude of the Thatcher government, and the wider state security apparatus, with its paid informers, towards any form of dissent. There were many 'enemies within' to be watched and dealt with, not just the miners or civil rights activists in Ireland but also ordinary trade unionists, CND members, Travellers, environmentalists and even OAPs and rose growers, such as Hilda Murrell.[70] Many buckled, others had their lives blighted and careers and families ruined. Mary remained undaunted.

She continued to support the work

An awkward looking Tony Blair is presented with a Cammell Lairds campaign t-shirt by Mary, at the GMB congress in 2006. He promised to investigate whether the convictions of the 37 Merseyside strikers were politically motivated. Unfortunately, the words never did translate into actions. ▼

GMB SAYS TIME FOR JUSTICE FOR CAMMELL LAIRD

www.gmb.org.uk

of the Irish Trade Unions for Unity and Independence, ITUUI. Together with MPs such as Chris Mullin, Clare Short and Diane Abbott, she continued to back the model resolutions brought to congress through the Labour Committee on Ireland, raising issues such as the use of plastic bullets and the withdrawal of British troops. A large number of labour movement activists had been galvanised into action in the bitter aftermath of the hunger strikes in 1981-82, while the 'Time to Go' movement gathered momentum, and the accompanying carnival held in Finsbury Park, in 1989, conjoined the 'Troops Out' campaign with wider discussions about cultural awareness, community cohesion and economic power within the Irish community in Britain.[71] However, it was the election of the Labour government in May 1997 with a sweeping majority and mandate that marked a watershed in Anglo-Irish relations and laid the ground for the 1998 Good Friday Agreement and a lasting peace in Ireland. The props fell away from the Ulster Unionists, whose MPs had enabled John Major to cling on to power for so long in return for holding-up

the peace process. Tony Blair regularly recalled his family roots in Donegal, the happy childhood holidays spent in Ireland before the Troubles, and the links between his own constituency in Sedgefield and the thousands of Irish migrants who had come, from the nineteenth century onwards, to work the coal seams in County Durham.[72] This was something that bound him and Mary together in a 'love-hate' relationship. They respected one another, and worked constructively together on many issues, not the least of which was Ireland. Mary would speak her mind to him, in both public and private, but, as Malcolm Sage remembers, in the midst of an over-crowded reception at the Labour Party conference in 2003, Blair, who would normally shoot-off immediately for another evening engagement, had spotted Mary at the very back of the throng. As soon as he had finished, he pushed 'through the packed room straight to Mary, and gave her a big hug and kiss followed by his wife, Cherie'. In a quick chat and after the Blairs had gone, Malcolm turned to Mary, telling her that 'you've impressed that guy!' 'That was how much respect she had from a

Prime Minister', he says. Though there might have been an air of political theatre involved, not least as Blair was embracing Mary, and by extension the GMB, at an event hosted by a rival union, Unite, it seems to have been based upon a genuine regard and affection.[73] When Mary lay ill in hospital, Blair came to see her and to wish her well. There were no cameras, there was no advantage to be had, or spun in the pages of the press. It was an act motivated by an undemonstrative sense of honour and a basic human decency that Mary, her friends and family all thought spoke well of him.

In a similar fashion, it is easy to overlook the achievement and the impact of the Good Friday Agreement in appraisals of Blair's governments.[74] However, the creation of an assembly at Stormont, a power-sharing framework that Sinn Fein, the DUP and UUP could all sign up to and participate in, and success in taking the gun out of Irish politics through the decommissioning of arms, were formidable accomplishments on the part of Mo Mowlam and the Labour government, achievements that had eluded all other British ministers and administrations since

'Proud to be a Wrecker': Mary grabbed the media spotlight at the TUC congress held in Blackpool, on 11 September 2002, by sporting a t-shirt that turned the words of the Labour leadership, criticising the unions, back upon them.

1969.[75] It was against this background that GMB London Region and the Battersea and Wandsworth trades council came together with local councillors in Kells, in County Meath, to consider ways of honouring Jim Connell and his work. Councillor John O'Shea, the former mayor of Lewisham, expressed his hope at the time that, as there were 'currently approximately 70,000 Irish people in Lewisham, not to mention other areas of London', then 'with a common bond, new friendships will develop and old friendships will be strengthened over the years to come'.[76] Tommy Grimes was a leading light in the initiative that sought to bring together communities in London and Ireland. Tommy, known affectionately as 'Tommy the Commie', was a big personality who wore his heart on his sleeve. He had begun his career with the Irish Baker's Union, of which Mary's father had been a member, before sitting on the executive of SIPTU and representing the Irish Labour Party on the district council in Kells. As such, it was little wonder that he and Mary had much in common and got on like the proverbial 'house on fire'.

Paul Kenny, who had become London Region Secretary after John Cope's retirement in 1991, and Steve Pryle, the future GMB chief press officer, then representing the Battersea and Wandsworth trades council, travelled to Connell's birthplace on St Patrick's Day 1997, meeting with local politicians and community leaders, and attending a rally on the site of a burial ground from the famine years. Paul spoke to the crowds under the folds of the Irish tricolour and the red flag. It was there that the plan was agreed to raise a memorial to Jim Connell in Crossakiel at a crossroads where he had delivered his last speech in Ireland, addressing a meeting of the Ballinlough 'Back to the Land Committee', in 1919. Funds were raised and Michael Keane, a young Irish artist, was commissioned to produce a bronze portrait of Connell to be set amid the newly raised stones.

Mary travelled to Ireland for the unveiling on Sunday 26 April 1998. Before a crowd of over 1,000 people, she was joined on the platform by Tommy Grimes, Ruairi Quinn from the Irish Labour Party, Des Geraghty of SIPTU, and Sean O Shea, the former Labour mayor.[77] As the band struck up the first bars of *The Red Flag*, Mary slipped out of a heavy overcoat draped over her shoulders as a barrier to the winds that whipped down the valley to lead the chorus, snatching a red banner from the crowd and brandishing it over the monument with gusto. The march to the monument became the high point of the annual Jim Connell festival and Mary was a frequent attender during its early years. On one occasion after a public services conference in Belfast, she took a last minute decision to take a coach load of delegates along. After the march and the speeches had finished and Billy Bragg had packed away his guitar, Euton Stewart from the Hendon Branch went to follow the others into the local pub. However, the presence of a Black man was a rarity in County Meath. For a moment all went quiet and all eyes settled upon him, before Mary and Barbara appeared through a gap in the sea of bodies at the bar, hailed him and called him over. The ice was broken, conversations began again and before anyone knew it, Mary was making sure that everyone in the pub was introduced 'to my good friend'. The commemoration was meant to break down barriers and bring people together and, on this occasion, it certainly did succeed. Jim Connell, himself an immigrant to London, would wholeheartedly have approved. Mary had an easy way of disarming people and challenging their prejudices in a way that won them over – no harsh words, but with plenty of reason backed by a cheerful manner and a ready wit.[78] As with the drinkers at Crossakiel, people hardly noticed when they'd been converted.

Socialism or cultural amnesia? The choice of the unions under New Labour

The Red Flag had renewed significance in the 1990s, as the apparatchiks and spin doctors of New Labour had determined that its singing should be dropped from the close of the party's conferences. As with much in 'New' Labour, it was not an original idea. Ramsay Macdonald had also tried to ditch the song more than seventy years before, offering through the *Daily Herald* a prize of £50 (a very considerable sum in 1925) for a song to replace it at the heart of the labour movement. Though there were well over 200 submissions, none was held equal to Connell's original

work. Its emotive appeal was such that it came to hold a symbolic value for both sides of the argument during the Blair years. Connell had been well aware that, unlike the French or the Irish, British radicals lacked popular, spirited songs that spoke directly to the people, gave them heart and spread a progressive political message. In setting *The Red Flag* to the tune of a well-known Scottish jig, the Jacobite *White Cockade* as opposed to the better known *Tannenbaum*, he was appropriating both a jaunty melody, ideal for marching to, and an earlier tradition of rebellion, sedition and dissent. Will Thorne's union, the future GMB, was only a few months old when Connell had written the lyrics, one evening, during a fifteen minute commute between Charing Cross Station and his home in London's New Cross, just before Christmas 1889. 'It immediately became popular … [by] the following Sunday the song was sung in both Liverpool and Glasgow', noted Tommy Grimes.[79]

Unfortunately, New Labour demanded a cultural and historical 'year zero' when it came to the trade union movement. It had Brit pop jingles, purposefully wrapped

in the red, white and blue of nationalism, rather than internationalist red. *D-Ream* were on hand to provide the platitudes of 'Things Can Only Get Better'. By way of contrast, the appeal to solidarity that

well recalls the triumphs past.
… gives the hope of peace at last,
The banner bright, the symbol plain,
Of human right and human gain.

demanded active participation and jarred with the fiction of social partnership. Unsurprisingly, the use, or the abandonment, of the song became a battleground. Though the leadership managed to have it dropped from conference in 1999, Mary used her position in the NEC to generate an ultimately successful campaign to have it restored. When all of their certainties were being eroded through presentational spin, the party's natural supporters required an article of faith and *The Red Flag* fitted the bill. However, at the dawn of the new millennium, the GMB was facing existential crises on every side and certainly needed reminding not to haul its own banner down. ∎

SAVING THE UNION

Contested ground, 2003-2004

John Edmonds' decision in 2003 to retire early as general secretary marked a watershed in the union's affairs. It served to throw Mary's position, as president of the GMB, into sharper focus as a symbol of continuity and as the means of expressing the views and feelings of grassroots union members.

She had worked closely and loyally with John Edmonds. They had respected one another and Mary appreciated that he listened to her opinions and never attempted to ride roughshod over her position as the representative of the laity in the union's highest counsels. 'At no time ever', she told congress, 'did this man say to me, "Mary you must do that"'. The trust was fully reciprocated by the general secretary and, more importantly,

by those whom she had given her life to serve.[1] Mary was not one to play fast and loose in politics. She never broke a mandate from her union, and never forgot that the members came first at all times. She was there to provide them with a voice and to enable them to participate fully in the internal democracy of their own union. 'You are the union', she told GMB delegates, 'this is your congress and you make the decisions'.[2]

After the euphoria of the Labour victory, it had been a gruelling few years for her, personally and politically. Commitments from government, on areas like rights for part-time workers or for the provision of school meals, were continually watered down and any progress in workers' rights was incremental and hard won. At the same time, though it was not

◄ Mary with GMB members and congress delegates picketing the AA offices in Newcastle, June 2005. Breaking congress in order to show solidarity to 431 sacked workers, many of whom were disabled, represented a profound sea-change in the way that the union dealt with employers and stood-up for its members. The GMB would never look back.

▲ Mick Graham, the National Officer, sets out the union's agenda for public services at a break-out session at congress. John Edmonds, Dick Pickering and Mary Turner share the platform.

generally known, Mary had been suffering from cancer and had undergone a major operation in 2001 to remove a tumour. It took her out of action for several months. Indeed, she had postponed an original operation in order that she should not miss chairing that year's GMB congress and throughout carried on as 'a real working shop steward and branch secretary'. As Paul Kenny told union members: 'She gets the call at 6 o'clock in the morning, just like many of you do. I have been to visit her when someone from the branch has come and, thinking this is someone who has come to see her, she discovered that they wanted her to give them some advice or to represent them from the hospital bed'.[3] Mary still managed to make light of it all, downplaying the seriousness of the surgery and noting that 'I know a great deal about the Health Service now'. What had helped get her through, she said, were the cards and letters she had received 'from ordinary members of our union who I never met in my life. That gave me the strength … to get well'.[4] The road to recovery was far from straightforward and was further complicated by the ailing state of the union itself.

Expensive but unworkable IT packages, failed property deals, an increasingly unserviceable cycle of interest repayments, and the threat to the union's pension fund occasioned by the transfer of more than £2.5 million in order to fund an ambitious rebuilding programme of the central office in Wimbledon, combined to leave the GMB with a net deficit by 1997 of more than £5 million.[5] Moreover, the servicing ethos of the union seemed incapable of attracting new members, while the traditional range of benefits on offer were growing ever more expensive to deliver, adding to the union's growing list of financial woes.

Yet, between 25 and 30 per cent of membership loss was said to have been as a result of 'unhappiness' with the union and the fact that members 'have little or no contact from us'.[6] If were not bad enough, the growing accusations of the bullying of staff at head and regional offices made headlines and caused the morale of the GMB's own employees to plummet along with its public image. *Private Eye* predicted that 'the days of the GMB appear to be numbered' as the union 'suffers from a poverty of ideas, as well as cash … with the most likely outcome being takeover

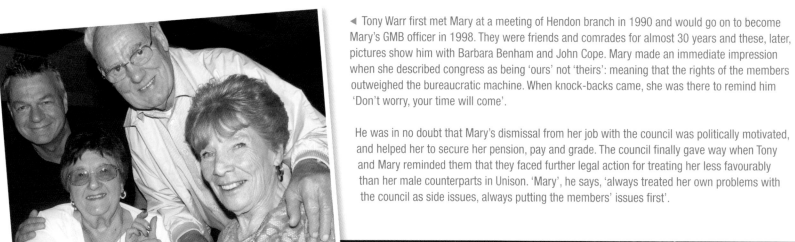

◄ Tony Warr first met Mary at a meeting of Hendon branch in 1990 and would go on to become Mary's GMB officer in 1998. They were friends and comrades for almost 30 years and these, later, pictures show him with Barbara Benham and John Cope. Mary made an immediate impression when she described congress as being 'ours' not 'theirs': meaning that the rights of the members outweighed the bureaucratic machine. When knock-backs came, she was there to remind him 'Don't worry, your time will come'.

He was in no doubt that Mary's dismissal from her job with the council was politically motivated, and helped her to secure her pension, pay and grade. The council finally gave way when Tony and Mary reminded them that they faced further legal action for treating her less favourably than her male counterparts in Unison. 'Mary', he says, 'always treated her own problems with the council as side issues, always putting the members' issues first'.

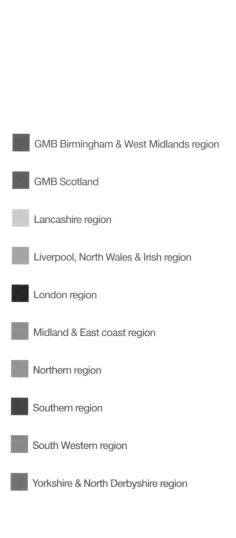

GMB Birmingham & West Midlands region

GMB Scotland

Lancashire region

Liverpool, North Wales & Irish region

London region

Midland & East coast region

Northern region

Southern region

South Western region

Yorkshire & North Derbyshire region

◄ The ten GMB Regions at the turn of the millennium.

by another union, such as the T&G'.[7]

In such circumstances, it was hardly surprising that the election for the post of general secretary was hard fought. The overt political content was remarkably subdued, with largely ad hoc organisations gathering around both candidates. These were based upon regional differences and personal powerbases as opposed to the more common broad left or right-wing alliances that dominated the electoral process in other unions.[8] Paul Kenny stood on an organising agenda and on his record in London where the region had grown under his stewardship from 67,000 members in 1999 to 83,000 members in 2003.[9] His rival, Kevin Curran, the Northern Region secretary, gained the approval of Polly Toynbee in *The Guardian* as a representative of the 'sensible left' and was thought to be closely allied to Gordon Brown. As the candidate closest to the former leadership, he was expected to continue both John Edmonds' arms-distance relationship with New Labour and his approach towards servicing the membership.[10] In the event, Paul Kenny gained far more nominations from the branches in the run-up to the election and

appeared to have greater support in the regions, but the result declared in April 2003 seemed to show that the contest was far less close than had been thought. Curran took 60,590 votes to Kenny's 32,954. Some activists scratched their heads and some complained that the electoral addresses had not been uniformly presented, with Curran's professionally typeset while Kenny's was cribbed and cramped on the page. The margin, though, seemed conclusive and John Edmonds handed over to Curran at the GMB Congress held that June, with the strangely prophetic comment that the union carried with it 'a health warning. Kevin, I should warn you that the job of general secretary is like no other. Stage by stage, inch by inch, you become public property'.[11] Some in the Winter Gardens at Blackpool might have been forgiven for thinking that he was handing over a poison chalice rather than the keys to the office.

Equally disconcerting was Curran's somewhat flat and awkward acceptance speech. 'I need in particular with you', he began,

'to do the following things: Get to work on our finances, get to work and

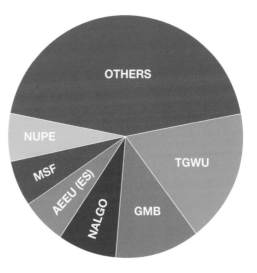

◄ The GMB delegation to the Labour Party Conference, September 1995: John Edmonds, Dick Pickering, Allan Wylie (on the second row) and Mary Turner, applaud the leader's speech. Optimism was in the air. The Tory Party was tearing itself apart over Europe and Labour was poised to make a return to power in the name of the many, rather than the few.

have a good look at ourselves, get to work helping this union grow and organise, get to work ... ensuring that we are democratic, transparent and open, get to work on giving you and our members the union you all deserve, get to work on making this union a union for the twenty-first century'.[12]

That process of reflection suddenly became withering criticism, when, just weeks after taking office as general secretary, Curran received a letter from the GMB's bank, the Unity and Co-operative, which, it was subsequently claimed and leaked to the press, 'set out in no uncertain terms the case for a financial meltdown at GMB based on [a] lack of financial control and unrealistic planning'.[13] It was this spectre, warning of a complete collapse into insolvency, which was used by the new leadership in order to justify all of the expedients that followed.

Not so expert, expert advice

Outside consultants, including Gerry Toner of Aspire HBSD Ltd., were brought in at considerable expense to provide the union with a 'health check' and to suggest ways through its financial and administrative impasse. Circulated in March 2004, Gerry Toner's report can reasonably be thought to have been written in order to frighten members of the CEC with its forecasts of doom. It was particularly disingenuous towards the administrative and managerial record of John Edmonds who, after all, had preferred the more polished courtier Curran to the rough diamond that was Kenny, and had forwarded his career accordingly. Even when safely ensconced in power, it is never a good idea to bite at the hand that once fed you.

The report gave an unvarnished view: 'The GMB has slipped from a position as one of the big four unions in terms of membership, income and assets. The income level is steady, the membership declining slowly and the assets have been depleted dramatically by short-sighted and weak management'.[14] The performance and vision displayed by Amicus and the T&G were praised, to the detriment of with the GMB as it has failed to control expenditure in an increasingly diverse and uncoordinated structure'.

More damning still was the conclusion that

'the GMB is a classic example of ... a decaying organisation with structures that have failed to maintain the health of its finances or the strategic direction of the union ... The main executive body, the CEC, is unrepresentative of the members as they are, or of any future membership. The congress is not representative of the membership as it has a large returning cohort of the same faces and names. Sub-committees of the CEC are peopled by the same faces year after year'.

▲ Mary's natural ground: the congress hall in Blackpool, June 1994.

the GMB, and it was significant that the desirability of a merger strategy was prominently noted:

'All of the major unions have adopted a "merger", i.e. takeover, strategy mopping up the mainly smaller and medium sized unions. In the main, these mergers have been amicable and then the parent has enforced disciplines on the newly acquired sibling. Again, this has not been the case

The recommendations of the report included the rewriting of the union's rule book, a reduction in the number of the regions, greater centralisation of control and a fundamental overhaul of congress. It was a case of attempting to achieve political ends through administrative means. This became crystal clear when the consultancy report highlighted the point that 'a major

'Mary can see you!': A familiar sight for GMB congress delegates over the years as the union's president looks for a show of hands in the hall. ▶

weakness in the union's structure is the mixing of the democratic process with the management of resources'.[15] This, in effect, was suggesting that the majority of the union's ills came from the ability of elected lay representatives, that is the president, CEC and congress delegates, to have oversight of the union's affairs. By removing democracy from the union, the managerial apparatus of the union would be able to run the organisation more 'efficiently', for its own ends and untroubled by the scrutiny of the union's own members. In short, the failure of the GMB, in the 1990s, was put down to an inability of departmental heads to overrule the decisions of regional secretaries, councils and congress. All that was needed was the provision of greater bureaucratic powers and 'better information to be effective managers'.[16] 'The effectiveness of Congress is in doubt', declared the report's findings, 'if it is ultimately responsible for decisions to protect the union's assets and take the union forward. In each of these cases it has failed absolutely. It is taboo to make such statements publicly for fear of retribution as the culture of the congress and its delegated bodies is dominated by overly dramatic responses to protocol in substitution for sound management and policy making'.[17] The answer being touted was that congress should be shorn of much of its power and become a virtual 'rubber' stamp for the union's administration as it could not be trusted to take informed decisions and to safeguard the union's finances.

The threat to congress and to union democracy

Congress had already been scaled back to a biennial meeting and was increasingly being seen by the union's senior management as an expensive luxury that the GMB could well do without. The move was not new. John Edmonds had argued, in the early 1990s, that, as the 'GMB had stable values and enduring policies – the purpose of congress should not be to dig up the branches every year, shake them and replant them'.[18] Sectional conferences could assume some of its functions, as, according to one CEC member, activists felt more affinity with them and they were 'closer to issues they personally relate to'. Congress,

itself, he said, was 'a monolithic structure with a narrow base'.[19] For Mary, however, the congress would always remain the supreme governing body of the union and the essence of its democracy and sense of political legitimacy. Without the input of the laity, who paid their subscriptions and for which the union existed, everything else was pointless. The removal of the annual congress ensured that the discussions and decisions around documents like the Toner report, or the continued existence of the GMB itself, could take place without being debated on the floor of congress. It was possible that a merger deal with Amicus and the T&G might be put before the next congress, scheduled for 2005, as a fait accompli. This made more urgent the need for Mary and the CEC to voice the concerns of the membership in discussions with the union's leadership. However, the location of authority within the union was becoming more opaque by the minute.

Two parallel bodies were created to discuss the projected changes to the union and any merger. The first was a 'Task Group', led by Kevin Curran as general secretary, and included Debbie Coulter, the new deputy general secretary, Mary

Turner, as president, and Malcolm Sage, the newly elected vice-president. As such it balanced the interests of lay and official membership, and contained those who had a democratic mandate, as all had been elected by GMB members. However, this was accompanied by the creation of a second body, the grandly, if somewhat nebulously, named Commission 2004, which consisted of fourteen members all hand-picked by the general secretary. Not all were GMB members. Some represented outside consultancies, brought in on the pretext of their expertise. Everything was up for discussion and liable to change. A fresh review of finances urged a restructure. It was tasked with identifying 'unproductive areas of expenditure' and seems to have envisaged further cutbacks in staff numbers and a major retrenchment. The sale of the head office was suggested, together with a plan to hire space in central London from another union. Employees worried about their jobs. Already suffering from low morale amid the much-reported climate of bullying, they looked at the projections for the move and realised that only a handful of desks for a 'secretariat' were required. It didn't take them long to figure out that the functions of the national office were going to be stripped out, prior to a merger, through massive job cuts. Seasoned activists criticised the proposals on different grounds, realising that once the national office went and the GMB was sharing desks, as the client and paying guest of another union, its identity would quickly evaporate. Rather like the story about the lobster being quietly lulled to sleep by the slow ratcheting up of temperature in the cooking pot, the GMB was in danger of being boiled alive without ever realising it or putting up a struggle.[20]

Self-inflicted wounds

The stated object was to 'balance the budget' in 2004, which would have required a saving of some £5 million. This could only be accomplished through voluntary early retirement, the sale or closure of the union's national college in Manchester, the sale of the Wimbledon office and the reduction of staff at national office to a rump. Something in the region of 110 to 150 job losses were projected across the regions.[21] The cutbacks were put before the CEC when it met on 28 October 2003, and encountered fierce opposition not least

from Mary, supported by Malcolm Sage. Mary always made it her habit, whenever arriving for a union meeting, to be early and to spend time talking to everyone from the cleaners, secretaries and staff to the officers and regional secretaries. She therefore knew well in advance of the plummeting morale among full-timers, of the plans and of the bitter opposition to the manoeuvres. As a consequence, she led the CEC in blocking the proposals for redundancies. The new general secretary had been 'turned over' by his own executive in his first full meeting and, blaming Mary for the defeat, determined neither to forgive nor forget. The battle lines were well and truly drawn. Henceforth, the circle of advisors around the general secretary would view her every utterance with suspicion. She was an obstacle to their plans, one they thought should be removed as quickly and as quietly as possible. As their campaign developed over the successive months, it was characterised by a dismissal of Mary as '*only* a dinner lady' and by a sneering contempt for her background and lack of formal education. On more than one occasion, it would bring the normally mild mannered, invariably courteous, John Cope

to a state of fury in her defence.[22] However, it was indicative of wider changes within the labour movement under New Labour, whereby young, ambitious and invariably black-suited graduates, fresh from PPE courses, flooded into officer and policy roles as a means of personal advancement. A decade earlier and they would have been Conservatives, but as New Labour now appeared as the 'natural' party of government, it seemed like the perfect vehicle for many who simply sought a career in politics. The abler ones found safe seats under Blair, the less able or less well-connected, looked to the trade unions and the TUC, often without particularly understanding what a union was or how it functioned. As Mary once observed, it was a case of 'New lamps for old'. But it did serve to foster an attitude bordering on contempt for lay members and their representatives. It certainly blinded Mary's critics within the union to her ability and to the deep wellsprings of support that she enjoyed amongst the actual membership. Like so many others down the years, her opponents underestimated her to their own cost.

The blistering defeat by the CEC had

convinced Curran that that body needed, wherever possible, to be sidelined or circumvented. A number of advisory committees were established, creating multiple centres of power and influence within the union. Policies could then be formulated and decisions taken without ever coming before the congress or the CEC. This offered the prospect of centralising power in the hands of the general secretary, without recourse to the regions. The price was the destruction of internal democracy and accountability to the members. Rapidly, the pre-meetings held by these advisory bodies began to impinge upon the time allotted for CEC meetings and caused the deliberations of lay members to be pushed further back, or off the agenda entirely. This was judged necessary if the ambitious plans to merge the GMB with Amicus and the T&G were to move forward smoothly and speedily.

The plans for the new super-union promised a great deal. In theory, it would have over 2.5 million members with 80 per cent of them concentrated in the private sector and with combined assets approaching £200 million. Politically, it offered the prospect of a parliamentary group of 300 Labour MPs and it would be by far the largest affiliate to both the party and the TUC. Industrially, the consultation documents envisaged an investment of 10 per cent of its membership income, estimated at some £20 million each year, into organising and recruitment campaigns. On paper, this seemed highly appealing. Had it been simply a matter of an amalgamation between the GMB and the T&G, it seems likely that a merger deal could have been quickly forced

Mary Turner and Kevin Curran leading the GMB delegation in voting at the TUC congress, 14 September 2004.

through. The two unions represented a predominantly blue-collar membership, often already rooted in the same sectors and individual workplaces, and had very similar rulebooks. Having explored such a merger a decade before, it did not appear as a 'bolt from the blue' or as a major shock to the system. However, the third prospective partner, Amicus, represented a very different proposition. It possessed a markedly different industrial culture, angled specifically towards skilled workers and professionals, and had a track record for ruthless acquisition policies. As a consequence, the GMB's negotiating team were far more wary of their opposite numbers in Amicus than those in the T&G delegation. Moreover, while those two unions had no financial imperative driving them towards a merger strategy and were motivated largely by shared political and industrial intent, the GMB was being pushed to the negotiating table by the worsening state of its finances and by falling membership rolls. Worse still, Amicus and the T&G knew it. This led to the sense among the CEC delegates that the other two unions were setting the tempo of change and were operating on

the basis that the smaller union, the GMB, had nowhere else to go and no other option than to acquiesce in whatever was offered. There was a fear, articulated on the CEC by Mary, that Amicus and the T&G were simply seeking to grow their base through the acquisition of the GMB, which risked being rapidly assimilated and forgotten within

▲ Establishing the line: Tony Woodley, the general secretary of the T&G, puts his point across to Kevin Curran during the debate on the Iraq War at the Labour Party Conference on 30 September 2004. It was never in any doubt that when the unions merged the T&G section would have the upper hand.

the structures of the new body, Unite. An awful lot was being taken for granted and on the basis of trust. Kevin Curran could expect to become a joint general secretary, alongside Derek Simpson and Tony Woodley. It was believed at the time that he harboured hopes for a political career under the patronage of Gordon Brown. But what would become of the GMB after the existing unions were formally merged in 2010? No one could see a candidate from the junior partner challenging for the leadership. The best that could be hoped for was that the GMB might strengthen the T&G's hand in any tussle with Amicus. Most likely, it would have simply flickered out after a few years, disappearing from the industrial landscape while a handful of its senior leadership remained within the newly created behemoth.

◄ Cutting the ribbon on a new bicycle that was one of the GMB's gifts to a special school in Blackpool, 17 June 2009. Mary and the GMB firmly understood that they were part of the wider community and that, after all, there really was such a thing as society.

Crisis and catharsis, 2004-2005

It is never a good idea to negotiate from a position of weakness but this was exactly what the GMB was doing in 2004. The organisation seemed starved of ideas, bereft of any will for self-preservation, and stripped of the power to act in the interests of its own members. This was emphasised that winter, when workers at Asda's distribution centre in Washington, Tyne and Wear, dramatically voted against recognition of the GMB. The company, backed by its new parent corporation Walmart, had launched a hard-hitting public relations campaign against what it claimed were the excesses of GMB officials, in particular, the behaviour of Robert Parker, the Scottish regional secretary, and of Nick Anderson, the former Northern regional secretary, who had departed under a cloud several years earlier.[23] The result of the ballot in Curran's own region, with workers effectively rejecting the union, was a terrible humiliation, especially in what had once been the GMB's stronghold of the north-east. It was what came when you did not put your own house in order. More trouble was simmering, threatening

to boil over, as the first industrial tribunals regarding claims of the harassment and bullying of women staff came to be heard. Two very able and courageous GMB women, Maxine Nixon and Giovanna Holt, had been subjected to appalling levels of intimidation at the hands of the Lancashire Region secretary. The union's own legal team reported to Kevin Curran that the evidence was so damning, so overwhelmingly in favour of the women, that there was no hope that any kind of defence could be mounted. Rumour and counter-rumour flourished, but it seems clear that some of those implicated in the Lancashire Region felt that they were about to be 'cut loose' and betrayed by Curran after they had, in their eyes, delivered the election for him in return for a promise that the bullying and harassment charges would be 'made to go away'. In an attempt to deflect attention from the tribunals and as an act of revenge, a dossier alleging all manner of irregularities was sent to Mary Turner, as the union's president, in advance of the meeting of the CEC in October 2004. Suddenly the whole rotten house of cards began to tumble.

It is conceivable that nothing might have

◀ Fighting Back: Paul Kenny declares the strike by 900 workers at the Lindsey Oil Refinery to have the union's official backing, at a mass meeting at Killingholme, 23 June 2009. Rachelle Wilkins is on the left of the picture, while Bob Grimley and Les Dobbs carry one of the union's historic banners. The atmosphere that day was electric. The dispute centred around the undercutting of wages and conditions by subcontractors and was not helped by Gordon Brown's comments about 'British jobs for British workers'. It was fortunate that the GMB was there to hold the line against attempts by the far right to hi-jack the dispute for its own ends. In particular, Phil Whitehurst, one of the GMB stewards, was instrumental in halting the spread of BNP propaganda and preventing gate rushes.

been done about the allegations. After all, their source was not a particularly pleasant or edifying one and in an atmosphere reminiscent, as one GMB officer put it, of 'the end scene in *Reservoir Dogs* when everyone is pointing guns at everyone else and blasting away', it might have not been thought expedient to bring the union further into disrepute.[24] That would certainly have been the easy way out. The GMB had become Mary's life. She had faithfully carried out mandates from general secretaries, at the Labour NEC and the TUC Congress, even when she did not necessarily believe in them. It was part of a sense of collective responsibility and out of respect for the union's wider democratic processes. However, this was something entirely different. The allegations pointed to wholesale electoral fraud in the course of the 2003 election on behalf of Kevin Curran's campaign, with ballot papers collected en masse, often being returned in the names of lapsed or deceased members, and with evidence

of external funding for the campaign, including from employers. Mary felt that it was her duty that, come what may, she should put the materials before the union's lay representatives at the CEC. As the documents 'came from the barristers and QCs dealing with a case on behalf of the GMB and others', Mary needed time to 'take it all in' and considered that she 'had to allow those who were being accused to reply to those allegations as I believed that was only fair'.[25] She would put a recommendation to the executive at the December meeting that an independent inquiry should be established. The CEC could then decide how to best proceed. 'From that moment', she said, 'my life became hell'.[26] The memory was still raw when we discussed the case six years later. There was no light-hearted aside this time, no jokes or funny stories recalled in order to get through the dark times. This was a matter of a fierce fight to the finish, with no holds barred on the part of the general secretary and his supporters

in their attempt to bring Mary down. Her eyes, which were her most striking feature, ever lively and expressive, flickered, shot through with the pain of the memory of those days, but also with a steely resolve, a resolve that was born out of the sense that she was right and that she had done that which she had known to be right. No, there were absolutely no regrets.

'I had months of harassment and interference in the process of establishing the inquiry', she remembered, 'and bullying to the point that I put it in writing that it had to stop, but it did not'.[27] Every conceivable pressure was brought to bear upon her from the supporters of the leadership. Threats and slander when cajolement and flattering failed. They went through her branch accounts, a favourite trick used by Tom Williamson and David Basnett to destroy many a troublesome or left-wing chair. Many branches, understaffed and overworked, very often with treasurers who were not particularly adept with figures, were known to be sloppy with their bookkeeping. As ever, Mary's branch books came back with a clean bill of health. When that didn't work, a whispering campaign began. IT was never Mary's strong point and she never used email if she could possibly avoid it, preferring the phone call and face-to-face contacts with members. In 2004, it was hard to think of her switching on a computer, logging onto a website, or searching the internet. But word got back to her that there was a website and an email strand that was making all kinds of allegations about her conduct and that of her husband, Denny. 'Maybe the worst part for me', Mary said, 'was that my family witnessed what was happening' and that her husband, who had only ever been quietly supportive of his wife's beliefs and endeavours, was now being dragged into a battle that was not of his own making.[28] Some people may think that others will behave, or react to events, in exactly the same way as they do themselves. Some in the general secretary's camp expected others to possess the same flaws as they did. Mud, after all, sticks and by throwing enough of it they might put doubt into the minds of some CEC members. On a more visceral level, they calculated on Mary's age as she was past retirement, the invasiveness of her cancer, and Denny's own ill health. As they kept

telling themselves and others, she was just a dinner lady, and far from their social or intellectual equal. They could out-think and outfight her and, if that took too long, they might grind her down, breaking her resolve together with her health.

Mary asked herself whether this was all there was. She had given her life to the union and operated on a set of assumptions and values that were now being challenged and shaken to their core. This was no longer about fighting the enemy, organising and recruiting members, improving lives; it was about turning in on oneself, being smeared by those whom, while you might have disagreed with them, were supposed to believe in the very things that you did. Except that it was now obvious they did not. She was clear, in her own mind, about what needed to be done and confident in her resolve to put everything before the executive. It was for the union to decide. But the union was not the bureaucracy, the

paid servants, careerists and time-servers too used to expense accounts and their comforts. It was the membership, who faithfully paid their dues, did what were often hard and unpleasant jobs for low pay, were treated badly by managements, and risked what little they had when they stood up for what was right in the workplace. Paying their subs was an act of faith and trust, it meant that money that could have been used for a night out or to buy a child a toy, was going to the union in the hope that it would, ultimately, make life better for them all. Mary understood this because she knew them and was one of them. Though the union had provided her with enormous opportunities to travel, to learn, to walk among politicians and heads of state, it had never altered her essence: she was still the dinner lady from Brent, who had started down this road because she had sought to feed the kids in her school properly, and who had wanted young people to have

'I had months of harassment and interference in the process of establishing the inquiry, and bullying to the point that I had to put it in writing that it had to stop, but it did not'

Throughout all the difficulties of 2004-05, as the union fought for its dignity and survival. Mary was fortunate in having the loyal and able support of the GMB's vice-president, Malcolm Sage. She thought the world of him and he remembers her as 'one wonderful lady'. They are pictured together, here, at Plymouth, 8 June 2008. Martin Smith and Phil Davies stand behind them. ▶

jobs. It was because she was 'just' a dinner lady that she did what she did. There would be no shameful compromises, no deals done in corridors to make uncomfortable things and people simply go away. It would all be put out into the open and the members could decide. She had faith in them.

The December meeting of the CEC was held at the National Union of Teachers headquarters in King's Cross and was, as could be expected, highly charged. On the platform, Curran rounded upon Mary and berated her in front of the delegates. What was happening was tearing her union apart and, with it, her very essence. Her slight shoulders rounded, as the baying volume from the general secretary grew louder in her ears, drowning out the murmurs from the CEC and, unbidden, tears came and her whole frame shook. The members of the CEC, so long derided, sidelined and taken for granted, took notice too. For some of them, the arguments to begin with had seemed too legal, too complex, and procedural. They were there as unpaid volunteers who gave their time, energy and industry to the union in order to get things done. It was often a frankly boring and thankless task. But now everything came into stark focus. They noticed Mary's obvious distress, they noted the demeanour of the general secretary. A dull rumble rose from the floor and grew into a thunder of disapproval. Malcolm Sage was there for Mary, at her side as vice-president. A vote was taken to launch a legal inquiry to examine 'serious allegations of breaches of the union's rules … in the 2003 election'. One regional secretary left his seat and ran down the aisle waving his order paper and shouting that the CEC 'couldn't do that!' But no one paid attention. The deputy general secretary, Debbie Coulter, who was not subject to the allegations at hand, looked down upon a fixed point upon the floor and said nothing at all. Curran swept from the hall, 'never' as one of the CEC delegates who was present recalls, 'to return'.[29]

The investigation was led by Phil King, a senior partner of Thompsons Solicitors. Officers, staff and lay members who had volunteered statements were interviewed.

The work of an initial inquiry led by John Hand QC was then merged with two internal reviews.[30] Matters had been complicated by the general secretary's attempts to interfere with the course of the investigations. He even argued that, as he was also the treasurer of the GMB, he should see the QC's initial findings before signing off any cheques, even though he was the one being investigated. A letter was published by the *Independent* which was thought to have been sent by him to the QC's clerk, stating that the general secretary was 'the only person in the union authorised to conduct the correspondence of the union and to incur legal costs in matters such as this'.[31] It was left to Malcolm Sage to give what was probably the most succinct account of what transpired next. 'There was no power struggle in the CEC. The things that happened actually happened through Kevin and the friends of Kevin. We received allegations. The allegations were then examined. Unfortunately, Kevin kept interfering with those investigations after being told on several occasions by the CEC [not to interfere]. However, he wouldn't listen'.[32] As a consequence, the

CEC issued a warning for him to 'cease and desist' and demanded an apology. None was forthcoming and when he turned down the offer of taking leave, he was suspended from office on full pay until the inquiry returned its findings. Debbie Coulter, the deputy general secretary, agreed to step in to cover his duties, despite a threat of an injunction from Curran's lawyers. In a game of brinkmanship, it was Curran who backed down, opting to resign and to take early retirement rather than to wait for the findings of the inquiry to be made public.[33] It was probably just as well that he did, for the report's conclusions were damning. It found that there was a 'breach of the union's rules and by-laws' in four specific areas: in the wrongful publication and distribution of election material; in the establishment of a website; the possession of a Post Office box number to and from which ballot papers flowed; and that 'there is clear evidence that one candidate (Kevin Curran) had financial and other support from external organisations'.[34] These latter, as Mary pointed out, included donations from 'employers and suppliers'. She added that 'if there is one cardinal sin that no shop steward or representative of this union should never permit it is to be in the pockets of the employers'.[35] 'Never, never again', she said, 'do we want to see people at a senior level trying to bring this union into disrepute, people who are more interested in their own self-advancement than our members' interests. People who aspire to high office should do so for the advancement of their members' interests, not their own. That has to be our bible from now into the future … Let me remind them and others … this union is not for sale to employers or anyone else. It is our union!'[36]

'We can hold our heads up high and say we are the GMB'

'To say that the last year has been traumatic would be an understatement', Mary told union members, and it 'would be true to say that the last two years have tested not only me but also the vice president and the CEC as a whole'.[37] There was one last piece of unpleasantness, as another flurry of 'poisoned pen' letters were circulated among delegates before the start of the GMB's congress in June 2005. However, they were to be dealt with very publicly. Paul Kenny, who, as

the most senior regional secretary and the candidate denied office through the flawed election, had been appointed as acting general secretary, read out the contents of the anonymous letters to the delegates, on the first morning of congress, together with his reply forwarded to the government's Certification Officer asking for them to be investigated forthwith and pledging the GMB's 'full co-operation'.[38] With a flourish, the envelope was sealed on stage, ready for despatch. The union would no longer fight itself in the shadows but would conduct its business in the full light of day, where it had nothing to fear. Delegates who might have been crushed by the wrangles, the uncertainties brought about by legal actions and the threat of merger, seemed curiously to take heart, to regain their confidence and their pride in the GMB as the congress wore on. The grassroots wanted no more truck with talk about forced mergers. 'We are the bloody GMB for Christ's sake!' called out Dougie Henry from Liverpool, North Wales and Irish Region, 'We are the union of the future!'[39] Andy Worth, from Midlands and East Coast, took up the sentiment that, provided the union adopted new organising

principles, 'the GMB has no need to merge and can remain independent'.[40] Sheila Bearcroft led a vote of thanks to 'our Mary', coining the phrase, and speaking for many when she commended her as one for whom 'The union comes first!'.[41] Congress had been pulled together at very short notice, not least through the efforts of Steve Pryle, who had secured and fitted out the venue in the Newcastle Arena in a matter of days. In a break with strict protocol, business was adjourned so the delegates could join members in picketing an AA call centre where management had just announced plans to cut 431 jobs and sack a large number of disabled staff. It was the first shot across the bows of employers, and hedge funding companies in particular, showing that the GMB was prepared to tackle them head-on. There would be no more sweetheart deals, money from business, or recourse to amalgamation and expensive consultancy reports. 'This is a great union', Mary told the members before they headed off to join the picket line. 'We can hold our heads up high and say: "We are the GMB, the true GMB!"'[42] For her, the union was now here to stay. ■

Synchronicity: Mary and Paul at congress, Brighton, 5 June 2011.

THE YEARS OF ACHIEVEMENT

The GMB@Work 2005-2015

It is often much easier to say what you are against than to say what you stand for. The dramatic fall of a general secretary, financial crisis and the predatory circling of two bigger unions necessitated a painfully honest assessment of the scale of the challenge confronting the GMB, if it was ever going to survive as an independent entity. As Mary said at the time, the 'union ran out of money and we were forced to think'.[1] If a merger was not what the vast majority of the membership wanted, and that certainly seemed to be the message from the floor of congress in 2005, then the GMB would have to set its own house in order, attempt to balance the books, and look at new methods of working and recruiting.

Steve Pryle, the union's giftedly mercurial press officer, liked to talk about 'fighting on all fronts, at all times'. This was certainly the case in 2005-06. The union was fighting for its survival. The success of congress in 2005, thanks in no small measure to Mary's authority, following and deft handling of procedure, had bought the GMB time. Curran's supporters were largely relegated to the sidelines, sniping in the press but having little sway in either the regions or at the centre, and no organic base within the membership. The union's new leadership could turn its attention to stamping out, once and for all, 'the bullying, gerrymandering, the seedy deals and, yes, even some corrupt practices that had gone down in previous regimes'.[2] By throwing Curran to the wolves, some of the guilty in Lancashire Region might have hoped to have saved themselves. However, the old ways of doing business were at an end. The judgment of the tribunal on the cases of discrimination ran to more than forty pages of findings and found senior figures in the region guilty on thirty counts against women officers and lay members. It was a damning indictment and quite the worst evidence of bullying and malpractice to be seen anywhere, not just in a trade union.

The banner ceremony marks the opening of every GMB congress, marking a moment when the union's past connects with its present, as the emblems of more than a century of struggle are paraded into the hall to the strains of William Blake's Jerusalem. Here, Mary Turner and Paul Kenny welcome the national banner onto the stage, Plymouth, 2 June 2013. ▶

▲ The presidium thanks the floor speakers. Mary Turner, Malcolm Sage and Kathleen Walker Shaw. Southport, 6 June 2010.

Indeed, the rot was so systemic that the view was taken that 'the whole region would have to go'. The report sent over to Mary put the view that 'it may lead us into some very serious stuff' if they were to act decisively to tackle the problem and sweep away what had been, since the days of J. R. Clynes and Charles Dukes, the regional powerhouse of the union. There was hardly a flicker of doubt: the union would have to clean itself up, whatever the cost. Now that they had begun, the process could not be halted and there could be no way back 'to the bad old days'. Mary, having seen the evidence, was '100 per cent behind' the decision to dismantle the region. After months of investigation, there was just a four-day discussion of the practicalities in Blackpool immediately prior to the 2006 congress, before the deed was done.[3] The region was split, with its Lancashire heartland being incorporated within what would become a new North West and Irish Region under Paul McCarthy, and its membership in Cumbria, heavily concentrated in the nuclear industry at Sellafield, was joined to Northern Region under Billy Coates. The lightning speed and the openness with which the affair was settled took the breath away, sent others scurrying for cover, and sent out a stark message that an institutional climate where discrimination and bullying were commonplace was now at an end. It also established that Mary, as president, and Paul Kenny, as general secretary, were a formidable partnership who

GMB
FOUNDED 1889
JARROW
HEALTH WORKERS
APEX
GMB working together GMB
GMB

meant every word that they said.

For the moment, the door was not entirely closed on the merger talks. The GMB needed time and, if there was a feeling that it had previously been railroaded in negotiations by Amicus and the T&G, there was now the dawning sense that it was the smaller of the prospective partners that was leading the others in a merry dance. As late as January 2006, the Amicus executive was still keen to press ahead with the planned merger and hopeful that the 'GMB will come on board with the merger'.[4] However, the GMB congress in June 2006 skilfully merged the issue of the adoption of an organising agenda with the calls to reject amalgamation. It became a case of 'either – or' and the union opted for independence and survival.[5] This was certainly assisted by the knowledge that the financial imperative that had driven the GMB to the table was lessening, month by month.[6] This was not just a matter of the freedom now afforded to the director of finance, Allan Wylie, to ensure fiscal prudence within the organisation. It was also the result of the rebuilding of the organisation from the ground floor

upwards. If the union was going to think about rejecting merger as a path, then it had to have something to put in its place. There was the recognition that:

'Our union … needs to adopt a radically different strategy on recruitment and organisation to grow and prosper. Membership growth must become the measure of every aspect of our work and we must re-build the link between recruitment, representing and retaining new members'.[7]

This fresh organising strategy, which had some of its roots in the long term work begun in London Region during the days of John Cope and continued under Paul Kenny's team, would eventually come to be known as *GMB@Work*, striving towards building the union as an 'Effective, active and strong workplace organisation, led and sustained by GMB Reps'.[8] This necessitated a very different approach from the top-down, excessively regimented structure that had existed hitherto within the union. It required trusting the members and empowering them to act as the union's motor for growth. First of all, though, they had to

be taken into the union's confidence and asked what it was that they, themselves, wanted to see happen on the ground. The consultation, undertaken in 2005-06 while all else was going on, found that members felt that the GMB

'should stop chasing rainbows, the endless search for the easy top-down bureaucratic or political solution to membership decline. We came to understand that partnership organising had failed us and confused our members over what the union stood for, and that government funded schemes like Union Learning could never deliver growth. Critically, we rejected merger as an unnecessary distraction that would only compound the complacency within the union and further obscure the scale of the membership challenge we faced in GMB organised workplaces'.[9]

Within those findings was a wider political critique that rejected almost the entire set of assumptions that had often been used to underpin ideas about the survival and continued development of the unions during the 1990s. The acceptance of partnership with employers (the lamb lying down with the lion) was the industrial reflection of New Labour's strategy of triangulation: a cosy fiction – to the benefit of the CBI but not necessarily of union members – that there was a commonality of interest between those who owned property and wielded the power of capital and those who sold their labour in the market place. Merger strategies mirrored the takeover practices of business, achieving economies of scale, usually though the sale of properties, the consolidation of assets and staff losses. They masked overall declines in membership, often creating phantom armies of members who existed only on the paper returned to the certification officer, but did nothing to address the actual causes of that decline. Lastly, the government's Union Learn programme injected vast amounts of public money into the TUC, helping to re-orientate the organisation towards training and skills and bolster the flagging further education sector. However, critics, not least of which was the GMB after 2005, suggested that New Labour's largesse was also a means of ensuring that the TUC was compliant. Shifting responsibility for reskilling workers onto the shoulders of the unions also allowed employers to dodge another one of their own responsibilities to let them pursue the maximum accumulation of profit.

By way of contrast, the GMB set out its belief that 'The main cause of our current decline is internal not external' and that the fundamental purpose of the GMB was 'not to manage decline' but to focus upon workplace organisation as a means to rebuild the union's membership.[10] This could only be achieved through a process of self-organisation. The GMB began by taking control of the training of its new and existing 'workplace organisers' and ended its reliance on outside organisations. From 2005, GMB training was delivered by GMB officers and workplace organisers using core course materials written and produced by the GMB, itself. It was now proposed that, as an article of faith,

'The GMB must always have a "claim on the table" ... Instead of waiting for management to propose changes and then responding, the GMB should have its own agenda and keep every employer on the back foot, responding to our members' demands ... Everyone at work should see

> **Long gone are the days when recruitment could be delegated to someone else. It's everyone's job and the future and size of the GMB is down to us, and us alone**

the GMB *as being a part of the workplace, and in it for the long term. We should replace short term "recruitment drives" with members regularly talking to non-members about what the union is doing. Not to sell the union – but to explain where we stand on issues where they work, why they should join and what they can do to support us'.*[11]

Furthermore, as Martin Smith, the National Organiser, told the GMB Congress, in June 2006: 'We need to build the union in every workplace not sell it on the high street. Because when we try to compete with the Prudential Insurance Company we start to look and sound like the Prudential Insurance Company more than the GMB'.[12] The maxim, now included in every workplace organiser's 'tool kit' and inside the cover of every GMB diary, was that: 'The employer has different interests than GMB members'. It was a simple message and a truth that should have appeared self-evident to every thinking trade unionist and labour movement activist. It succinctly drove a nail through the coffin of any cosy partnership agreements with employers, put an end to the notion that

you could separate the recruitment and servicing of members, with some officers building the union while others maintained it, and restated in simple, modern language the fundamental opposition of capital to the rights of labour. Words and ideas do indeed have power. The successful growth enjoyed by the GMB from 2005 did not happen by simple chance. It was achieved through thought, planning and the dedicated work of thousands of workplace reps who turned the theory into everyday practice.

The union emerged from its period of deep financial and existential crisis with fewer officers and resources than at any other time. However, by spending less and asking more of the union's workplace organisers, the GMB began to turn around decades of membership and financial decline. As a first step, tens of thousands of 'ghost members' were removed from the union's records in 2005, creating an accurate membership list in every workplace, branch, sector and region of the GMB. The establishment of the National Organising Team (NOT) served to bind the regions into a national strategy for organising, recruitment and retention,

instrumental in building a unity of purpose across the entire union. Moreover, the original team provided a pool of considerable organising talent, from which was drawn the next generation of regional secretaries: Paul Maloney, Southern Region; John Phillips, Wales and South West; Tim Roache, Yorkshire and North Derbyshire; Billy Coates, Northern; and Neil Derrick, Yorkshire and North Derbyshire.

As Paul Kenny told the members: 'Long gone are the days when recruitment could be delegated to someone else. It's everyone's job and the future and size of the GMB is down to us and us alone'.[13] It has to be remembered that in order to grow at all, the GMB needed to recruit some 90,000 members a year just to offset turnover, but, from very modest beginnings, the figures, reported to the general secretary every Friday morning, began to turn around.[14] This made everything else possible. The GMB established itself as one of a very small

The nine new GMB regions after reorganisation, 2012. ▶

GMB Scotland

GMB Northern region

GMB Yorkshire & North Derbyshire region

GMB Midland & East coast region

GMB North West & Irish region

GMB Wales & South West region

GMB Birmingham & West Midlands region

GMB London region

GMB Southern region

◄ Mary with George Dove, a young lad who spoke to congress about his fundraising campaigns to combat childhood diabetes, Southport, 6 June 2010. Mary was immensely proud of him and never forgot him.

group of unions that were growing in membership and influence during a period when legal restrictions and economic circumstances should have worked to the disadvantage, if not the outright destruction, of the unions. Reps and officials became increasingly in the habit of using every single pay claim, workplace issue and negotiation to involve members in the work of the union and to challenge non-members to join the GMB. It was a case, as Paul Kenny said, of acting in concert to 'build our strength where it matters – where people work'.[15]

Within this context, Mary was part of a wider movement to rejuvenate the union. She understood the impulse of activists instinctively, without needing to be told, enabled the crucial debates to be heard at the CEC and congress, and encouraged the grassroots to think and act, freely, for themselves. Due to her own background in the union and having fought her own way up rather than being appointed or anointed by the hierarchy, she was able to act as a conduit for, not a block to, members' own ideas and wishes. Mary could be formidable at the CEC, and was a stickler for the rulebook. But, in her case, this was

in order to permit democracy to flourish. The steely glance would be replaced by the smile and words of gentle encouragement for any delegate or member who genuinely wanted to know the answer to a question, or who was trying to find their way through a jungle of procedure and unfamiliar language. Over a decade or more at the women's conferences hosted by North West and Irish Region, she would sense if a member was nervous about their surroundings or frightened at the prospect of speaking in public, bring them up to the top table to sit beside her and confide: 'I'm not going to ask you to do anything … *yet* …'[16] It was a gentle introduction to the union and its work that left a deep impression upon members and brought many women, of different ages, forward and through the ranks. It was the same in her nurturing of those shop stewards that she took under her wing, as in her directness of approach to a teenage girl visiting congress for the first time, whom she fixed with a direct gaze and declared: 'This is the future of the movement right here in front of us!' That was the sort of moment that would never be forgotten, and which allowed others to see that the labour movement, often appearing as unfamiliar or off-putting territory, was open, welcoming and existed to help them, their families and friends. Similarly, Mary's personal authority helped to break down barriers to recruitment in other, less familiar or popular areas. If Mary could be won round by arguments for recruiting amongst tattoo artists or sex workers, then the wider GMB could, too. In this manner, never afraid of voicing unpopular sentiments, or giving voice to the marginal when she believed the cause to be just, Mary would brave the critics at the TUC women's conference in defending the GMB's decision to organise and recruit among members of the sex industry.[17] It was about as far from her natural constituency as she could get, but she instinctively understood what the GMB could, and should be, and had a consistent sympathy for those who found themselves marginalised, excluded or discriminated against. In this, she possessed a remarkable flexibility of thinking and the ability to step outside any preconceived ideas of what did, or did not, constitute the reach and constituency of the trade unions.

For her, the GMB was the only genuine general union at a time when, with some 8 million workers in precarious employment, this was precisely what the economy was screaming out for, and what the labour movement so desperately needed. She understood that the old craft sectors, which had sustained the union during the post-war period, were in permanent retreat and, quite simply, were never going to return to their former glory. In contrast, jobs such as care workers, cleaners, school teaching assistants, contractors, logistics and retail assistants, were essentially 'recession proof' as they could not be shipped abroad. These workers required protection and formed an enormous potential for recruitment and organisation that was not, as yet, being met by the unions. Mary was, initially, a little suspicious of moves to recruit among school teaching assistants, often drawn from a different class to her own school meals staff, and wondered about the lower 'Grade 2 rate' set for their union subscriptions. Yet, seeing that the problems besetting them as women and as part-time workers with thirty-eight week, term-time only contracts were substantially the same as her own branch members, she had no hesitation in getting behind the drive to recruit TAs. Overlooked and, indeed, shunned by the teaching unions, teaching assistants would become one of the fastest growing sectors for GMB recruitment over the next decade with some 70,000, predominantly women, joining the union.

Union growth & campaigns

With similar recruitment drives taking place in care homes and the union growing by almost 20 per cent over the decade after 2005, the face and the outlook of the union inevitably altered. In response, the eight existing industrial sections of the union were compressed into three less unwieldy groupings: Manufacturing, Commercial Services and Public Services. These more accurately reflected the composition of the union, and acknowledged the reality of contraction in the former FTAT and Tailor & Garment Workers' sections, where jobs had been increasingly outsourced to the developing world. At the time of their creation in 2006, Manufacturing accounted for only 14 per cent of the union's membership, while Commercial

Services held 32 per cent and Public Services 54 per cent.[18] By 2012, 45 per cent of members were now joining online, 80 per cent of members worked in service industries, almost 50 per cent were women and some 20 per cent worked within the school environment. As well as the TAs and care home workers, the union was now organising in the security industry, casinos, in the supermarkets and across the supply chain.[19] It was experiencing a growth in confidence as recruitment mounted and industrial victories were won. At the AA, a breakaway staff association was stifled. At Co-op Funeral Care and at Asda/Walmart, recognition was won. At Swindon's Great Western hospital, Carillion workers stood firm against intimidation and bullying. In each case, success came through 'not by sucking up to employers but by standing up for members'.[20] This was as true in the Amazon warehouses, where GMB activists attempted to organise in cellular structures, in conditions not dissimilar to the French Resistance, as it was characterised at the time, as it was in the struggles to save the A&E departments in North London's hospitals and tackle

the management at Medirest in 2014. At Medirest, part of the giant Compass group specialising in privatised meals services across the world, Mary was again on the picket lines. She stood alongside a predominantly Tibetan and Nepalese workforce and worked to draw in the support of local councillors and MPs, like Stephen Pound, who were prepared to, in the words of Dean Gilligan, 'move the campaign on to a whole different level'.[21] On this occasion, Medirest took fright at the thought of the spotlight being shone upon its affairs and moved to settle with an ethnic minority workforce that had been treated differently from its other workers and systematically underpaid.

At this point, the GMB became more than a purely reactive force. It sought to make common cause with other campaigning groups, such as UK Uncut, and tried to organise around those fundamental issues that threatened the livelihoods and well-being of members such as tax avoidance by the major global corporations like Amazon and Starbucks, off-shoring of finance, and the depredations of the private equity groups and hedge funds upon established

UK company pension schemes. It was a matter of the seeking the root cause of late capitalism's malaise, rather than just fighting the fires and repairing the damage caused by neo-liberalism. The struggle against the AA, which had laid off some 3,400 staff out of a total of 10,000 after being taken over by the private equity consortia of Permira and CVC, led the union, almost alone, to publicise the hawkish takeovers that were inevitably followed by stripping out companies' assets and pension funds.[22] When the economy was booming, in the late 1990s and early years of the new millennium, private equity consortia had used cheap credit to swallow up vulnerable companies. They rarely paid UK tax, cut thousands of jobs, and invariably off-shored the enormous profits accrued, often through raids on pension funds, in order to begin the cycle once again. Between 1997 and 2009, so many companies had fallen under the sway of private equity consortia that some 20 per cent of the total workforce were employed by them. As Paul Kenny explained at the time: 'Private investors, hiding under a cloak of secrecy and pretending to

GMB Private Equity Rogues Ga...

o.1
nds
e, TerraFir
n with wife
Rich List

Vote No. 1
Philip Yea

◄ A real rogue's gallery at the Glastonbury Festival, 24-29 June 2009. The asset-stripping chiefs of private equity were often a faceless bunch operating behind a veil of secrecy. The fact that the GMB could not source photographs of two of the eight CEOs that it targeted was telling, in itself. The union moved to 'name and shame' them and festival goers could vote for their own choice of the 'biggest rogue'.

be interested in building up the UK economy, are taking the taxpayer for a ride, while destroying jobs and leaving in their wake thousands of workers who saved for their pensions, without a pension and dependent on the state'.[23] Even *The Times* began to characterise private equity as a 'secretive industry'. The merger of the travel company, Saga, with the AA saddled the new company with £4.8 billion of fresh debt, while the three private equity owners, Permira, CVC and Charterhouse, scooped-up £2 billion in profits. Largely as the result of GMB's press campaign, helped by Mary's lobbying on the NEC and among Labour MPs, four of the leading figures in the private equity business (including Damon Buffini of Permira, whom Mary habitually referred to as 'Damon Buffoon') were hauled-up before the Commons Treasury Select Committee and questioned over their policy of asset-stripping.[24] Again and again during these years, the GMB warned about the spiralling debt created by these practices, the draining of the public purse through tax avoidance by global

companies and the super-rich, and the enormous volatility caused when currency speculators were permitted to bet on markets with impunity, moving practically limitless amounts of money around the globe almost instantaneously. The difficulty always seemed to be that New Labour was simply not listening. Peter Mandelson had already opined that he, and by extension the party, 'are intensely relaxed about people getting filthy rich', while Gordon Brown's response to the parliamentary inquiry into private equity was to appoint Damon Buffini to a new 'Business Council for Britain'.[25] In a similar fashion, his predilection for the Private Finance Initiatives, or PFI, begun under the Tory Major government but significantly expanded by New Labour, ensured that further public debt was being stored up for the future. Private firms were given charge of delivering capital and infrastructure projects including the building of new roads, schools and hospitals, in exchange for payments from the state, often to be continued over many decades. In 2009, the collapse of Metronet, the largest

Paul Kenny, general secretary of the GMB 2005-15, addressing the Labour Party Conference in Manchester, 27 September 2010. 'This great union of ours is growing. We fear no employer or politician. We exist to support and fight for the rights of working people … our communities and the vulnerable in our society'.

single contractor in the £30 billion PFI market, cost taxpayers £410 million and delayed upgrades to the London Underground. Echoing the GMB, the Office for Budget Responsibility warned that the schemes were 'a source of significant financial risk to government'.[26] However, nothing was done. The result was that the 2018 collapse of Carillion, one of the GMB's long term foes, cost the taxpayer more than £150 million after the firm defaulted on commitments to build a bypass and the Royal Liverpool and Metropolitan Midland hospitals. There was absolutely no joy to be had in being 'right' when the end result was that the union's own members suffered and the public treasury was effectively plundered in order to subsidise and satiate private greed.

This was never more the case than when the financial crisis of 2008, created by the recklessness of bankers and financial speculators, brought about the prospect of bank ATMs running out of money, wages going unpaid, and companies defaulting in their repayments to creditors. In the short term, billions of pounds of public money were committed to shoring up the banking system, with the Royal Bank of Scotland, Lloyds TSB and HBOS being effectively nationalised in an attempt to prevent them from going under.[27] In the long term, the 'credit crunch' was allowed to serve as the justification when the Conservative-Lib Dem coalition and then the majority Conservative governments imposed austerity, not, of course, upon the finance sector, but upon Britain's working people and the poor. 'The economic crisis was less of a surprise to us, the GMB, than to the financial wizards', Mary told union members. 'We warned about private equity profiteers who reap huge rewards without having to pay any tax while wrecking the lives of employees, and venture capitalists with huge pay-offs for failure'.[28] But, she said, 'contrast the way trade unionists who want decent wages and fairness at work are treated, with the way the reptiles who have destroyed our financial system are rewarded by failure. Government and ministers, and even the prime minister, seem far happier to listen to clarion calls from business and the City rather than heed any warnings or listen to any words of concern coming from the unions'.[29] Nothing better illustrated the fundamental disconnect of those years than the spectacle of a rejuvenated, campaigning GMB union again and again championing the cause of fiscal and public probity against the grain of a New Labour government that should have taken those very same interests to heart.[30] Just think what the GMB under Mary Turner and Paul Kenny might have been able to achieve had their instincts, morality and fight been echoed by a progressive Labour Party in government.

New Labour blues

It was not just the banking collapse that had New Labour on the run. An expenses scandal had hit Westminster, largely as the result of the investigative journalism of the *Daily Telegraph*. It revealed the extent to which MPs of all parties were using custom and practice in order to supplement their basic salary and to claim for all manner of luxury items. As Mary told GMB members: 'Because it happened on Labour's watch, the Labour Party is taking the brunt'.[31] Public anger turned into a heavy defeat for the party in the local government and European Parliament elections in May 2009. As the GMB was 'still coming to terms with the results', Mary expressed her sympathy for 'the hundreds of Labour councillors up and down the country who have lost their seats, it is not because of anything they have done but because of wrong-doing in Parliament'.[32] The expenses scandal encouraged, in Mary's words, the 'disillusion with politics and the political class [that] is at the heart of the political malaise destroying our political system' and was symptomatic of the disconnect between Labour in Parliament and its natural supporters.[33] The GMB's new regional network of political officers found union members at best apathetic and, at worst, openly hostile towards New Labour in the wake of the Gulf War. It was extremely difficult, after the government's second term of office, to fire any activist to join the party. Labour had been haemorrhaging votes in every election since 1997 and the behaviour of some of its MPs and ministers appeared to bear out the claims about being 'intensely relaxed' about the filth that accompanied the riches.[34]

New Labour loses its way: the GMB fights for Remploy & the soul of the party

Two New Labour MPs, who the GMB had long raised concerns about, were heavily featured in the *Telegraph's* investigation and were targeted for particular censure. Ben Chapman, whose selection as a parvenu MP Mary had warned about back in 1997, was revealed to have been paid £15,000 for a 'phantom mortgage' that had already been paid off, together with £94,000 in expenses between 2004 and 2008 for refurbishing his property in Lambeth. It included weekly payments for a gardener and architect's fees for a new conservatory, as well as £1,230 for a new fridge freezer.[35] According to a report in the *Telegraph*, he claimed that what constituted luxury was 'entirely subjective'.[36] In a similar fashion, James Purnell, a Blairite minister among those tipped to succeed Gordon Brown, was found to have avoided paying capital gains tax on his London flat – and to have charged the advice sought from an accountant on the deal back to the taxpayer. Martin Bell, the former Independent MP for Tatton, who had

made his name campaigning against parliamentary corruption, thought that it was 'yet another example of an MP playing the system to the limit within the rules that MPs themselves have set'.[37] Yet, as the Secretary of State for Work and Pensions, Purnell had recommended a 'tough' line on poverty, cuts to public services, and that lie detectors to be used to uncover benefit fraud by the poor. He had also pushed for the introduction of private companies to run US-style welfare-to-work programmes and had overseen plans to close the Remploy factories.

Remploy was an independent company that, amid the optimism that accompanied Labour's election victory in 1945 and the creation of the welfare state, had been founded to provide training and specialised employment for severely disabled people, many of them injured during the war. The first of these factories had been opened in north Wales in 1946. Many more followed across the country and provided a bespoke programme encompassing employees of all ages, giving worthwhile jobs for a workforce with different skills and levels of ability. For more than fifty years it had ensured dignity at work for a vulnerable sector of the population and enabled them, in turn, to contribute to society through their work. However, Conservative drives to privatise the more profitable sectors of the business in the mid-1990s were followed by New Labour's preparedness to tolerate a system whereby the number of able-bodied and well-paid managers within Remploy rose considerably, while the number of disabled workers fell by more than 900. In the wake of Blair's wars in Iraq and Afghanistan, there were no attempts to revitalise the factories through the provision of work for returning injured veterans, and spending cuts saw the slow erosion of the number of factories, a process championed by James Purnell. As Phil Davies said at the time, 'Remploy disabled people [are] helping and sharing the good and the bad times together. No other group of workers can offer this level of support to each other. No other group of workers are more loyal to the GMB trade union'.[38] Mary had become close to a young girl working at one of the factories, Tracey, and to her parents, who were under few illusions that she was likely ever to find another decent source of

employment once Remploy was closed down. Despite all the GMB's efforts, despite Mary's passionate appeals at the NEC and protests outside Labour Party conferences, it was a case of 'death by a thousand cuts' as the Remploy factories were picked off one by one. It may have been the Conservatives who began and finally finished the process, but New Labour starved Remploy of contracts, refused to help in the hour of need, and chipped away at both factory numbers and its central ethos. Thus, when Purnell stood down, refusing to meet with his constituents and local party in order to discuss his expenses claims, Mary noted that he 'did not have any problems with coming out and facing our Remploy members and shutting down their factories'.[39] 'Good riddance', was her verdict on him and the MPs like him.[40]

'Sometimes', she recalled, 'I have been one of the lone voices on Labour's national executive demanding action on a flawed, corrupt expenses system'.[41] It was a simple matter of morality. 'For me, it is not about what was in the rules, it was about what was morally right and

morally wrong. Those are my rules'.[42] The answer was for Labour to set its own house in order, just like the GMB had done. 'The NEC of the Labour Party', she said, 'has given the go-ahead for local parties that are not happy with the expense claims of their MPs to ask the NEC to begin the process of investigation … We need to clear out the MPs who have made money out of the expenses system'.[43] This raised the opportunity for deselecting corrupt MPs who did not possess core Labour values. If in more recent times, it has become common for the media to allege that Jeremy Corbyn's supporters and Momentum have sought to use deselection as a means to rid the party of its placemen and Blairite right wing, then it is worth recalling that it was the trade union movement, and the GMB, driven to frustration and despair through the PLP's intransigence and wide-eyed infatuation with the 'free market', that were pushing for 'trigger ballots' in constituencies a decade earlier. It also led the GMB to thinking about how to ensure the selection of parliamentary candidates more representative of those they were there to serve. As Paul Kenny said, 'Now is the time to reflect and elect 40 to 50 … fresh, real people, real trade unionists, people who actually know how much a pint of milk costs and what it is like to get on a bus, MPs driven by commitment rather than being worried about being driven by a chauffeur. We want our MPs to be MPs full-time, not as an add-on: one person, one job'.[44] Mary was very clear about what she wanted: 'The Labour Party would greatly benefit from more trade union candidates, who understand and can effectively represent their local constituencies'.[45]

'We will work to ensure that Labour returns to its traditional values and listens to us, because only the trade union movement can fight and work to ensure the election of a future Labour government. When we are asked to canvass, help stuff envelopes or speak up and vote for Labour, remember the decent and hardworking MPs who have worked for us, such as … Kelvin Hopkins and Angela Eagle, who have not exploited the expenses system. There are many good MPs like them'.[46]

There were some signs of hope. In Islington in 2006, the GMB had spearheaded a local campaign to overthrow a Lib Dem council that had pursued proto-austerity policies and imposed swingeing cutbacks on public services and schools. Gary Doolan, a close friend of Mary's and a one-time caretaker on the Clive Court Estate, had targeted the St. Peter's ward held by the council leader, Steve Hitchens, and fought on a very personal manifesto. 'Unless people experience poverty', he said, 'they don't know what it's like. Poverty always leaves a taste in your mouth so we must make a difference and make sure no one suffers like that'.[47]

Thinking the election was a foregone conclusion, Hitchens canvassed in other wards only to discover, on election night, that Gary had won friends on the doorstep, winning for Labour by thirty votes. Three years later, the whole borough came under Labour control. Mary was delighted and told the GMB: 'They won because they had socialist policies. They ran the free school meals issue and got back into power with a twenty-two seat majority'.[48] Gary explained that Islington now had 'free school meals for all children under the age

of 11 … free admission to sports centres for everyone under the age of 18 is now in place, and £100 off the council tax for people over the age of 65 is now in place … We are moving towards moving all of the privatised services back in-house'.[49] It was a highly successful and viable blueprint for a union anxious, as Mary said, to make sure that 'the voice or experience from the workplace, the communities of the council estates up and down the country' were registered and acted upon.[50] Furthermore, in Mary's view, it would 'do all the Labour leaders and councillors a great deal of good … to carry out socialist policies and not still live in the Thatcher years of privatisation'.[51] The GMB's councillors network was one practical development that suggested a way forward and Gary Doolan helped inform a strategy that sought to re-invigorate grassroots democracy in local government, holding councillors accountable, exposing instances of off-shoring funds by private contractors, and encouraging all Labour councils to bring their services back in-house. The logical extension of this was an expansion of the GMB's political department, led by Mary's close friend

▲ Internationalism in action: Andy Worth and Mary Turner in Cuba, visiting a Committee for the Defence of the Revolution and campaigning for the US government to free the 'Miami 5'.

▲ A new day, a new picket line. Mary Turner and Barbara Benham share a joke and join members from North West and Irish region on the front line.

Cath Speight, who joined her on the Labour NEC. In tandem, they worked to restore the party to its roots and to hold it accountable to the communities and ordinary party members it had appeared to leave behind.

No one had wanted the outcome but the lacklustre 2010 campaign resulted in the loss of ninety-one seats and, after thirteen years in office, Labour was out of government. The formation of a coalition between the Conservatives and the Liberal Democrats marked a sea-change and the beginnings of 'austerity Britain'. Henceforth, the GMB would have to operate in entirely new territory. 'This is not the final chapter in the history of Labour', Mary said in an attempt to rally the troops, but 'it may well be however … the end of New Labour. Going forward, GMB must ensure its vision and values are at the heart of the Labour Party'.[52]

'It would have been even worse without the tremendous work and support that the GMB and its activists gave in the constituencies. In some constituencies which appeared to have been abandoned by the party, our activists, officers and staff

Gary Doolan with Mary Turner. In the summer of 2012, Mary had presented him with the GMB's Gold Badge. It was a proud moment for both friends. Gary, after working his way up through the ranks of the union, to become a branch secretary and a long-standing member of regional council, was a real force for progressive change on Islington council. At GMB's national office, he soon proved himself to be an extremely hardworking, loyal and imaginative political officer: the epitome of all that was brightest and best in the Labour Movement. ▶

knocked on doors, delivered leaflets and supported the local campaigns. We turned the tide and won seats. We kept Labour out of third place. And it helped put the hated BNP back to the bottom of the dung heap where they belong … To all those in the country who voted Lib Dem thinking they would keep the Tories out, you let them in, straight through the gate and into Number 10. We warned that a vote for anyone else than the Labour Party would let the Tories in, and how right we were … now that the Lib Dems have tasted power they are not going to let it go, no matter what policies the Tories put forward'.[53]

Ironically, the election defeat had further served to entrench the union within the party, as eighty-four of the remaining Labour MPs, almost a third of the PLP, were sponsored by the GMB, and some 70 per cent of Labour's funding came from the unions, as New Labour's fair weather business consorts fled back to the arms of the Conservative Party.[54] The GMB was bitterly tired of the arrogance

that power had brought. When it came to electing a new Labour leader, the union's leaders baulked at the continued 'market speak' of David Miliband, the former Foreign Secretary, and recalled his dismissive attitude towards the union while in office. Members recalled that Ed Balls, the former Chancellor, had done himself few favours, not being available for the leadership hustings at the GMB congress but arriving a day later, to strut through Southport's Floral Hall, his black-suited advisors clearing a path through delegates, exhibitors and visitors to herald his arrival. By way of contrast, despite his diffidence and awkwardness under the media spotlight, Ed Miliband promised something different. He was open about not having a particularly clear idea about the unions and their functions, but he was concerned about how working people were suffering from austerity. Just as importantly, after years of spin and the expenses scandals, the GMB felt that here, at least, was somebody who was fundamentally honest and who could grow into the role.[55] Mary

was quick to present him with the 'GMB's shopping list', as

'we want a manifesto that represents the spirit of '45. Give us back our services robbed from us; stop privatising our public services; we need a massive house building programme; give us back our rail and utilities; get rid of the bedroom tax; take on the landlords; bring back fair rents; look after our young people and give them real work; and most of all give us back our trade union rights'.[56]

It may be that the full story of how the GMB moved heaven and earth to try and secure his election will never be told, but it then threw enormous resources, in terms of finance, thought and planning into the subsequent general election campaign of 2015. In particular, the GMB had been instrumental in building a bridge to the Liberal Democrats in the expectation that the election might once more result in a hung parliament and that, this time, the Lib Dems might prefer to change coalition partners and join Labour in government. Among the Lib Dems, it seemed that Danny Alexander had come to like the exercise of power and was keen to hang on to it, while Simon Hughes appeared to be someone the GMB and, by extension the Labour Party, could hope to do business with. A special resolution at the Lib Dem spring conference on the public services, subsequently threaded into their manifesto, made a deal possible.[57] At the same time, Labour's plans for a commission on work offered the GMB the basis for putting their policy aims for an expansion of housing, progressive taxation, an end to PFI, for school meals and the establishment of a £10 an hour living wage at the heart of a new government.

Certainly, there were difficulties. The GMB had needed to fight hard to secure the election of Iain McNicol as the party's general secretary, and was vindicated when he succeeded in turning around Labour' s finances and clearing the mountain of debt accrued during the Blairite years. The union had also to contest further attempts to cut its electoral involvement in the composition of the Labour conference, committees and the NEC. Plans for state funding appeared at best 'a big gamble' for Miliband's leadership and, at worst, spectacularly ill considered.[58] In particular, even though the GMB had 'not been knocked down in the rush with people taking up that opportunity' to join the party as affiliated members, the Labour leadership was fixated upon a complicated formula by which individual union members might be registered, paid for, and accounted. The objective was quite clearly to remove once and for all the influence of trade unions upon the policy and governance of the party, based upon the calculation that 'ordinary' members were likely to be more centrist than their leaders, and that that there was an untapped reservoir of potential membership within the unions that could be swiftly mobilised in order to make good the enormous financial shortfall likely to result under the new formula. The vision was of a mass party, based on individual membership that would be essentially passive as opposed to active in its governance. The reality was that, while this redrawing of the balance of power in the CLPs and at conference failed to ignite great interest in 2014-15, it laid the institutional framework for the Corbyn revolution, which succeeded in delivering a mass membership party, with a strong activist base. Be careful of what you wish for, Paul Kenny had once warned the party in a BBC interview, as 'Father Christmas might come early'.[59] What came was a far more militant, left-wing membership which outflanked the comparatively modest demands of the unions on most issues after 2015, those painful, incremental changes made to Labour policy in order to attune it to the hopes, aspirations and needs of working people.[60] Neither the unions nor the PLP had seen it coming and were struggling to keep up. Yet it was precisely this sense of democracy as empowerment that translated into action over and above the casting of a ballot every few years, that was increasingly coming to underpin the

GMB's own ethos and annual congress and which, in many ways, was Mary's foremost achievement.

The president at congress

Hayley and her friend Lyndsey sat on Wigan Station and watched the cavalcade approach. Southport was a pain to get to on public transport ever since Dr. Beeching had ploughed up the main train line back in the 1960s. Now it meant changing trains and stations, and crossing a busy road before arriving at the other platforms. Mary led the way, followed by Barbara. Behind them a thin line of GMB members and officers, some in suits and jackets, some in congress T-Shirts, threaded its way through the taxi queues and up the steps, carrying all manner of suitcases, plastic bags, rucksacks and congress souvenirs. The biggest and most prominent of these cases was Mary's own, a bright pink behemoth, manoeuvred aboard the train by helpful hands as attempts were made to cram luggage into any available space on the overcrowded, swaying Virgin carriage. The two girls somehow found a seat and, as the excited hubbub of conversation rose in volume, as all sorts of foil-wrapped sandwiches appeared out of bags and were handed around, together with miniature vodka bottles and tonics, they were encouraged to join the impromptu party. Neither knew terribly much about unions but what they did know had certainly not prepared them for a president who used public transport, who sat with her members in standard class, and who would talk to, and involve, anyone who cared in a discussion about everyday life, and how it was affected by politics, that was anything but dry, dull and theoretical. By the time they swayed, somewhat unsteadily, onto the concourse at Euston, amid fond farewells, they had learned an awful lot about the GMB and its work, and had gained a sense that not all political figures behaved in the same way. Some, it seemed, were very down-to-earth and, well, thought Hayley, 'normal' and fundamentally 'alright'. Unions were almost 'exciting'!

It was not surprising. Mary, after all, was happiest with the members. Congress was her natural stage. Penny Robinson told delegates how things worked under her chairing of proceedings:

'If this is your first Congress, believe me, Mary will have noticed you and will make sure she has reassuring and encouraging words for you. If you struggle at the rostrum, do not worry. Mary will be right next to you, encouraging and helping you, something delegates who have been here before will have seen on many occasions. It does not stop once Congress is over. I can tell you from personal experience, if you have your own work or health issues, Mary will be the first on the phone offering support and encouragement, always looking out for others. That is her nature'.[61]

Yet, as Linda Lord reported:

'There is another side to this red-headed, Irish, Gemini … Mary Turner, President of the GMB, can point out the error of their ways to congress delegates who should know better. They are told in a very measured, no-nonsense, humorous way that clearly says, "Don't push it"'.[62]

Kevin Maguire, of the *Daily Mirror*, concurred: 'She's a superb chair of the annual conference, defusing rows with a little laugh and the respect for her rulings

◀ Denny was always there at Mary's side. Here, he is with Mary when she was awarded the MBE from the Queen, 12 February 2010.

is a tribute in itself to the respect in which the GMB President is held'.[63] Mary was no respecter of high-flown titles, moved to slap down blatant electioneering for union posts from whatever quarter it came, and could be withering when she felt that the GMB was being patronised. At the hustings for the Labour Party leadership in 2010, there were deep intakes of breath from the platform when a Birmingham delegate rose from the floor to ask the candidates: 'Before becoming a professional politician what job did you do and what life experience would you bring to the job of leader of the Labour Party?' David Miliband replied first, all smiles, outstretched palms and Blair-like tugs to immaculately white cuffs. 'My first ambition', he said, 'was to be a bus conductor when I was four-years-old ...' He expected an 'Aah!' of simple-minded affirmation from what he took to be a simple-minded, unsophisticated, audience. What he got was a razor-sharp, lightning-quick retort from the union's president: 'Well, you would have lost that job, wouldn't you, a bit quick?'.[64] It brought the house down. It was clinical and cutting, and there was no way back for him after that.

This said, on other occasions Mary could be supremely diplomatic even when provoked. The petulance and bad temper displayed by Vince Cable after the mild barracking he received from delegates, after he had threatened the unions with sequestration was met with calm and equanimity. Mary made sure to keep the show on the road. Even as he attempted to storm off the stage in a fit of pique, she remained dignified, returned him to centre stage and presented him with a gift from the very union he had just offered to destroy.[65] He might have no manners, but the GMB certainly did.

Protests by young members were quite a different case. Keir Greenaway, then one of the union's youngest branch chairs, well remembers Mary's ability to act as a positive channel for dissent:

'At my second GMB conference [in 2012], Mary had somehow got wind of Holly Smith's idea to hold up a banner when Danny Alexander [then the Chief Secretary to the Treasury in the coalition government] was on stage. I don't know how, as the paint was barely dry on the bed sheet, but nothing really ever got past Mary. I was told that Mary wanted a word

with us and so, therefore, expected to get pulled and given a telling-off.

I think she surprised us all when she told us to get on with it and that she would expect nothing less. All she wanted was for us not to interrupt proceedings. She managed to show off three of her great character traits: indomitable activist spirit, that she could relate to any member of the union including the Bolshie young members, and that she was a brilliant chairperson'.[66]

Mary never forgot a face, a name or a story. It was a remarkable, and often uncanny, gift. Years later, when looking through some photos, she came across images from the Southport congress and of the eleven-year-old lad, George Dove, who had talked to delegates about his battles with type one diabetes and his sponsored walks across the east Midlands in order to raise funds for the insulin pump that would mean that he no longer needed to inject insulin with a needle three times a day.[67] 'You know he did it', Mary said with a glow of pride, 'he got his pump'. She forgot no one, once congress was over and the hall cleared, and often followed up the stories and stayed in touch with

and file also remembered and took her to their own hearts. As her granddaughter, Lisa discovered, when at congress:

'She could not walk more than a few feet without someone stopping her for a chat, some support or advice. If we were leaving the hotel at 8 p.m., I would have to make sure that I was pulling her out of the door at least an hour and a half beforehand otherwise we would be eating our evening meal at midnight, which Nan would then class as having her breakfast'.[69]

The importance of congress to the GMB, or of Mary to congress, cannot be overestimated during those years. It was, after all, the union's parliament. 'After years when congress and branches were undermined and attacked, which resulted in the abolition of annual congress', the first thing the new union leadership under Paul Kenny and Mary Turner had done was to restore it as an annual body and to reaffirm its powers as the GMB's supreme authority, while the CEC was changed to an all lay member assembly.[70] It was now an article of faith that 'involving more lay members in our parliament is worth every

speakers, such as young George – 'a smashing lad' – to see how they, and their campaigns had progressed.

In a similar fashion, when a congress delegate, Edna Greenwood, was taken sick, Mary thought nothing of taking off in a car, driven by Paul McCarthy, the North West and Irish regional secretary, immediately after the close of the day's congress session in order to travel for more than two hours to visit her in hospital. She was back, fresh as a daisy, in time for the start of the next morning's business, having done more than 300 miles in a round trip, thinking nothing of it and having barely drawn breath.[68] It was simply what you did as a union member. It was scarce wonder, then, that the rank penny. Let's never, ever, get fooled again with the idea that abolishing congress or diluting the power of lay members to make policy is a good way of travelling forward. Congress is worth everything we have put into it'.[71] However, as Paul Kenny explained in 2010, 'Now, we must go further. We must expand congress and bring more lay delegates into the decision-making parliament'.[72] This entailed a move from a system, unchanged for almost seventy years, whereby the congress ratio was one delegate for every 2,000 members to one where there was one delegate for every 1,500. At a stroke, it served to expand lay member participation at congress by over 25 per cent. Paul considered that: 'We need that wider participation for a variety of reasons and we need to use the expansion of that democracy by bringing in a series of appointments to this congress through regional committees to deal with some of the equalities [issues] in the make-up of delegations, and our representational bodies'.[73] This was in order 'to fill those gaps so that we can make sure we get proper representation of women, ethnic minorities, young people, LGBT, disabled

Mary was awarded the TUC's Gold Badge in recognition of a lifetime's service and achievement, by Brendan Barber, the general secretary of the TUC, at Brighton, 12 September 2012.

The election of a Conservative-Lib Dem Coalition government marked the beginnings of the policy of austerity and consigned millions of British people to misery and poverty. The TUC organised a mass protest as a 'March for an Alternative', in London, 26 March 2011. The eagle-eyed will be able to spot Mary Turner, Paul Kenny and Andy Worth from among a sea of familiar GMB faces and banners.

[workers], to make sure that certain geographical areas [throughout] the union are covered and not excluded', and also to ensure that certain trades and skills were not missed out.[74]

These changes to congress were very much in line with the new equalities policies that were being driven forward, often by the self-organising groups known as SOGs at the base of the union. In time, these would grow to include GMB Shout, GMB Race, GMB Young London and GMB Sisters. The work of the SOGs enabled members to organise in the workplaces around the implementation of policies that directly affected them, such as domestic violence, mental health, and 'from menstruation to menopause', while at the same time providing support to Trans workers, and challenging racist behaviour and hate speech. Taranjit Chana is in no doubt that:

'Mary Turner embraced the very essence of equality by ensuring that class, gender and race were always on the agenda. Her passion for ensuring equality, fairness and justice for under-represented communities and groups ensured that their voices were heard in the corridors of power. Every

meeting with Mary Turner left you even more inspired. When she spoke at London Region's inaugural women's conference, you could hear a pin drop. She made you feel that you belonged and were never alone'.[75]

This gift for inclusivity was felt particularly strongly at congress, and at the annual President's Night when the union was allowed to let its hair down, with a covers band usually on hand to fill the dance floor until the early hours of the morning. It was a chance for the union's reps, whose grinding, often hard and unglamorous work sustained and grew the union, to be acknowledged by a president who always had time for them, and where they, and their families, could enjoy themselves amongst their comrades. As one delegate from Yorkshire and North Derbyshire put it, 'Congress, like no other gathering of GMB members, revitalises and reboots our union activity and re-affirms our resolve to fight harder for the likes of our members'.[76] The attainment of an 'expanded, vibrant, challenging, inclusive … congress' was, itself, a symptom of a growing confidence.[77] It is far easier to preside over a docile and cowed body whose only purpose is to

rubber-stamp decisions by a leadership, than to enable discussion and the flow of ideas. In this way, Mary's chairing of congress was key to the process of change, and to bringing on all those who announced themselves as 'first-time delegate, first-time speaker' to have their say and make their mark. Indeed by the time that the GMB met for the 2015 congress in Dublin, there were some ninety first-time speakers ready to bring motions to the floor.[78] This necessitated trust on both sides of the equation and the mature realisation, on the part of the GMB's executive, that there were going to be times when relinquishing control to enable a greater sense of openness meant that the leadership was going to lose votes and be 'turned over' by congress delegates. That was the very nature of democracy. It came with the territory, and was a very different world from that inhabited by the union a decade before. In a very short space of time it had been rebuilt from the bottom up; its membership was increasing year upon year and renewing itself at its base. There was, indeed, the sense of new freedoms and possibilities, that 'We can trust ourselves a little bit … trust our values. The GMB is a growing, democratic and independent union and we must stay that way'.[79]

The honour to serve the people

Mary's influence stretched far outside the congress hall and her own union. On one occasion a phone call in the early hours of the morning was from the police attempting to stop a suicide. The distraught man had been asked to whom he wanted to talk. Although he had never met Mary and didn't belong to the union, he was aware of her work helping the different communities and ethnic groups across Brent. In his desperation, Mary's was the only name, the only beacon of hope, he could think of. The local police found her number and, apologetically, got her out of bed before dawn. It was all very different from the attentions of the Special Branch at Brighton all those years before. Mary rubbed the sleep from her eyes and didn't think twice about rising to the occasion. She talked the man round, effectively saved a life, and then, without much of a pause, continued with her union duties.

These, too, had expanded. She could

be found at 'Save Our Hospitals' events, where she spoke alongside Labour MPs but from a very personal perspective: that of having recently been an NHS patient.[80] She campaigned tirelessly against the resurgence of the hard-right and the return of fascism, warning that 'there is a chill spreading across Europe that was liberated from Nazi rule sixty-five years ago, as right wing extremist parties are gaining ground. We all share the horror of seeing racists like Nick Griffin and his henchman, Andrew Brons, elected to the European Parliament'.[81] And she celebrated when union sponsored candidates swept away the BNP's vote and counter-demonstrations routed the English Defence League in Britain's major cities. Together with Sheila Bearcroft, who had just become president of the TUC, she participated in a candle-lit vigil outside the US embassy in Grosvenor Square, in support of the campaign to free the Miami Five, Cubans who had been jailed for combating CIA-sponsored terrorism.[82] She met the jailed men's wives and would see them again when she toured Cuba, together with Andy Worth and Paul McCarthy, visiting collective farms,

state enterprises and the Committees for the Defence of the Revolution, at a time when the US blockade of the island and the sting of sanctions were being used in an attempt to impoverish the ordinary people and bring the country to its knees. Internationalism was close to her heart. She forwarded both practical and political aid to Cuba after her return home, remained in touch with the families of the Miami Five (who were eventually freed in December 2014 after a campaign spearheaded by unions throughout the world), and invited representatives of ICAP, the Cuban organisation for international friendship, to attend GMB congresses.[83] If the example of Cuba had impressed her, then so too had the labour movement in Malta. She was the guest of the Maltese Labour Party, together with Gary Doolan and Malcolm Sage, during their election campaign in 2013 and spent the best part of a week shuttling from one rally or meeting to another across the isle. At a time, pre-Corbyn, when popular enthusiasm for the Labour Party at home was muted to say the least, all three GMB delegates were re-invigorated by the experience of mass participation in street

rallies that took on the aspects of a fiesta, with young people much in evidence and with Mary delighting in addressing the crowds that thronged the squares of Valetta.

Mary had also been at the forefront of the 'Put People First' demonstration, held to coincide with the 2009 G20 summit in London, when thousands marched to demand action on poverty, climate change and jobs. 'I did not meet any bankers, private equity bosses, or tax haven gangsters on that march', she said. 'Instead, I marched with the ordinary people of Britain who are furious with the bankers and chancers who exploited the flawed financial system for their own ends while creating a global financial crisis which our children, grandchildren and generations to come will pay for'.[84] The march further emphasised the gulf that separated the fears and concerns of the vast majority from New Labour's preparedness to sup with neo-liberalism and the new global elites, the less than 1 per cent at the top holding sway over more than half the world's wealth and resources. The financial collapse had already seen the banks tottering on the

Mary with Dave Prentice, the general secretary of Unison, at the head of the protest against Welfare Cuts, 10 April 2010, on the way to the rally at Trafalgar Square.

edge of the abyss, and Mary was one of the many who urged that another, socialist and environmentally sustainable world was possible.

She allowed no separation between her role as an activist and as a member, or chair, of official committees. In essence, this was her great utility and strength. Her consistent championing of nutrition and its role in the betterment of children's lives did much to inform the 2009 publication of a joint document produced by the GMB and the Child Poverty Action Group, *Raising the kids: Stop in-work poverty*. It also brought her to the attention of the professional body that represented nutritionists, the BDA. The organisation had a long history, stretching back over eighty years, and represented a membership that was over 98 per cent women. Its leadership, and previous presidents, had often been drawn from the ranks of very senior medics, academics and health service professionals. However, through her campaigning work, the BDA had become aware of Mary's passion for, and knowledge of, the territory and, as Andy Burman the chief executive officer explains, there was a growing realisation

within the organisation that it needed to be far more active in the promotion of health and nutrition in the early stages of life.[85] Mary seemed like the ideal ambassador, who could combine practical experience and personal passion with the ability to organise campaign groups and to gain the ear of government ministers. There were exploratory meetings with Paul Kenny and Mary and it quickly became apparent that there were no conflicts of interest between the two organisations. Indeed, there was a mutual synchronicity between the GMB and the BDA in terms of their commitment to changing social policy in order to improve the health of the nation, in general, and that of the young, in particular. Mary was elected as the honorary president of the BDA in 2010, and from that moment on, it was felt, 'almost gave the organisation the permission and the confidence to go out and organise and campaign on a number of new platforms'.[86] She would regularly attend the BDA's conferences and both fascinate and 'inspire a younger generation of dieticians, who could now feel that they were part of something larger, and feel what it was like to know someone who

had to really battle to get anywhere in life'. She was instrumental in promoting areas such as the representation of women and BAME members within the BDA and in launching the national 'Dieticians' Week', to take place at the beginning of every July. For Mary's own part, it was the fulfilment of long-term interests and beliefs begun many years before in voluntary night school classes in food hygiene and nutrition while working in the school kitchens at Salusbury Road. In this way, everything that she did was done well and with a consistency that could eventually break down banners and achieve results. If Mary had a quick turn of phrase, or was good at dreaming up an appropriate slogan, then these were always informed by knowledge and principle. She would take a quiet pride that, though she had never stopped being a 'dinner lady', her opinions and ability was now being sought and recognised by the professional experts in the field. At the Labour Party conference, held in Manchester in 2010, BDA members were amazed at the ease with which Mary could call over leading Labour MPs and shadow ministers to their table. Some trotted over dutifully and just offered platitudes, but some, like Diane Abbott, whom Mary had known since she was young, stayed to offer constructive help and support. Mary's own legacy was a culture change in the organisation. 'Now', says Andy Burman, 'whenever we are confronted by a problem, we think to ourselves "what would Mary do?"'[87] The decision of the BDA in 2017 to take the Children's Food Trust under the organisation's wing is seen as a direct product of Mary's influence upon the BDA's practice, while their trade union award was posthumously renamed in her honour.

Other awards and honours were forthcoming. In 2010, she was awarded the MBE 'for services to trade unions' in the New Year's Honours List. That February, she was at Buckingham Palace, together with Denny and their children, John and Denise, to receive the decoration. She accepted it, she said, not on her own behalf but on that of every single member of the GMB. 'I love this union and its members and it's a privilege to do what I do', Mary told the *Daily Mirror's* Kevin Maguire. 'What I've achieved is because of GMB and I'll never forget who we are and where we're going'.[88]

Four years later, the union celebrated its 125th anniversary in Canning Town Hall, the site where the union had been founded by Will Thorne on what was then waste ground and to where Keir Hardie had returned, in triumph, after being elected as Labour's first MP. Glittering lights illuminated a hall draped in banners that told the story of the GMB's early years and its work in the borough, while Mary, together with Unmesh Desai, a Labour councillor and GMB member, were on hand to unveil a meeting room, named in honour of Will Thorne. There was a carol concert performed by local children belonging to a community music project that had been sponsored by the union, watched appreciatively by Ed Miliband and his staff. There was, of course, the obligatory late night dancing but there was also serious business and seriously good news. The union had long been campaigning for justice for the Cammell Laird workers, victimised and wrongfully imprisoned by Thatcher's government in 1984. When, at the time, the national union had shown little interest in the case and given the lads short shrift, Mary had championed their cause in the GMB. It was a source of pride to her that night that justice seemed, at last, to be in sight. A delegation led by Eddie Marnell, Paul McCarthy and Kathleen Walker Shaw returned from Brussels with the news that the EU Parliament had heeded their petition and found that the UK government did, indeed, have a case to answer. The GMB and its members had come a long way in a comparatively short time, from ruin to a thorough-going resurgence. 'When we embarked on that journey, in 2005', Paul Kenny had already reminded the union's members, 'it was to reclaim and re-establish the GMB and we knew that we had many, many difficult tasks that lay before us. We knew that we had to re-establish financial discipline and replace the financial mismanagement of the past. We knew we needed organisational change to halt membership decline … Most of all, we knew we needed re-establishment of the trade union morality and decency in order to triumph'.[89] That triumph was, in large measure, Mary's own. Amid the Christmas celebrations at Canning Town Hall it seemed that the union had at last come home. ■

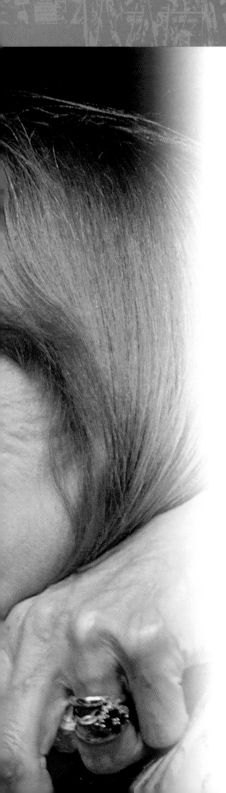

LIVING FOR OTHERS

The GMB fights and cares for all

'The GMB doesn't just care about one group of people', Mary told her members, 'it cares for all. As long as you have the principles of caring, that's all that matters'.[1] The union's North West and Irish Region had been acting on that, hosting a number of 'Justice' conferences that brought together a range of different campaigns, all fighting to obtain judicial reviews over miscarriages of justice, or to have iniquitous legislation overturned.

They included the Shrewsbury 24, the Cammell Laird workers, the anti-Blacklisting campaign, and the Sophie Lancaster Foundation; but prominent among them, and rooted in the region, was the Hillsborough Families Support group. In the aftermath of the death of 96 fans, and the injury of more than 700 others, at a football match at the Sheffield stadium in

◄ Hearts worn on the sleeve. Mary embraces Sue Roberts and Margaret Aspinall from the Hillsborough Families' Support Group, Bournemouth, 7 June 2016.

April 1989, the police had fed false, highly emotive and misleading stories to the press, which were amplified in the pages of the *Sun*. It was left to the bereaved families to pull together, initially with few resources and little in the way of popular support, and then to seek redress and the truth from the authorities. Private prosecutions failed but a second coroner's report, which had taken two years to compile, was released in April 2016, which overturned the errors contained in an initial report into the deaths of the fans. It found that there had been 'unlawful killing' and laid the blame squarely upon the failures of the West Yorkshire police and the emergency services. Against the background of this fresh coroner's report, two leading figures within the support group, Margaret Aspinall, who had lost her son, and Sue Roberts, who had lost her brother, were welcomed to address the GMB's congress by Mary Turner.

As Jeremy Corbyn had said the previous afternoon, Hillsborough was the tragedy of 'a working-class community traduced by the media, lied to by officials, dishonestly

Mary Turner with Barbara Plant (who would eventually succeed her as president of the GMB in June 2018) at the TUC 'Rally against the Cuts' and lobby of parliament, central London, 19 October 2010. Kathleen Walker Shaw and the, then, London regional secretary, Paul Hayes, stand behind them. ▶

damaged by allegations of their behaviour during that dreadful day' and had sparked a twenty-seven-year-long struggle for redress by the families.[2] It was a story of courage and persistence amidst heartbreak and government intransigence over what increasingly had been exposed as a cover up. 'The ordinary people are the ones who stood by us for all of those years', explained Margaret Aspinall, 'when the establishment was trying to bring us down and down and down, and we were determined to make sure that we got the truth'.[3] The terrible truth revealed by the second coroner's inquiry was that many of those crushed in the pens could have been saved if the police and the emergency services had done their job. Fans, like Margaret Aspinall's eighteen-year-old son, James, who had left home cheerfully with his mate that morning, off to

see his first away game, need never have died. 'He was in the ground at a quarter-past one', his mother said. 'I didn't find out that James had died until six o'clock the following morning'.[4] It was a direct, personal tale of a mother's love and loss. It was also the tale of justice denied and gained through organisation, determination and fighting spirit. As such, it was one that touched an immediate, raw chord with everyone in the hall.

During the post-war period, the union's congresses had been highly regimented affairs, dry, clinical and overwhelmingly male. They union had believed it could carve a niche for itself within a corporatist state as a willing partner with governments, as little more than a wage-broker. Community campaigns and expressions of grief that was still raw had not been part of the union's approach. Now, all of that had changed, with these struggles being

Braving the winter's chill: Mary speaking to strikers on the picket line at Chemilines, London, 16 December 2008. The workers at the pharmaceutical company – predominantly Asian and female – had voted unanimously to take strike action in a pay dispute. In an echo of the Grunwick strike, the company responded by issuing 25 redundancies. ▶

Mary was intensely proud of her Irish background and the GMB's congress, held in Dublin, in many ways represented a home coming. Michael D. Higgins, the President of Ireland, delivered a barn-storming speech that brought the union's delegates to their feet. Immediately afterwards he was pictured alongside Mary. Paul McCarthy, GMB North West & Irish region secretary, and Sheila Bearcroft, regional president of GMB Wales & South West, are in the background, 8 June 2015. ▼

linked to the wider campaigns that the GMB was pursuing. The union now existed, as Paul Kenny had once said, 'to challenge and change'. Certainly, Mary saw it as one continuous thread of struggle bringing people together in order to achieve what was right, and, by so doing, to refashion the whole of society. This was a particularly hard task when faced by a hard-right Conservative government committed to imposing austerity on working people. 'They are trying to bring us to our knees', she told delegates, 'but we will not bow to you [the Conservatives] or anybody else. We will fight for what we believe in, and that is justice, justice for them and justice for those who have gone before'.[5]

That then was Mary's credo, a call to action based upon fundamental principle, one founded upon compassion and an extraordinary sense of empathy for those who had suffered an injustice or a loss. 'No words of mine', she told congress,

'can ever explain or understand what these wonderful people have had to go through for twenty-seven years. By listening to Margaret, I believe that it is still going on … They paid the price of their children,

brothers, sisters and uncles ... I am proud to know them, I am proud that they are standing on my union's platform, and I am extremely proud of the region which has kept this going – Paul McCarthy and the North West and Irish Region'.[6]

It was, she thought, both a 'dreadful and lovely' experience to hear the women's stories. After presenting them with a gold medal from the GMB to mark their achievements, she made sure that she handed the congress chair over to Malcolm Sage so that she might spend time with them backstage, talk to them and be there for them.[7] Her concern, and that of the GMB, did not start or end with the gaze of the public and the glare of the congress hall lights.

The story of the Hillsborough families was particularly poignant as family, whether it was her immediate relatives, or her wider trade union 'family', was incredibly important to Mary. Everything else was built upon those rocks. Yet, Mary had lost Denny, her great pillar of support, on 25 August 2015 after a long illness. Dementia is a particularly savage condition, remorselessly stripping away memories and

the essence of self like so many layers of peel, progressively distancing the sufferer from those closest to them. After almost sixty years of happy married life, it was particularly devastating in the case of Mary and Denny. It was, said Mary, simply 'a dreadful, dreadful disease' and 'caring for those with dementia and Alzheimer's is a twenty-four-hour, not an eight-hour day'.[8] No one would have thought any the less of Mary had she, at this point, chosen to step back from the union's affairs and to have thought of her own self. But she determined to continue looking after Denny alongside her duties in the branch and as union president. In this, she had the full support of her family and also of Gary Doolan, who would often act as chauffer, ferrying her to and from her many meetings, and would try to insist that somewhere along the way, she should also eat properly and look after herself. Though she had given up smoking, Mary's diet consisted of various protein shakes and her favourite jellied eels. Her own cancer was back again. She was paper-thin. One union member commented that, even with her overcoat draped over her shoulders as everyone gathered around her outside in the street after a meeting in

Nottingham, 'it looked as though a single gust of wind would blow her away'.

Though there could be no disguising her physical frailty, the fires still burned bright. The personal was also political. So Mary became a strong campaigner for the Alzheimer's Society, 'a cause very close to my heart'. The family were to raise more than £20,000 for the charity through various events and sponsored walks.[9] It was a recognition of the respect and affection she was held in that hundreds of union members packed the church for Denny's funeral mass. They understood his own, steady, often unnoticed support to Mary over the years and that he, too, had contributed to the success of GMB, permitting 'his' Mary to become 'ours'. That Christmas, the family flew off to Mexico for a two-week holiday spent in the sun. Mary spent a large part of the flight occupied with teaching her great-grandchildren to play the hands of cards that she had once enjoyed with her husband. For their own part, Jess, Katie and Hallie recalled their Nan's sense of fun and knack for always taking them somewhere new, interesting or exciting. Back at home, she was 'always there to cheer us up', would be on hand to help with homework, and would enjoy sharing 'her dearest memories' with them 'while drinking continuous cups of tea' and trying to tempt them with the 'delights' of jellied eels. There would regularly be eighteen of the family sat around the table for Christmas dinner. Sunday lunch was a big family tradition, with Freddy, Mary's great-grandson, always trying to be the last one in the kitchen with her, and all of the children looking to the drawer where the sweets would be kept for 'afters'.[10] In a society increasingly atomised, with parents increasingly out at work and children consumed by mobile phones and games consoles, Mary's family remained cohesive and, in a way, acted as its own cheerful little collective. It was a remarkable achievement in that commitments to labour movement activism often have the effect of driving partnerships, marriages and families apart. It was Mary's rare ability to 'have it all', to juggle her commitments and to make one feed into another as a logical extension, a case of practice fitting with the movement's ideals. This was based on incredible levels of dedication and sheer hard work, and on her own support systems, through Denny and the wider network of family and friends.

Those family and friends, including some closest to her in the GMB trade union, among them Gary Doolan, Cath Speight and Lesley Stansfield all came together, on 16 March 2017, for a party held on her home turf, in Whelan's Irish pub in Cricklewood, to celebrate her investiture with the CBE. 'It was a wonderful honour, really wonderful', reflected Malcolm Sage, then with a hint of sadness added 'It's just a shame that it couldn't have been given just that bit earlier so that she could really have enjoyed it'.[11]

Living in austerity Britain
Throughout the months following Denny's passing, so many of the themes of the struggles that had hallmarked Mary's career resurfaced and presented new challenges. After a decade at the helm of the union, Paul Kenny had decided that the time was right to retire and had been succeeded by Tim Roache, the Yorkshire and North Derbyshire regional secretary. As Jeremy Corbyn was to tell the GMB's new general secretary, a union had never been passed on so smoothly and in such good condition. After ten years of continual membership

growth, the GMB had resolved the financial difficulties that had dogged it in the 1990s and now possessed an organising culture that was capable of sustaining those gains despite changing work patterns and the casualisation of many jobs. Indeed, in acknowledging the reality of 'a broken labour market' and engaging with the new precariat, the union was shown to be capable of bucking the trend of decline during the years of austerity. It even published ambitious plans for delivering 750,000 members by 2020.[12] However, while the internal health of the GMB had never been stronger, the union was operating in an unrelentingly hostile political environment. The Conservative government was using the banking collapse of 2008 as a justification for the imposition of austerity upon the poorest sections of society and for making further stinging cuts to essential public services.

The already fragmented school meals service was, unsurprisingly, one of those areas designated for destruction. This was due, in no small measure, to the failures of New Labour to act upon the issue when it had had the chance. The Acheson Inquiry had, after all, pinpointed the link between

Mary Turner and Cath Speight, GMB National Political Officer, sat together on the
NEC of the Labour Party over many years. Here, they cast the GMB's votes at the Labour
Party Special Conference on the 'reform' of the party's links to the trade unions, ExCel
Centre, London, 1 March 2014. While the party tinkered with its own internal bureaucracy
in an attempt to pander to right-wing critics in the media, the GMB and its members,
such as Mary and Cath, fought every day for the return of a Labour government.

poverty and deprivation, particularly in early life and later ill-health and mortality. The publication of the Green and White Papers, *Saving lives: Our healthier nation*, in 1998 and 1999, respectively, urged a 'whole school' approach to encourage the adoption of healthier diets for the nation's children. The plans for breakfast clubs and, in 2000, the launch of a new nationwide fruit scheme, whereby every nursery and infant school child between the ages of four and six would be entitled to a free piece of fruit each day, were developed as a direct result of Mary's lobbying on the NEC and were very much in line with her thoughts on early years nutrition. However, New Labour's unwillingness to use direct taxation as a progressive instrument in the engineering of social policy, and its timidity in confronting vested commercial interests, meant that food poverty was not systematically addressed. The school meals service was not restored to its pre-1980 status and national nutritional standards were not imposed upon privatised suppliers.[13] Even where healthy options were offered, the pressure upon schools to offer 'choice' and commercial concessions in order to gain fresh income streams led

to the provision of fast-food alternatives, in the form of pizzas, burgers and chips, and in the installation of vending machines in school corridors, dispensing chocolates, crisps and fizzy drinks. That Mary Turner had to be 'launched' as the expert in the field onto Charles Clarke as the Secretary of State for Education from 2002 to 2004, or that she achieved few concessions

> **This government are trying to restrict our political fund to stop members having a say in politics while fat cats in the City of London use their slush funds [and] hedge funds to prop up their Tory friends … We need our political fund to continue the fight**

from him and from New Labour, was a sad reflection upon the PLP. It was noted in the party's traditional heartlands, as the votes of 'natural' supporters haemorrhaged away.[14] On a local level, some Labour councils tried to do their best. The new leader of Brent Council, Muhammed Butt, for instance, had promised in 2013 to look into healthier menus in the borough's schools. Mary's continued pressure in advance of the

2014 local government elections certainly encouraged a number of Labour-controlled councils to either safeguard, or increase, the quantity and quality of their provision of school meals.[15] No doubt knowing of Mary's work and conscious of the prime-time media coverage of 'turkey twizzlers' in *Jamie's School Dinners*, which had aired between 2004 and 2006,

the Liberal Democrats, as part of their manifesto for the 2010 general election, gave a commitment to introduce free meals for infants. They saw the policy implemented as part of their role in David Cameron's coalition government, from 2010-15. It must have been galling in the extreme, for Mary to see her ideas, rejected or watered down by New Labour, so assiduously, if selectively, harvested by the

Conservative-Lib Dem government.

Yet, the results of the coalition's drive to austerity were there in the accompanying growth of food banks, in the causal link between poor diet through food poverty and the rise in cancers, heart disease, childhood obesity and diabetes.[16] This was a new, breadline Britain, where GMB families, though in work, found themselves struggling to feed their families, pay the gas bills, fill their cars and pay the rent. Major supermarkets began to report that one in five of their customers went without, at least once a week, in order to keep their families fed. Numbers of working people relying upon food parcels trebled, while there was a steep rise in the numbers of the homeless upon the streets. Having long since dropped the Liberal Democrats when the Conservatives won an absolute majority in 2015, and having called a snap election in the hopes of wiping out a bitterly disunited Labour Party, Theresa May's Conservative government announced in its 2017 election manifesto that it would replace the commitment of the coalition government (which the Tories claimed had cost £1.2 billion since 2014) to free hot school meals and cold breakfasts. A life's work in campaigning for healthy school meals for all the nation's children seemed, once more, to be in danger of being undone by an incoming Conservative government. At the same time, the Cameron and May governments after 2015 renewed the attack upon the trade unions. Again, the feeling was that they might complete the work that Margaret Thatcher had begun, with fundamental alterations to the way that unions handled the recruitment and retention of membership and governed their own internal democracy. Initially, the government threatened major changes to the way union dues were collected with the abolition of check-off, whereby union subs were taken directly at source, alterations to enrolment in the political fund making members opt-in, as opposed to opting-out, supplemented by further legal restrictions on the right to strike. 'They are coming after our very right to organise and defend ourselves', Mary said, warning that the Trade Union Act of 2016:

'is a direct attack on me, on you, on our union, on our movement and on our politics. And it's nothing to do with them. What we democratically decide … is nothing to do with this government. The contractual arrangements we have with employers is our business, not theirs. Who our union – which was there at the founding of the Labour Party – chooses to support politically is our business and nothing to do with them. This government are trying to restrict our political fund to stop members having a say in politics while fat cats in the City of London use their slush funds, hedge funds, to prop up their Tory friends from Eton … [but] we need our political fund to continue the fight whichever government is in [power]'.[17]

TUC protests, a lobby of Parliament which Mary attended, and a rally in Westminster Central Hall, proved largely futile gestures, though some traction was gained in the House of Lords. Far more effective was the growing fear, rather too late in the day, of Conservative ministers that the EU referendum of 2016 might be lost and that trade union support might be enough to make the difference through rallying the votes of working people. As a result, there were some concessions before the act was passed in 2016, most notably in regard to check-off. But the increased stringency on strike ballots and picketing became law, saddling unions with the legal obligation of letting employers know a fortnight in advance of balloting, and stipulating that a threshold of 50 per cent of membership participation in the ballot had to be reached before a strike could legally be called. This removed the more usual democratic mandate to achieve a simple majority (as in the EU referendum and in parliamentary elections) and weighted the result in favour of the apathetic. A failure to turn out in a ballot now actually counted more than a vote against industrial action. These changes rendered British trade unions the most circumscribed in the Western world and rendered collective action all but impossible, save for very particular circumstances.

If anyone was still kidding themselves that the parties had become indistinguishable, then the commitment in the Conservative 2017 manifesto to significantly alter the way in which care was provided and charged for Alzheimer's patients should have provided a sufficient degree of instruction. Charges for social care would now take the value of an individual's property into consideration. Those whose homes were valued at more than £100,000 would have to pay towards their care. With average house prices, especially in London and the south of England, far outstripping that, it meant that the state was effectively laying claim to the homes of the elderly and the afflicted in the form of a 'dementia tax'. Taken together with Conservative plans to remove the 'triple lock' on pensions and to place a cap on winter fuel allowances, this was a veritable assault upon the elderly and the vulnerable. Mary, who knew more than most of trying to ease the decline and passing of a loved one with as much comfort, dignity and compassion as was possible, was enraged by this 'attack on carers who look after their loved ones saving you [i.e. the state] millions over the years … I have a great deal of feeling for anyone, irrespective of who they are, getting this terrible, terrible disease. You [i.e. Theresa May and the Conservative government] intend to rob them of their homes and leave them without'.[18]

New Labour had peddled the fiction, comfortable and useful to the rich, that the age of ideologies was at an end and that the lamb might, indeed, lie down with the lion. The return of a majority Conservative government had now witnessed the explicit return of neo-liberal ideology. Stripped of David Cameron's earlier notion of the 'Big Society', it was hungry, ruthless and acquisitive, aiming to strike a knockout blow while Labour was brought low through its own divisions and by the public disloyalty of many of its own MPs towards its leadership. It was against the background of the looming snap general election that the GMB reassembled for its 100th congress in Plymouth.

'I am here because you willed it'

The congress, conceived as a celebration of the GMB's longevity, was somewhat muted, not least as proceedings were cut back from the usual five days to barely three in order that delegates might get back in time to campaign before polling day, just as they had in 1983. Many predicted gloom and doom, accepting both the media predictions that Labour would be reduced to a mere rump of 150 or fewer MPs, and that the calling of the election was a masterstroke by Theresa May which would see the Conservatives return in triumph. Defeatism, however, was not in Mary's

◄ Mary with those closest to her, family and friends, at a reception given in her honour, in North London, after she had received her CBE from the Prince of Wales, 16 March 2017.

nature. Her health was poor, the returning cancer had her in its grip. Over the last year, she had had to delegate some of her branch duties and Malcolm Sage had taken over the chairing of the CEC when she was too ill to attend. Some had expected her to stand down but she was there, sure enough, at the December 2016 CEC, wagging a finger and teasing the delegates that 'don't think I don't know what you've been up to while I've been away!' – and above all she was there at her union's congress.

'It has not been an easy year', she admitted in her opening address. 'I have been like a cat with nine lives, although I only have five left now!'.[19] However, she pledged that 'you can bet your bottom dollar I will be steady in keeping congress moving' and, of course, she did precisely that. There was still that Mary look that said in no uncertain terms 'don't you push it', the support and words of encouragement for the 'first time delegate, first time speaker' and the unbreakable bond of affection between her and the membership that crackled and sparkled across the auditorium.[20] She couldn't stay up as late, apologised profusely for not being able

to attend all of the regional events as she always had in the past, and relied upon the support of her granddaughter, Lisa, to look after her. But she remained in control of the congress, determined to attend an afternoon session that recalled her friend and colleague, Jo Cox, the MP murdered by a right-wing extremist, and breathed heart into delegates dispirited by the thought of the coming election.

She had, she told the delegates, still been trying to put her speech together at 1.30 a.m. that morning, while in the hotel room the news broadcasts had pumped out images of Theresa May's comfortable, confident, privileged face. 'Don't be fooled', she told the hall, 'Listen to her words'.[21]

'They want to sell our NHS and saddle our young people with debt. They want to take food from our kids' bellies and lay-off thousands of hard-working school catering staff, and support staff, this year. I was a dinner lady and this union fought to get healthy free school meals. Well, Mrs May, we will fight you again. We fought Thatcher on the milk and we will fight you!'[22]

The GMB had much to be proud of:

'We have achieved a lot over the years, an eight-hour day, minimum wage, fighting to save our NHS, we were the first to raise issues on the mis-selling of pensions, the crisis in care homes, the first to highlight those who have raided company pension schemes'.[23]

Now, to the activists themselves and to the coming election:

'It is people like you who built our union. It is you who keep it growing today. We have a past to hold dear and we are proud now we have a great future ahead … No one but us will deliver that [Labour vote] to support our movement, and our colleagues deserve that right. Go out on the doorsteps and speak to people. In our branches we owe it to our members. The Tories who told you to buy your house on right-to-buy now want to take it away if you care for people with dementia … let's go out there and fight for a Labour government. Thatcher never broke us and I am bloody sure May won't either!'[24]

Congress responded with a standing ovation and, later, Sheila Bearcroft spoke for many when she paid tribute to Mary's record in 'breaking down the barriers of vested interests that held back so many able and talented female activists for so many years' through her 'indomitable spirit'. 'You really are the jewel in the GMB crown. You have your own style when discharging the role of National President and in chairing congress. You have that rare ability to show that you care for everyone in the GMB … may you continue to represent all that is good and decent in our great union'.[25] Mary had already provided delegates with a statement of her core conviction that: 'This congress belongs to you. You are the sole owners of this congress. I will make sure that will stand as long as I am in this chair', but she returned again to the theme.[26] The annual congress was the bedrock of the union's industrial democracy, to be owned and shaped by the lay members, those whom the GMB existed to protect, to further and to serve. She could no longer hide her own frailty, but in weakness there was strength. 'This is a job I love to do' she told her people. 'I am here because you have willed me and I have willed to get here'.[27] From the congress floor her name was chorused and a delegate called-out an impromptu: 'Three cheers for Mary Turner!', which was taken up by everyone just before the delegates joined in the singing of *The Red Flag*.[28]

All the elements of Mary's life combined and were amplified by those verses: the solidarity, the call to action and activism, and the essence of the union's original motto, settled upon by the Beckton gas workers more than a century before, of 'Love – Liberty – Fidelity'. The combination had sometimes seemed incongruous, especially during the hardnosed years of Clynes, Bondfield and Williamson. Yet the conjoining of dedication and faithfulness to the cause of liberty, and the appeal to love as an abstraction, that nevertheless comes unbidden, without the need for words or discussion, seems to sum up both the nature of Mary's career and her relationship with those that she spoke for and represented. It was a formidable achievement, one that could not be repeated, learned, bottled or sold, and it was all the more remarkable and precious for that. As so many said, both then and subsequently, Mary was unique, 'the most significant woman trade unionist of her generation'.

The last 'hurrah'!

Every last scrap of Mary's energy had been saved up for her congress duties. The journey back was gruelling, as the adrenalin faded and the cycle of hospital appointments resumed. Yet, that Thursday night, 8 June, provided its own surprises when, contrary to all expectations, Labour was not wiped off the electoral map. Without spin and gloss, the party had gone to the country with a progressive socialist manifesto and had clawed its way into the Tory majority, gaining 30 seats and denying the Conservative Party an overall majority in Parliament. It gave the lie to the idea that the left was unelectable, and dealt a knock to the idea of 'triangulation' in Labour politics, and a heavy blow to the ambitious coup conspirators within the PLP who actually seemed dismayed that Labour had survived the night. Mary was, first and foremost, a Labour loyalist. If you cut her, she always said, she 'would bleed GMB', but the Labour Party, from her father's example, was also encoded in her DNA. It was ever the 'people's party' and the political wing of the industrial movement. She knew full well what misery a total defeat would have brought at the polls for her own membership and she recognised just what had been achieved by the party under Corbyn. The lack of an overall majority effectively put an end to the 'dementia tax' and it also helped to ensure that the Conservative manifesto commitment to scrap free hot school meals and the provision of cold breakfasts for children could not be enacted. The dawn was breaking, even though you were sometimes unaware of it. On the morning of 9 June 2017, as the news came flooding in, Mary drew strength from the thought that the fight had not been in vain. The school meals service, though diminished, would survive and her own legacy, under a future Labour government, might be permitted to take root. Who said that voting never changed anything? Yet, Mary knew that democracy was not simply a matter of casting a vote once every five years and then sitting back and letting others do the work for you. It was about constantly campaigning, yourself, for what you felt was right, and taking that forward into every sphere of your life. That was what the GMB was good at, and it ensured that even in her last days Mary was to be found putting those principles into practice.

She could not, and would not, stop doing. On the way to her hospital appointments, she found out that her regular cab driver was distraught over his father's death, over the Easter weekend. He wanted the old man to be buried, according to Islamic custom, within the space of twenty-four hours, but everyone at the registrar's was either on holiday or not answering the phone. Mary made a call to Parvez Ahmed, the mayor of Brent, and a solution was quickly found.[29] In similar fashion, once at hospital, she would take a break from the oxygen mask pressed to her mouth, in order to handle calls from members anxious for advice. Having spoken with them, the mask could be slipped back on, or the treatments could begin. Family and members of the branch would keep her company through the long hospital evenings. BBC *Question Time* was always a highlight of the weeks when she was kept in for treatment, as, says Lesley Stansfield, 'It gave her something to shout at'.[30] Even at the end, when she had returned home and was receiving respite care, she was to be found, propped up in bed, compiling long lists of 'must do' things and advice for Penny Robinson and Gary Doolan to take to heart and to follow,

making sure that everything was going well for Cath Speight, Kathleen Walker Shaw and the union. She never ceased, or tired, of thinking of others.

GMB members heard of her passing, on 19 July 2017, when Tim Roache, the union's general secretary, sent out an email and press release, breaking the sad news that Mary 'was gone', but affirming that 'she has left behind a union that will ensure the values and principles she fought her whole life for will always endure'.[31] It captured, perfectly, what the union thought and felt at that moment. Mary had died peacefully, several hours earlier, surrounded by her family. Exceptionally, in the case of a trade union activist, as opposed to a leader, the news was run on TV broadcasts and her obituary appeared not just in the pages of *The Guardian* and the *Independent* but also in the establishment columns of the *Daily Telegraph* and *The Times*. Watching the cortege wind its way through Kilburn's streets, packed with well-wishers wanting to pay their respects, her daughter, Denise, was struck by the thought: 'Didn't the girl do well'.[32] The vast Church of the Sacred Heart was packed to capacity for the funeral service led by Fr Terry Murray. While it was

GMB

◄ Comrades at the close of the GMB's 100th congress, Plymouth, 6 June 2017: Malcolm Sage, Kathleen Walker Shaw, Mary Turner, Tim Roache and Ida Clemo.

undoubtedly a very public occasion, with the leader of the opposition, prominent MPs, former ministers and leading trade unionists all in attendance, alongside GMB activists, it was also intensely personal as the family, that had meant everything to her, children, grandchildren and great-grandchildren, all paid their own tributes. There were memories of kindnesses, both big and small, of holidays, good times shared, and always of the warmth of Mary's love.[33]

The weather had turned grim that morning. It seemed like winter had settled over north London rather than it being a summer's day. Under darkened skies and lashing rain, a large crowd encircled the plot, in Kensal Green Cemetery, where Mary was laid to rest alongside Denny. The sleet drummed down upon a sea of umbrellas, the ground turned to mud underfoot; close by an officer from another union hummed Jim Connell's *Red Flag* in remembrance of other days spent at Crossakiel. There was a simple 'Goodbye, Mary' from Paul Kenny as he leant over and dropped his rose into the open grave. It fluttered, red for a second, before being swallowed up by the darkness of the earth. A stream of silver heart shaped balloons glinted against the grey as they were sent up into the heavens, one for each member of the family, each carrying its own memories, thoughts and prayers. Farewells were said, the cold pinched, the damp seeped into every pore. At last the crowd dispersed, having taken its leave of one who had meant so much to so many different people.

A poem folded away, kept among Mary's private papers, might serve as her credo. There is, it said, 'the inner thing' in every one, that had been there since the time of slave revolts in ancient Rome to 'frighten Lord and King'. It was there to break free 'through pitiful Paris streets' in order to storm the walls of the Bastille. Uncomfortable, often ignored or despised, it is the universal idea that embraces liberty, economic justice, and the moral authority embodied in working people:

It is there in every race …
It screams in tyrants' eyes
It has reached the peaks of mountains high
It comes searing cross the skies,
It lights the dark of this prison cell
It thunders forth its might
It is the undauntable thought, my friend
The thought that says I'm RIGHT.[34]

How often had Mary had recourse to those words, and held onto that sense that she was, indeed, 'right' throughout the course her career, when facing down callous managers, rapacious landlords, politicians and union leaders who had forgotten the very cause in which they served? In every case those words and that sense had stood her well. For hers was a life that was well lived, of achievement, of love, light, and of laughter. It is one that defies all the usual clichés of political biographies. There were no 'what ifs', 'buts' or regrets, when it came to Mary. You will look in vain for tales of tawdry sell-outs or compromises of principle. She did not sacrifice her family life on the altar of political expediency, as so many others have done. Certainly, politics was not dry stuff when Mary was around. She was not a saint, and never pretended to be: as one of her comrades put it, 'if she had've been, she'd have been no damned use to us!' However, Mary, unlike so many political figures, was not personally ambitious. Her career had been a long one with a slow, incremental rise, gaining experience all the while that she could put to good use at the negotiating

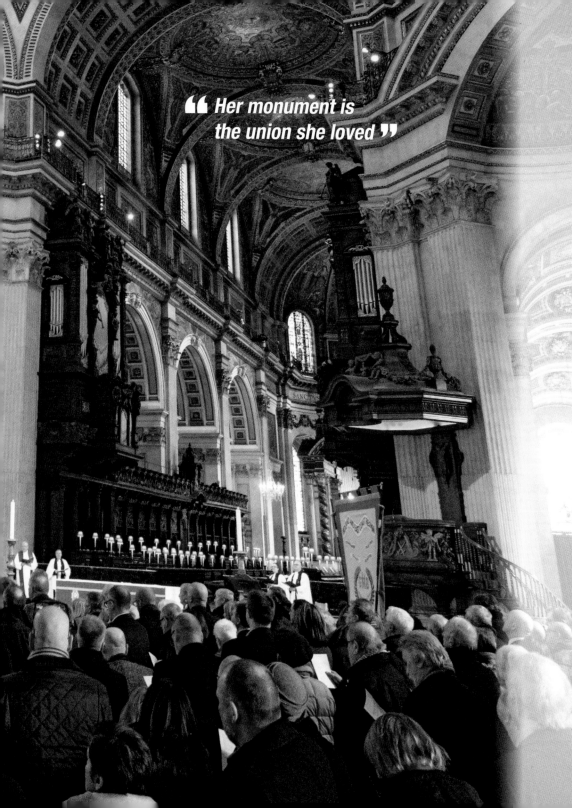

> **" Her monument is the union she loved "**

◀ A Last Farewell: the GMB's National and Regional banners are processed through St. Paul's Cathedral at the beginning of the Service of Thanksgiving held in her honour, 27 February 2018. In his welcome address, the Rev. Mark Oakley, the Canon in Residence, spoke of Mary's 'commitment throughout her life to the values of Socialism' and reminded the large congregation that she always spoke 'for ordinary workers, being the voice of those without privilege or power'. Outside, a snow storm swirled and turned the City white.

table, and always in the service of her members. The ambition that did course through her veins was of a different kind, fierce, passionate and raw but in the service of those she represented as a champion of the low-paid, the part-time, the casualised, the excluded, and the woman worker. She existed to help to secure justice and equality, to realise a full sense of humanity and to unleash the potential that lies within everyone. Her monument is not one set in stone: it is the union that she loved. While it exists and continues for fight injustice, 'Our Mary' can never be said to have truly passed: for she is there in its every victory, in the words of every new delegate who comes hesitatingly to the rostrum, in the spirit on every picket line when the winds blow chill, and in the belief that, through collective action, there is a better world to be won for the good of us all. She is there in every beat of the GMB's heart. ∎

Acknowledgements

The GMB, at its best, is a family union. A family that can sometimes disagree amongst itself, feud and fume, but one which also, when it comes together, unites in love and solidarity to achieve great things. It was an honour and a pleasure to have worked for it during the time of Mary Turner's and Paul Kenny's stewardship.

The trade unions have, since the 1980s, suffered from a crisis of visibility. Their stories and, especially, those of their lay activists are nowadays rarely told or recorded. This was never more marked than in the case of Mary herself. While she was a household name for GMB members and often pressed for autographs or more latterly 'selfies' with delegates at Congress – as 'Our Mary' who needed no other explanation – and while news of her death was broadcast on the bulletins of the major TV channels in Great Britain and Ireland, her career and achievements have barely registered in academic treatments of the recent history and development of the labour and trade union movements. You will look in vain for references to her in the indices of the vast, tome-like chronicles and memoirs published in the wake of New Labour or within specialist accounts of the role of women in the trade unions. Even Lewis Minkin's exhaustive account of the Labour NEC during the Blair years only accords her three brief mentions. There may be a reason for this, in as much as she, as a working-class activist, forever living in the moment of industrial and political struggles, rarely wrote for the newspapers and never for academic journals. When she was interviewed, it tended to be within a very specific context, usually the local politics of Brent or the campaigns waged by the GMB over the best part of four decades. As such, she tended to go under the radar of historians and academics, and I think that she rather liked it that way.

It was Harriet Harman MP at Mary's wake in August 2017 who first expressed the need for a book on her life. Warren Kenny and the London Region of the GMB decided to act upon her call by commissioning the biography that you now hold in your hands. Over the following pages you will see the list of those branches, organisations and ordinary members who contributed their hard-earned money to see that the book was published and, in this way, it is truly a 'people's book': a tribute to Mary Turner from those to whom she dedicated her life and endeavours.

Though the opinions contained within the covers of this book and any errors or omissions therein are those of the author, this book has been shaped and made possible through the goodwill, friendship and assistance of a large number of people. First and foremost are Mary's family, without whose involvement and support this would not have been possible. Namely: her children, Denise Folwell and John Turner; her sister, Meg Kavanagh; her grandchildren; Lisa and Anthony Folwell, Louise, Jack and Katie Turner; and great-grandchildren, Jessica and Millie Jo Bacon, Hallie Francis, Freddy, and Dennis Folwell. Lisa Folwell was unfailingly helpful in always being on hand to answer questions, access family photographs and provide the fund of family stories without which this book would have been well-nigh impossible.

Her 'Nan' would have been incredibly proud, as she was of all her family.

The following all gave their time and help with interviews and other materials for the book, for which I am extremely grateful:

Martin Allen, Barbara Benham, Peter Berresford Ellis, Andy Burman, Taranjit Chana, Brian Collins, Martin Collins, Bob Crosby, Francis Devine, Jack Dromey MP, Simon Fletcher, Dean Gilligan, Keir Greenaway, Charlotte Gregory, Alan Grimes, Anne Grimes, Sue Hackett, Harriet Harman MP, John Haylett, Paul Kenny, Warren Kenny, Bruce Kent, Richard Leonard MSP, Ken Livingstone, Richard Lynch, Seamus McDonagh, John McLean, Anni Marjoram, Olivia Pryle, Penny Robinson, Malcolm Sage, Bert Schouwenburg, Martin Smith, Cath Speight, Lesley Stansfield, Euton Stewart, Brian Strutton, Maria Sulis, Byron Taylor, Kathleen Walker Shaw, Tony Warr, Lord Larry Whitty, and Andy Worth.

Lawrence & Wishart remains a beacon in the world of radical, independent publishing. Katharine Harris oversaw the book's commissioning while Katharine Fletcher took it through the production stages to completion. Sally Davison was, as ever, the ideal proof reader and editor.

Lynette Cawthra at the Working-Class Movement Library and Jeff Howarth at the TUC Library were, as ever, incredibly generous and helpful with their time, materials and expertise. Their institutions represent two of the brightest jewels of the British labour movement. Without them, the institutional memory of unions like the GMB, and of lives like Mary's, would be irrevocably lost to us. They are national treasures and the movement would do well to view, and to support them, as such.

In similar fashion, Ida Clemo was always on hand with the available documentation and her own encyclopaedic knowledge concerning the GMB's institutional structure and administration during the period covered by Mary's career. Andrew Wiard has chronicled the recent history of the GMB through his unsurpassed photographs of demonstrations, marches, strikes and congresses. Each one combines the eye of the artist with the journalist's true instinct for reportage and intent to inform the historical record. ▶

Acknowledgements: Making history

▶ Julie Brown's professionalism and expertise produced the splendid design that enhances those images, and which has lent the book its own particular look and feel.

On a personal level, my thanks go to: Sean O' Brogain, Melissa Seims, Christina Harrington and Becky Stocks, whose friendship was a constant throughout. Similarly, my thanks are also due to the kindnesses of Julianne and Richie Emborg, firm members of GMB Durham branch, and my hopes are that their son, Niky, likes his 'Uncle John's' new book!

There is one last mention.

Gary Doolan was unfortunately not able to contribute to the book in the way that he would have wished. He was the best of union officers, and the most loyal of friends and comrades to Mary and to Paul Kenny, as well as to myself and a host of his other colleagues in the GMB. Always bursting with ideas, energy and life, he liked a good scrap on behalf of his members and was the very essence of the union. Like Mary, he was Labour 'through and through' but unlike her, his was a promise that was never destined to be fully realised. Mary's death hit him particularly hard. In the midst of his chemotherapy treatment he made sure that he came to her memorial service at St. Paul's, as a simple debt of honour and as a mark of the deepest affection, on a day when a sudden and unseasonable chill crept into every corner and crevice of the cathedral. Outside on the steps the snows had started to fall and to swirl, forming in drifts and soon blotting out a pale sun. It had taken the last reservoirs of his strength to make the journey and sit through the celebration of Mary's life. He wouldn't have wanted it to be any other way. Wrapped in the folds of his overcoat, and with a still-firm handshake as he climbed into the back of a black cab, he passed out of my own vision and life.

So, in a way, this book represents his story and monument too, just as it does for every faithful GMB activist who stands, or has ever stood, beside their union through the bad times and the good, but remains always true in their comradeship. ■

John Callow, 8 February 2019

Acknowledgements

Donors to the book project

This book was made possible by donations from the GMB's rank and file members, individual branches, regions and activists. It could not have been published without the support of the following:

GMB CWU Branch
GMB Harlow Gas
GMB Ipswich and District
GMB Barking (B10)
GMB Redbridge R27
GMB Barking & Dagenham (B11)
GMB Huntingdon and Wisbech
Received in cash congress bucket collection
GMB X47 Holborn Apex
GMB H46 Hounslow
GMB Scotland
GMB Milton Keynes M20
GMB Central Wembley C22
GMB Barnet Public Services P06
GMB Camden Apex X19
GMB British Airways Hatton Cross X31
GMB Islington/Haringey I35
GMB East Dereham
GMB Cambridge 2
GMB London Region/Regional

Committee
GMB Beds County B44
GMB London Stores L54
GMB Hendon H30
Warren Kenny Donations 2018
GMB Hillingdon H37
GMB King's Lynn 1 K17
GMB Essex Public Services
GMB Plaistow
GMB Glasgow 29
GMB Luton Branch (L45)
GMB Norwich General
GMB Norfolk Public Services
GMB British Airways LHR (diary donation)
GMB City of London (diary donation)
GMB London Security (diary donation)
GMB Thames General
GMB Heathrow Cargo
GMB Havering

GMB Stanstead Airport
GMB Barnet PS
GMB BA Hatton Cross
GMB Energy Central
GMB East Dereham
GMB A37 Aviation Security
GMB North West London
GMB Securicor 1
GMB Unite M23
GMB Huntingdon CFTAT
GMB Braintree and Bocking
GMB Salstream
GMB Silvertown Sugarworkers
GMB Tower Hamlets
GMB Waterworks Branch
GMB London Volunteer Servers
Workers' Beer Company - Events, Bars & Catering Finsbury Park. *This event was organised by Paul Kenny and Ida Clemo.*

Photo credits

Barbara Benham
91, 164

Brent Archives
16 (bottom)

Stefano Cagnoni (reportdigital.co.uk)
170

Jim Connell Society
116

Cuba Solidarity Campaign
163

Lisa Folwell & the Turner Family
8, 10, 11, 14, 16 (top), 17, 18, 19, 20-21,
23, 26, 28, 29, 56, 57, 61, 84 (left), 85

GMB Hendon Branch
32, 73, 109

GMB London Region
40, 41, 43, 66, 81, 88-89, 92, 94, 97, 100,
101, 104, 105, 112, 124, 125, 126, 127,
128, 130, 131, 151, 165

John Harris (reportdigital.co.uk)
134, 135, 171

Jess Hurd (reportdigital.co.uk)
158

TUC Library
42, 46, 47, 50, 55, 60, 68, 76, 77, 84 (right)

Andrew Wiard
Front Cover, ii, 6, 34, 35, 97, 118, 119, 122,
136, 138, 141, 144, 146, 147, 152, 156,
168, 172-173, 176-177, 180, 182, 183,
184, 191, 192, 196, 198-199, 200-201

Philip Wolmuth (reportdigital.co.uk)
187

Abbreviations

AEEU Amalgamated Engineers and Electricians Union, 1992-2002

Amicus The rebranded union formed from the merger of the AEEU and the EETPU, 2002-2007

APEX Association of Professional, Executive, Clerical and Computer Staff

AUEW Amalgamated Union of Engineering Workers

BAME Black, Asian and Minority Ethnic

BDA British Dietetic Association

BNP British National Party

CBE Commander of the British Empire

CBI Confederation of British Industry

CCT Compulsory Competitive Tendering

CEC Central Executive Committee of the GMB, from 1976 onwards

CND Campaign for Nuclear Disarmament

COHSE Confederation of Health Service Employees

CPAG Child Poverty Action Group

CPGB Communist Party of Great Britain, 1920-91

CWU Communication Workers' Union

DUP Democratic Unionist Party

EDL English Defence League

EETPU Electrical, Electronic, Telecommunication and Plumbing Union

EU European Union

FTAT Furniture, Timber and Allied Trades Union

GLC Greater London Council

GLEB Greater London Enterprise Board

GMB Originally the General, Municipal and Boilermakers' Union but by the 1990s rebranded as a logo for the union as opposed to a set of initials

GMBATU General, Municipal, Boilermakers and Allied Trade Union (acronym adopted in 1982 after the merger between the GMWU and the Boilermakers' union. It was rapidly shortened to 'GMB' and was generally accepted as such from 1989 onwards, when the union merged with APEX)

GMWU General and Municipal Workers' Union, 1924-82

HR Human resources

ILEA Inner London Education Authority

ITUUI Irish Trade Unions for Unity and Independence

LEA Local education authority

LGBT Lesbian, Gay, Bisexual and Transgender

MBE Member of the British Empire

MSF Manufacturing, Science and Finance Union

NATKE National Association of Theatrical, Television and Kine Employees

NATO North Atlantic Treaty Organisation

NATSOPA National Society of Operative Printers & Assistants

NEC Labour Party, National Executive Committee

NHS National Health Service

NOD National Organising Department (of the GMB)

NOT National Organising Team (of the GMB)

NUS National Union of Seamen

NUPE National Union of Public Employees

NUPGE National Union of Public and General Employees (Canada)

NUTGW National Union of Tailor and Garment Workers

PPE Politics, Philosophy, Economics

RMT Rail, Maritime and Transport Union

SIPTU Services, Industrial, Professional and Technical Union (Ireland)

SOG Self-organising groups

TAs School teaching assistants

T&G Transport and General Workers' Union

TUC Trade Union Congress

Unite Britain's largest union, forged from the merger between the T&G and Amicus in 2010

USDAW Union of Shop Distributive and Allied Workers

UUP Ulster Unionist Party

WEEP Work employment on employer's premises

YOP Youth Opportunity Programme

Endnotes

Chapter 1

1 Corbett, W., and Nolan, W. (eds), *Thurles: The cathedral town*, Geography Publications, Dublin, 1989, pp5, 22-24.
2 Meg Kavanagh (née O'Brien), interviews with the author, 16 June 2018 and 17 January 2019.
3 *Ibid.*, 16 June 2018.
4 Dunne, C., *An unconsidered people: The Irish in London*, New Island, Dublin, 2003, p2.
5 Buckley, M., cited in: Walter, B., *Outsiders inside: Whiteness, place and Irish women*, Routledge, London, 2001, pp150-151.
6 Dunne, *op. cit.*, p5; Whooley, F., *Irish Londoners: Photographs from the Paddy Fahey Collection*, Grange Museum/Sutton Publishing, Stroud, Gloucestershire, 1997, p5.
7 *GMB Working Together,* April 1991, p15.
8 Dunne, *op. cit.*, p60.
9 Jack Dromey MP, interview with the author, 13 September 2018.
10 Kavanagh, interview, 16 June 2018.
11 Whooley, *op. cit.*, p48.
12 Dunne, *op. cit.*, p98.
13 Kavanagh, interview, 16 June 2018).
14 *Ibid.*
15 Maguire, K., 'GMB's First Lady', *GMB Candid*, Spring 2010, p13.
16 Callow, J., *GMB@Work. The story behind the union, 1889-2012*, Evans Mitchell Books, London, 2012, pp355-356, 358-359.
17 Kavanagh, interview, 16 June 2018.
18 *Ibid.*
19 TUC, 'Mary Turner, winner: Women's Gold Badge', *Congress Events,* TUC, London, 2012, p43; GMB, *Mary Turner: Biography*, GMB, London, 2014, f1.
20 Sykes, C. C., Area Manager, 'Jackson, the Tailor', reference for Miss M. O' Brien, 15 May 1958, 1f.
21 Anon., 'Moving into "Paradise" from the "Hell" of Granville Road', *The Kilburn Times*, 1 March 1963, p17.
22 *Ibid.*; Barbara Benham, interview with the author, 16 June 2018; Cath Speight, interview with the author, 15 January 2019.
23 Denise Folwell, interview with the author, 16 June 2018.
24 Anon., 'They held a party in spite of critics', *The Kilburn Times*, 25 December 1964, p3.
25 Walsh, J., 'The dinner lady who succeeded in a male-dominated movement', *Times Chronicle Series*, 6 February 1992, p11.
26 Maguire, *op. cit.*, p13.
27 Folwell, interview, 16 June 2018.

Chapter 2

1 GMWU, *Report of the Sixty-Fifth Congress. Pavilion Theatre, Bournemouth, Sunday 18 May to Thursday 22 May 1980*, GMWU, London, 1980, p637.
2 Anon., 'Mary Turner', *The Times*, p56; Callow, *GMB@Work*, p354.
3 Hayman, K., 'Dinner lady joins Labour top brass', *The Times Chronicle Series*, 12 October 1995, p5.
4 Callow, *op. cit.*, p355.
5 GMWU, *Report of the Sixty-Fifth Congress*, p442.
6 Callow, *op. cit.*, pp255, 258-261; Lane, T., and Roberts, K., *Strike at Pilkington's*, Collins/Fortana, London, 1971, *passim*.
7 Larry Whitty, interview with the author, 7 January 2019.
8 Anon., 'John Cope – London as eel pie', *GMB Journal*, June 1986, p19.
9 GMB, *GMB – Britain's General Union. Proceedings at the Annual Congress. The Brighton Centre, Brighton, 4-7 June 2007*, GMB, London, 2007.
10 Dromey, J., and Taylor, G., *Grunwick: The workers' story*, 2nd edition, Lawrence & Wishart, London, 2016, pp121-125, 128-135, 151-161, 165-179; Rogaly, J., *Grunwick*, Penguin Books, Harmondsworth, 1977, pp9-

15, 19-21, 185-187.
11 GMB, *Report of Congress 2003. Winter Gardens, Blackpool, Sunday 8-Thursday 12 June*, GMB, London, 2003, p160.
12 Barbara Benham, interview with the author, 16 June 2018.
13 Cope, J., 'Fight Against Privatisation', *GMB Journal*, December 1983-January 1984, p6.
14 *Ibid.*, pp6-7.
15 Warner, D., contribution to *Mary Turner, 1938-2017: Memories of an amazing and inspirational woman*, GMB, London, 2017, final folio.
16 GMB, *Report of Congress 2003*, p159.
17 GMWU, *Report of the Sixty-Fifth Congress*, p636.
18 *Ibid.*, p637.
19 Klein, N., *The shock doctrine: The rise of disaster capitalism*, Penguin Books, London, 2007, p52.
20 Rumsfeld, D., quoted in: Klein, *op. cit.*, p116.
21 Klein, *op. cit.*, p135.
22 Haylett, J., 'Roast dinner welcome – The London Borough of Brent welcomes the jobs marchers today', *Morning Star*, 2 June 1983, p2.
23 Beckett, F., *The battle for London*, Pluto Press, London, 1985, pp78-79.
24 Jack Dromey, interview with the author, 13 September 2018.
25 Bevins, A., 'Charity campaign "is political"', *Daily Mail*, 29 April 1981; War on Want, *Press Release*, 29 April 1981.
26 TUC, *People's March for Jobs, May '81: Official Souvenir,* TUC, London, 1981, p2.
27 *The Guardian*, 28 May 1981.
28 Jack Dromey, interview with the author, 13 September 2018.
29 Livingstone, K., (foreword), *A Tribute to the People's March for Jobs*, 2nd edition, News Line Magazine, London, 13 June 1981, p58.
30 Stanley, J., 'Thunderous reception for jobs protestors',

Morning Star, 29 May 1981, p1. See also: Benn, T., *The End of an Era: Diaries, 1980-90*, ed. Winstone, R., Arrow Books, London, 1992, p133.

31 *TUC, People's March for Jobs, May '81, Official Souvenir*, TUC London, 1981, p4. George Melly, the veteran jazz musician and bohemian stalwart of many left wing causes performed alongside Pete Townsend, a former member of the Young Communist League, Viv Albertine and The Slits, and Aswad.

32 Andalo, D., 'Rock in the Park: Welcome to the Republic of Brixton', *South London Press*, 5 June 1981, p38.

33 'Prior denies blame for jobless and rules out more financial aid', *The Guardian*, 2 June 1981, p1.

34 Ezard, J., '100,000 join jobs march finale', *The Guardian*, 1 June 1981, p1.

35 Warman, C., Routledge, P., and Evans, R., 'Tories not to blame, Prior tells marchers', *The Times*, 2 June 1981, p2. See also: Murray, A., 'The leaders must build on the march', *Morning Star,* 1 June 1981, p1.

36 *Ibid.*

37 Anon., 'Jobs Express train', *GMW Journal*, September 1981, p23.

38 GMWU, *Report of the Sixty-Seventh Congress*, p442.

39 Thurland, A., 'Too old but too young', *Labour Herald*, 20 November 1981, p12.

40 Anon., 'Mary Turner. Union activist who began by defending the interests of dinner ladies in Brent and rose to become the President of the GMB', *The Times*, 21 July 2017, p56.

41 *Ibid.*, p56.

42 Anon., 'Express success… But Thatcher persists with her cruel policy', *GMW Journal*, Christmas 1981, p9; TUC, *Jobs for Youth Campaign: Accommodation in Greater London for the Weekend of the 27-29 November for 2,000 Young People*, TUC, Press Release, 26 November 1981; Anon., 'Here's Bread for the Jobless …', *Wembley Observer*, 4 December 1981, p5.

43 GMWU, *Report of the Sixty-Seventh Congress, Congress*

Theatre, Eastbourne, Sunday 23 May to Thursday 27 May 1982*, GMWU, London, 1982, p441.

44 Callow, *GMB@Work*, p356; Barbara Benham, interview with the author, 16 June 2018.

45 Harford, B., and Hopkins, S. (eds), *Greenham Common: Women at the wire*, The Women's Press, London, 1984, pp1-2, 11, 19; Kent, B., *Undiscovered ends*, HarperCollins, London, 1992, pp171-175; Postgate, O., *The plain man's guide to the Bomb*, The Menard Press, London, 1982, pp11-13, 17, 19-21; Bruce Kent, interview with the author, 7 January 2019.

46 This alliance became even more marked with the 1983 People's March for Jobs, where the rallies became intertwined with those of CND. See: Sanders, J., 'No ifs, No buts – Give us jobs now', *Morning Star*, 25 May 1983, p5.

47 Anon., 'Thatcher sees young jobless', *Daily Telegraph*, 1 December 1981; Merritt, J., 'She gave us no hope', *Daily Mirror*, 1 December 1981, Felton, D., 'No hope from Thatcher, say the young', *The Times*, 1 December 1981.

48 Morton, A., 'No-hope Maggie shuns jobs plea', *Daily Star,* 1 December 1981.

49 Anon., 'Inside left – Jobs for youth', *City Limits*, 20-26 November 1981.

50 GMWU, *Report of the Sixty-Seventh Congress*, p441.

51 Brent Trades Council, *Marchers – We won't let you down*, Brent Trades Council, London, 1983, p1.

52 *Ibid.*, p1.

53 Benn, *End of an Era*, p265.

54 Haylett, 'Roast dinner welcome', p2.

55 Gostwick, M., 'Jobs crusade on its way', *Morning Star*, 25 April 1983, p1.

56 Wintour, P., 'Respectability goes on the march', *The Guardian*, 23 May 1983, p2.

57 *Ibid.*

58 GMB, *Report of the First Congress. Spa Grand Hall, Scarborough, Sunday and Monday, 5-6 June 1983*,

GMB, London, 1983, pp305, 328.

59 *Ibid.*, p328.

60 Basnett, D., 'Defence: Unions must prepare for a new onslaught of Thatcherism', *GMB Journal*, June-July 1983, p2.

61 Boilermakers' Union, unpublished Executive Council Report, 1983, 1f., Mary Turner Papers.

62 GMWU, *Report of the Sixty-Seventh Congress*, p442.

63 Gopsill, T., and Andersen, R., 'On the sidings: Responses to unemployment', *The Leveller*, no. 69, 13-26 November 1981, p2.

64 Anon., 'Inside Left – Jobs for Youth', *op. cit.*

65 Motion 102, Hendon Branch, London Region, Congress 1982.

66 GMWU, *Report of the Sixty-Seventh Congress*, p442.

67 *Ibid.*

68 Beckett, F., *The Battle for London*, Pluto Press, London, 1985, p8.

69 *Ibid.*, p87.

70 Popular Planning Unit (GLC), *Jobs for a Change*, no.5, January 1984, p4.

71 Blunkett, D., and Jackson, K., *Democracy in crisis: The town halls respond*, The Hogarth Press, London, 1987, p166.

72 Beckett, *op. cit.*, p9.

73 Livingstone, K., *You Can't Say That: Memoirs*, Faber and Faber, London, 2011, pp247-248, 261. Labour took 84 of the council seats, with 4 each secured by the Conservatives and the Liberal/SDP Alliance.

74 Ken Livingstone, interview with the author, 14 January 2019. ▶

Chapter 3

▶ 1 See, for example, Lord Cooper's part in the debate in the House of Lords on In Place of Strife, as reported in the *GMWU Journal*, Vol. 32 no. 4, April 1969, p3.

2 *GMWU Journal*, Vol. 32 no. 5, May 1969, pp4-5.

3 Anon., 'Congress Report', *GMWU Journal*, Vol. 33 no. 6, June 1970, p18. J. Twist, one of the delegates from Sutton Oak branch on Merseyside, was more direct. He described the GMWU as 'a bloody awful union' and castigated it for cosying up to the establishment, ibid. on Merseyside, was more direct. He described the GMWU as 'a bloody awful union' and castigated it for cosying up to the establishment, *ibid*.

4 Anon., 'Trade unions – Still for men only?', *GMWU Journal*, Vol. 35 no. 3, March 1972, pp18-21; Anon., 'Do men at TU meetings sneer at women?', *GMWU Journal*, Vol. 35 no. 5, May 1972, p21; Anon., 'Servicing the shop floor', *GMWU Journal*, Vol. 35 no. 6, June 1072, pp8-9; Anon., 'Women's champion', *GMWU Journal*, Vol. 36 no. 9, September 1973, p15. Marian Veitch was described as being 'never a Women's Lib. enthusiast' and as possessing 'Cold eyes and a waspish tongue'.

5 Shaw, P., 'The growing power of the army in skirts – When housewife turns shop steward she'll need more than charm', *GMWU Journal*, Vol. 32 no. 8, August 1969, pp20-21; Olga Mean quoted in Anon., 'Congress Report', *GMWU Journal*, Vol. 32 no. 7, July 1969, p8.

6 Untitled panel, *GMW Journal*, May-June 1982, p2.

7 Larry Whitty, interview with the author, 7 January 2019.

8 *Ibid*.

9 Barbara Benham, interview with the author, 16 June 2018. You can also see Mary telling one version of these stories at the 2012 GMB Equalities Conference: https://www.youtube.com/watch?v=koXe6lX71bw.

10 Paul Kenny, interview with the author, 21 January 2019.

11 Basnett, D., 'The Lost 100,000', *GMWU Campaign Report*, December 1981, p1.

12 The vote was won by a 3:1 margin in the GMWU and by 2:1 in the Boilermakers' Society. Anon., 'Success: Members vote a big "Yes" for merger', *GMW Journal*, October-November 1982, p1; Basnett, D., 'New union is born', *GMB Journal*, December 1982-January 1983, p2.

13 Willman, P., Morris, T., and Aston, B., *Union Business: Trade union organisation and financial reform in the Thatcher years*, Cambridge University Press, Cambridge, 1993, p141.

14 Cope, J., 'Lay activists swamp London conference', *GMW Journal*, January-February 1982, p15.

15 Paul Kenny, interview, 21 January 2019; Cope, J., 'Our Mary gets MBE', *GMB Candid*, Spring 2010, p8; Anon., 'Union welcomes new members to Central Executive Council', *GMB Journal*, December 1983-January 1984, p11.

16 Anon., 'The cook who came in from the cold', *GMW Journal*, January-February 1982, p5; Anon., 'Welsh march against Tories', *GMW Journal*, August 1981, p11; Anon., 'Our new directions', *GMB Journal*, October 1987, p11; *GMB Journal*, February 1986, p2; *GMB Direct*, Issue 29, November-December 1996, p15.

17 GMB, *Report of the Second Congress*, p477, *GMB Working Together*, January 1990, p10.

18 GMB, *Report of the Second Congress, Princes Theatre, Torquay, Sunday to Friday, 3-8 June 1984*, GMB, London, 1984, p477.

19 *Ibid*., pp477-478.

20 *Ibid*., p460.

21 Walsh, J., 'The dinner lady who succeeded in a male dominated movement', *Times Chronicle Series*, 6 February 1992, p11.

22 Anon., 'John Cope – London as eel pie', *GMB Journal*, June 1986, p19.

23 Paul Kenny, interview, 21 January 2019.

24 *GMB Journal*, February 1986, p2; Anon., 'Political fund ballot: GMB's magnificent triumph', *GMB Journal*, July-August 1985, p1; Larry Whitty, interview, 7 January 2019.

25 Hurley, C., and Riley, S. (eds), *Recipe for change: A good practice guide to school meals*, Child Poverty Action Group, London, 2004, p13; McMahon, W., and Walsh, T., *Filling the gap: Free school meals, nutrition and poverty*, Child Poverty Action Group, London, 1999, p6.

26 Hurley and Riley, *op. cit.*, p13; Orrery, J., *The dinner lady: Change the way children eat for life*, foreword Oliver, J., Transworld Publishers, London, 2005, p34.

27 Anon., 'End of School Meals', *GMW Journal*, April 1981, p27.

28 Anon., 'Dinner ladies' jobs in jeopardy under Social Security Bill', *GMB Journal*, June 1986, p7.

29 Dibb, S., 'Food for thought', *GMB Direct*, Issue 1, February 1992, p19.

30 Hurley and Riley, *op. cit.*, pp9, 15; Dowler, E., Turner, S., and Dobson, B., *Poverty bites: Food, health and poor families*, Child Poverty Action Group, London, 2001, p12.

31 GMWU, *Report of the Sixty-Seventh Congress*, p499.

32 TUC, *Report of 121st Annual Trades Union Congress, 4-8 September 1989*, TUC, London, 1989, p.473.

33 Orrery, *op. cit.*, p10.

34 Since the 1960s, academia has expressed an increasing interest in recovering untold stories and 'hidden' histories, particularly among disadvantaged or ethnic minority groups. However, there is a paucity of material available that deals with the experiences of women's work in town halls, the school meals service, and in the lower grades of the health service, since 1945.

35 Brent Trades Council, *Unemployment in Brent*, Brent Trades Council, London, May 1982, p7.

36 *The Brent Worker, Newsletter of Brent Council Manual J.C.C.*, No. 2, Spring 1985, p1.

37 Turner, M., 'Fighting to keep school meals on the menu', *Morning Star*, 20 July 1982, p4.

38 Anon., '"Our Mistake" – Council tells meals ladies', *GMW Journal*, April-May 1982, p10.

39 Anon., 'I.T. hears claim from Devon dinner ladies', *GMB Journal*, July-August 1983, p11.

40 Anon., 'Dinner ladies' dismissal case makes legal history', *GMB Journal*, October-November 1983, p15.

41 Anon., 'London borough scraps school meals', *GMB Journal*, March-April 1983, p5.

42 The Brent Education Committee reported, on 5 January 1981, that government cutbacks meant that the authority would be forced to recover 110 per cent of its provision at Kilburn Polytechnic and 140 per cent at Willesden College of Technology. 'Seventy per cent of this cost', the committee laconically observed, was the 'overhead' of 'labour'. However this was dressed-up, Mary knew full well that it meant redundancies and the shredding of the service. See: London Borough of Brent, Education Committee, *Report No. 286 of the Director of Education*, 5 January 1981, ff1, 3, 5.

43 TUC, *Report of the 123rd Annual Trade Union Congress, 2-6 September 1991*, TUC, London, 1991, pp344-345.

44 TUC, *Report of the 123rd Annual Trade Union Congress*, p345.

45 Thomson, 'Lorraine's poverty trap', *GMB Working Together*, December 1991, p11.

46 Holmes, K., 'Eat your greens', *GMB Direct*, Issue 24, January-February 1996, p6.

47 *Brent Union News*, April 1988, p8.

48 *Ibid.*

49 *Brent Union News*, September 1984, p9.

50 *Brent Union News*, February 1984, pp5, 11.

51 Callow, J., *GMB@Work*, p358.

52 Anon., 'Action warning over food safety', *GMB Working Together*, October 1989, p13.

53 Maguire, K., 'GMB's First Lady', p13.

54 Holmes, *op. cit.*, p6.

55 *Ibid.*

56 *Ibid.*

57 Maria Sulis, interview with the author, 16 January 2019.

58 Hayman, K., 'Dinner lady joins Labour top brass', *Times Chronicle Series*, 12 October 1995, p5.

59 *Ibid.*

60 Darley, A., 'Tories regain control at Brent town hall', *Kilburn Times*, 16 February 1995, p1.

61 Anon., 'Private firm will run school meals', *Brent Leader*, 3 August 1995, p3.

Chapter 4

1 Lisa Folwell, email to the author, 23 January 2019.

2 Anon., 'True to form: Mary plays mum to the marchers', *GMB Journal*, June 1986, p19.

3 *Brent Union News*, Winter 1984-85, p5.

4 *Ibid.*

5 GMB, *Report of the Fifth Congress, London, 22-25 June 1987*, GMB, London, 1987, p505.

6 Harman, H., *A woman's work*, Allen Lane/ Penguin Books, London, 2017, p44.

7 Anni Marjoram, interview with the author, 11 January 2019.

8 Anon., 'NEC plans for women "flawed"', *The Guardian*, 1 October 1987, p5.

9 Hetherington, P., 'Leadership rebuffed on Ministry for Women', *The Guardian*, 29 September 1986; Harman, H., *The century gap: Twentieth century man – Twenty-first century woman*, Vermilion, London, 1993, pp171-172

10 GMB, *Report of the Third Congress, Opera House, Blackpool, 2-6 June 1985*, GMB, London, 1985, p416; GMB, *Report of the Fourth Congress, SPA Grand Hall, Scarborough, 1-5 June 1986*, GMB, London, 1986, p449.

11 Anni Marjoram, interview with the author, 11 January 2017; Harman, *A woman's work*, p141. See also: Harman, *The century gap*, pp127-128, 165-168.

12 GMB, *Report of Congress, 2003. Winter Gardens, Blackpool, 8-12 June 2003*, GMB, London, 2003, p49.

13 See, for example, the academic study he co-authored in retirement: Tutchell, E., and Edmonds, J., *Man-made: Why so few women are in positions of power*, Routledge, London, 2016.

14 GMB, *Report of the Second Congress*, p477.

15 *Ibid.*

16 Maguire, K., 'GMB's First Lady', *GMB Candid*, Spring 2010, p12.

17 Mary Turner, copy of reply to an advert in the *Kilburn Times*, 16 October 1974, 1f.

18 Ken Livingstone, interview with the author, 14 January 2019.

19 Wintour, P., '"Love me or leave me", Livingstone tells Brent', *The Guardian*, 18 July 1989, p6.

20 Linton, M., 'Support for PR surprises Labour', *The Guardian*, 31 July 1989, p2; Wintour, op. cit.

21 Livingstone, K., *You can't say that: Memoirs*, Faber and Faber, London, 2011, p315.

22 Livingstone, *op. cit.*, p488; Anon., 'The steps to reconciliation', *The Guardian*, 17 December 2003, p9.

23 Malcolm Sage, interview with the author, 3 October 2018.

24 Edmonds, J., 'Dick Pickering, 1942-1996', *GMB Direct*, Issue 29, November-December 1996, p2.

25 Two years later she would be returned, unopposed: *GMB Direct*, Issue 22, September-October 1995, p14.

26 *GMB Direct*, Issue 32, July-August 1997, p9.

27 *Ibid.*

28 *GMB Working Together*, September 1989, p9.

29 Anon., 'Skills Centre trainees receive certificates', *Times Chronicle Series*, 11 June 1992, p11.

30 *GMB Working Together*, April 1991, p15.

31 Anon., 'United Kingdom: More nuclear weapons per square mile than any country on earth', *GMW Journal*, July 1981, p8.

32 Anon., 'GMB joins the CND: Against executive wishes', *GMB Journal*, July-August 1985, p11.

33 *GMB Working Together*, October 1989, p13; *GMB Working Together*, July-August 1990, p9; ▶

▶ *GMB Direct*, October 1992, p14.

34 Fraser, K. M., *Same or different: Gender politics in the workplace*, Ashgate, Brookfield, USA, 1999, pp31, 78, 102, 110, 129, 154, 163, 177, 199, 220; Boston, S., *Women workers and trade unions*, revised edition, Lawrence & Wishart, London, 2015, p362. For an academic study that seems entirely disconnected from the unions as Mary Turner understood and experienced them, see: Ledwith,S., and Hansen, L. L. (eds), *Gendering and diversifying trade union leadership*, Routledge, London, 2013.

35 Routledge, P., *Mandy: The unauthorised biography of Peter Mandelson*, Pocket Books, London, 1999, pp113-115, 118, 269-270; Smith, A., *Faces of Labour: The inside story*, Verso, London, 1996, pp311-312.

36 *GMB Working Together*, July-August 1990, p7.

37 *Ibid.* p.5.

38 Undy, R., *Trade union merger strategies: Purpose, process, and performance*, Oxford University Press, Oxford, 2008, p117; *GMB Working Together*, February 1991, p5.

39 GMB, *Culture change in the GMB: CEC special report to congress*, GMB, London, June 1999, p5; *GMB Direct*, February 1992, p1; *GMB Direct*, October 1992, p13; GMB Direct, Issue 9, July-August 1993, p8; GMB Direct, Issue 13, March-April 1994, p4.

40 Willman, P., Morris, T., and Aston, B., *Union business: Trade union organisation and financial reform in the Thatcher years*, Cambridge University Press, Cambridge, 1993, pp142-143.

41 *GMB Direct*, Issue 26, May-June 1996, p13; Anon., 'Clause Four change defended', *GMB Direct*, Issue 21, July-August 1995, p7.

42 Fabian Society, *A new constitution for the Labour Party: The report of the Archer committee*, The Fabian Society, London, June 1993, p5; McIlroy, J., 'The enduring alliance? Trade unions and the making of New Labour 1994-1997', p540; Beech, M., and Lee, S. (eds), *Ten years of New Labour*, Palgrave/Macmillan, Houndmills, Basingstoke, 2008, pp38, 71-72; Seldon, A. (ed.), *Blair's Britain, 1997-2007*, Cambridge University Press, Cambridge, 2007, pp4, 35, 164-165, 214-225, 274-277.

43 Kampfner, J., *Blair's wars*, Free Press, London, 2003, p351.

44 Anon., 'Blair's strategy mapped out', *GMB Direct*, Issue 21, July-August 1995, p7.

45 *Ibid.* p8.

46 McIlroy, *op. cit.*, pp542, 544.

47 Anon., 'Political fund ballot: GMB's magnificent triumph', *GMB Journal*, July-August 1985, p1.

48 *GMB Direct*, Issue 29, November-December 1996, p15.

49 Hayman, 'Dinner lady joins Labour top brass', p5.

50 Beech, M., and Lee, S. (eds), *Ten years of New Labour*, Palgrave/Macmillan, Houndmills, Basingstoke, 2008, p125; McIlroy, *op. cit.*, p.546.

51 McIlroy, *op. cit.*, p546.

52 Anon., 'Trouble with the press, a voting fiasco and the union reps who kept quiet', *The Guardian*, 30 March 2001, supplement p4.

53 *Ibid.*

54 L. Minkin, *The Blair supremacy: A study in the politics of Labour Party's management*, Manchester University Press, Manchester, 2014, pp248, 255.

55 Robinson, T., *No cunning plan: My story*, Sidgwick & Jackson, London, 2016, p372.

56 Jack Dromey, interview with the author, 13 September 2018.

57 Liverpool Echo Reporter, 'Wirral South MP Ben Chapman to quit over expenses scandal', *Liverpool Echo*, 21 May 2009.

58 White, M., 'Labour selects diplomat', *The Guardian*, 28 November 1996, p10.

59 *Ibid.*

60 Keith Harper quoted in: *GMB Direct*, Issue 29, November-December 1996, p8.

61 *GMB Direct*, Issue 30, January-February 1997, p5.

62 Penny Robinson, interview with the author, 8 October 2018.

63 Beech and Lee, *op. cit.*, p122; Dowler, E., Turner, S., and Dobson, B., *Poverty bites: Food, health and poor families*, CPAG, London, 2001, pp80-81.

64 *GMB Direct*, Issue 32, July – August 1997, p7.

65 Walshe, N., 'Jim Connell: A biographical sketch', *Saothar*, no. 24, 1999, p96.

66 Boyd, A., *Jim Connell: Author of the Red Flag*, Donaldson Archive/Socialist History Society, Oxford, 2001, pp12, 20-22, 25-27, 29, 39-45; Grimes, T. (ed.), *Jim Connell, author of "The Red Flag"*, Memorial unveiling, Crossakiel, 26 April 1998, Jim Connell Society, Slane, 1998, pp3, 8-9.

67 Livingstone, *op. cit.*, pp185-188, 224-225; Ken Livingstone, interview with the author, 14 January 2019.

68 Walker, L. (ed.), *Madge Davison: A revolutionary firebrand*, Shanway Press, Belfast, 2011, pp11, 13, 15-16, 19, 25-26, 33-34, 54-55, 65, 76-77.

69 Anni Marjoram, interview with the author, 11 January 2019; Martin Collins, interview with the author, 14 January 2019.

70 Murray, G., *Enemies of the state*, Simon & Schuster, London, 1993; Scott, L. V., and Jackson, P. D., *Journeys in the shadows: Understanding intelligence in the twenty-first century*, Routledge, New York, 2004; Cook, J., *Unlawful killing: The murder of Hilda Murrell*, Cecil Woolf, London, 1985. See also: Gee, M., *Grace*, Abacus, London, 1989.

71 Collins, interview, 14 January 2019.

72 Coogan, T. P., *Wherever green is worn: The story of the Irish Diaspora*, Arrow Books, London, 2000, p125.

73 Malcolm Sage, interview with the author, 3 October 2018.

74 For example, one academic study of Blairism gives the Irish peace process barely a paragraph and the reader will look in vain for Mo Mowlam in the index:

Beech and Lee, *op. cit.*, pp74-75.

75 Rawnsley, A., *Servants of the people: The inside story of New Labour*, Hamish Hamilton, London, 2000, pp123-126, 128-136, 138-142; Seldon, *op. cit.*, pp515-526.

76 Grimes, *op. cit.*, p10.

77 Boyd, A., Devine, F., and Grimes, T., 'Norah Walshe and the rescue of Jim Connell', *Saothar*, no.24, 1999, pp91, 93.

78 Euton Stewart, interview with the author, 23 November 2018.

79 Grimes, *op. cit.*, pp12-13.

Chapter 5

1 GMB, *Report of Congress 2003, Winter Gardens, Blackpool, 8-12 June 2003*, GMB, London, 2003, p5.

2 *Ibid.*, p5.

3 *Ibid.*, p159.

4 *Ibid.*, p7.

5 GMB, *Culture Change in the GMB*, p6.

6 Staff Representatives Committee GMB/Amicus, *National office proposals for costs savings*, GMB, London, 6 November 2003, ff3, 6.

7 Callow, J., *GMB@Work*, p344.

8 Daniels, G., and McIlroy, J. (eds), *Trade unions in a neo-liberal world*, Routledge, London, 2009, p153.

9 Kenny, P., *Growth, accountability and democracy*, Election address, GMB, London, 2003, p3.

10 Murray, A., *A New Labour nightmare: The return of the awkward squad*, Verso, London, 2003, pp91-92; Daniels and McIlroy, op. cit., p182.

11 GMB, *Report of Congress 2003*, p46.

12 *Ibid.*, p671.

13 Toner, G., *The Future of the GMB*, unpublished consultation document, Aspire HBSD Ltd, London, March 2004, f1

14 *Ibid.*, f1.

15 *Ibid.*, f56. The present author has removed the spelling and other mistakes in the original document, for example 'the health of finances' rather than 'of the finances'. For a highly expensive report, it was decidedly slipshod and heavy with jargon that dazzled rather than informed.

16 *Ibid.*, f36.

17 *Ibid.*, f40.

18 *GMB Direct*, August 1992, p18.

19 *Ibid.*

20 Staff Representatives Committee GMB/Amicus, *National office proposals for costs savings*, f8; Ida Clemo, interview with the author, 8 October 2018.

21 Curran, K., *Letter to full-time officers of GMB and MSF and to elected employee representatives*, 14 November 2003, ff1-3.

22 Penny Robinson, interview with the author, 8 October 2018.

23 Clement, B., 'Union is dogged by bullying and harassment allegations as leadership battle lines are drawn', *Independent*, 10 February 2003.

24 *Ibid.*

25 GMB, *Report of Congress 2005*, p3.

26 *Ibid.*

27 *Ibid.*

28 *Ibid.*

29 Bob Crosby, interview with the author, 12 December 2018.

30 GMB, *Report of Congress* 2005, p54.

31 GMB, CEC Minutes, 15 March 2005.

32 GMB, Report of Congress 2005, p56.

33 GMB, *CEC Minutes*, 19 April 2005; *GMB, Report of Congress 2005*, pp53-54.

34 GMB, *Report for the CEC of the GMB of the internal investigation into the 2003 election of the General Secretary and 2004 election of the Deputy General Secretary*, GMB, London, 10 February 2006, p.5, 107-112. Mary's own view was that: 'If I was innocent of allegations that had been made in that report, I would have been banging that door down today [in congress 2005] to get in here to put my case. Think about it colleagues!' Furthermore, she noted: 'I wish to make it abundantly clear that the ex-general secretary was given the opportunity to respond to the serious issues raised by the investigation and chose not to do so, even on a one-to-one basis with Phil King'. See: GMB, *Report of Congress 2005*, p61; GMB, *GMB Congress 2006*, p9.

35 GMB, *GMB Congress 2006*, pp9, 61.

36 *Ibid.*, pp9-10.

37 *Ibid.*, p9.

38 GMB, *Report of Congress 2005*, p83.

39 *Ibid.*, p45.

40 *Ibid.*, p42.

41 *Ibid.*, p4.

42 *Ibid.*, p61.

Chapter 6

1 GMB, *Report of Congress 2005*, p3.

2 GMB, *GMB Annual Congress 2010*, Day One, p24.

3 Paul Kenny, interview with the author, 21 January 2019.

4 Callow, J., *Change the world: The history of Amicus: A union of a new type, 2002-2007*, Lawrence & Wishart, London, 2011, p236.

5 GMB, *GMB Annual Congress 2006*, pp44-45.

6 NOD, *GMB@Work. Presentation to full time officers*, GMB, London, 1 December 2006, f3.

7 GMB, CEC *special report: GMB@Work workplace organisation*, GMB, London, June 2006, p2.

8 *Ibid.*

9 Smith, M., *GMB@Work: Growth, accountability and democracy in GMB*, GMB, London, 2011, f2.

10 GMB, *CEC special seport: GMB@Work*, p4.

11 *Ibid.*, p.2.

12 Smith, M., draft of speech to the GMB Congress, seconding the Special Report GMB@Work on behalf ▶

▶ of the National Organising Team and the CEC, June 2006, f4.

13 Kenny, *National Organising Department*, f1.

14 NOD, *GMB@Work. Presentation to full-time Officers*, GMB, London, 1 December 2006, f3.

15 Kenny, P., *National Organising Department – General Secretary's report to congress*, 2012, draft ms., f1.

16 Kathleen Walker Shaw, interview with the author, 3 April 2018.

17 Martin Smith, interview with the author, 16 April 2018; Buckley, C., 'Business big shot', *The Times*, 23 June 2006, p47.

18 NOD, *op. cit.*, f11.

19 Hawkes, S., 'Union says 3i handling of traffic wardens not the ticket', *The Times*, 24 February 2007, p49.

20 GMB, *GMB Annual Congress 2009*, Day Two, p113.

21 Dean Gilligan, interview with the author, 17 January 2019.

22 Hawkes, S., 'GMB Camel Ride', *The Times*, 26 March 2007, p38.

23 Kosman, J., *The buyout of America: How private equity is destroying jobs and killing the American economy*, Portfolio/Penguin, New York, 2009, pp159-160.

24 Kennedy, S., and Hawkes, S., '3i makes profit of £240m from partial sale of NCP', *The Times*, 15 March 2007, p55; Hawkes, S., 'Permira chief faces union', *The Times*, 26 March 2007, p38; Hawkes, S., and Butler, S., 'Unions ask Health Secretary to intervene over Boots takeover', *The Times*, 14 April 2007, p.59; J. Bolger, 'Boots Plays Down Rumours over Pensions Dispute', *The Times*, 4 June 2007, p41; Kennedy, S., and Hawkes, S., 'MPs widen net and call two more private equity groups to account', *The Times*, 27 June 2007, p53; Walker, M., 'Row over CVC five's £250 million payout', *The Times*, 15 October 2007, p46; GMB, *GMB Annual Congress 2009*, Day One, p10.

25 Kennedy and Hawkes, 'MPs widen net', p53.

26 Davies, R., 'Public-Private Partners: End of the road for PFI contracts after collapse of Carillion', *The Guardian*, Budget Supplement, 30 October 2018, p2.

27 Mullin, C., *Decline and fall: Diaries, 2005-2010*, ed. Winstone, R., Profile Books, London, 2010, pp264-265, 271-273; Brown, G., *Beyond the crash: Overcoming the first crisis of globalisation*, Simon & Schuster, London, 2010, ppxvii-xx, 3, 21-5, 37-50; Seldon, A., and Lodge, G., *Brown at 10*, Biteback Publishing, London, 2010, pp139-147, 159-179; Hughes, C. (ed.), *What went wrong Gordon Brown?* Guardian Books, London, 2010, pp159-167.

28 GMB, *GMB Annual Congress 2009*, Day One, p11.

29 *Ibid.*, p.10.

30 Buckley, C., 'Darling attacked by both business and the unions', *The Times*, 10 October 2007, p56.

31 GMB, GMB Annual Congress 2009, Day One, p12.

32 *Ibid.*, p9.

33 *Ibid.*, p12.

34 Seldon and Lodge, *op. cit.*, pp262-270; Rawnsley, *The End of the Party*, pp645-652.

35 Swaine, J., 'Ben Chapman over claimed £15,000 on mortgage: MPs expenses', *Daily Telegraph*, 18 May 2009; Liverpool Echo Reporter, 'Wirral South MP Ben Chapman to quit over MP expenses scandal', *Liverpool Echo*, 21 May 2009; Press Association, 'Ben Chapman becomes first Labour MP to stand down over MPs expenses', *The Guardian*, 21 May 2009; Mullholland, H., 'Is Ben Chapman a Labour bellwether?', *The Guardian*, 18 May 2009. See also: Mullin, *op. cit.*, p230.

36 Swaine, *op. cit.* See also: Mulholland, H., 'Ben Chapman refuses to "repay a penny" of £15,000 claim on paid-off mortgage', *The Guardian*, 18 May 2009.

37 Seldon and Lodge, *op. cit.*, pp274-276; Rawnsley, *op. cit.*, p477; Hasan, M., 'Good riddance to James Purnell', *The Guardian*, 19 February 2010; Drury, I., 'James Purnell – the "Sideburned Schmoozer" who milked his expenses', *Daily Mail*, 5 June 2009; Prince, R., 'MPs' expenses: James Purnell becomes latest to quit parliament following scandal', 20 February 2010; Prince, R., 'James Purnell "Claimed expenses on flat partly paid for by his girlfriend"', *Daily Telegraph*, 4 May 2009.

38 Callow, *GMB@Work*, p388.

39 GMB, *GMB Annual Congress 2009*, Day One, p12.

40 *Ibid.*

41 *Ibid.*, p11.

42 *Ibid.*, p12.

43 *Ibid.*, p9.

44 GMB, *GMB Annual Congress 2009*, Day Two, p111.

45 *Ibid.*, p211.

46 GMB, *GMB Annual Congress 2009*, Day One, p12.

47 Gulliver, J., 'Gary Doolan: Requiem for a fallen hero', *Camden New Journal*, 20 September 2018.

48 GMB, *GMB Annual Congress 2010*, Day Two, p226.

49 *Ibid.*, p254.

50 GMB, *GMB Annual Congress 2009*, Day One, p10.

51 *Ibid.* p105.

52 GMB, *GMB Annual Congress 2010*, Day Two, p213.

53 GMB, *GMB Annual Congress 2010*, Day One, pp7-8.

54 Coates, S., 'Brown hopes to charm party's disgruntled pay masters', *The Times*, 11 September 2009, p13.

55 Paul Kenny, interview with the author, 21 January 2019.

56 GMB, *GMB Annual Congress 2014*, Held in Capital FM Arena, Nottingham, 8-12 June 2014, GMB, London, 2014, p11.

57 Paul Kenny, interview, 21 January 2019.

58 Paul Kenny, interview with Sarah Montague, BBC1 *HARDTALK*, 17 July 2013.

59 *Ibid.*

60 Corbyn, J., (foreword), *For the many not the few: The Labour Party Manifesto 2017*, Labour Party, London, 2017.

61 GMB, *GMB Annual Congress 2017*, Day One, f40.

62 GMB, *Report of Congress 2003*, p7.

63 Maguire, K., 'GMB's First Lady', *GMB Candid*, Spring 2010, p13.

64 GMB, *GMB Annual Congress 2010*, Day Two, p269.

65 Watson, R., and Lea, R., 'Strike control would prevent total public service shutdown', *The Times*, 7 June 2011, p7.

66 Keir Greenaway, email to the author, 24 September 2018.

67 GMB, *GMB Annual Congress 2010*, Day One, pp92-94.

68 Paul Kenny, interview with the author, 21 January 2019.

69 GMB, *GMB Congress 2018*, p5.

70 GMB, *GMB Annual Congress 2009*, Day One, p22.

71 *Ibid*, p23.

72 GMB, *GMB Annual Congress 2010*, Day One, p25.

73 *Ibid.*, p25.

74 *Ibid.*, p28.

75 Taranjit Chana, email to the author, 28 January 2019.

76 GMB, *GMB Annual Congress 2010*, Day One, p29.

77 *Ibid.*, p25.

78 GMB, *GMB Congress 2015. Held in City West Hotel, Conference & Events Centre, Dublin, 7-11 June 2015*, GMB, London, 2015, p41.

79 GMB, *GMB Annual Congress 2010*, Day One, p25.

80 Anon., 'Save our hospitals', *GMB Candid*, Spring 2013, p28.

81 GMB, *GMB Annual Congress 2009*, Day One, p10.

82 GMB, *GMB Annual Congress 2009*, Day Two, p86.

83 GMB, *GMB Annual Congress 2009*, Day One, p3.

84 *Ibid.*, p11.

85 Andy Burman, interview with the author, 19 November 2018.

86 *Ibid.*

87 *Ibid.*

88 Maguire, *op.cit.*, p12.

89 GMB, *GMB Annual Congress 2010*, Day One, p24.

 Chapter 7

1   GMB, *Congress 2016, Bournemouth International Centre, 5-9 June 2016*, GMB, London, 2016, Day One, f37.

2   *Ibid.*, ff.407-408. For a comprehensive account of the disaster and the early days of the campaign, see: Scraton, P., Jemphrey, A., and Coleman, S., *No last rights: The denial of justice and the promotion of myth in the aftermath of the Hillsborough Disaster*, Liverpool City Council, Liverpool, 1995.

3   GMB, *Congress 2016*, Day Three, f46.

4   *Ibid.*, f48.

5   *Ibid.*, f61.

6   *Ibid.*, f60.

7   *Ibid.*, ff63, 78.

8   GMB, *Congress 2017, Held in Plymouth Pavilions, Plymouth, 4-6 June 2017*, GMB, London, 2017, Day One, f34.

9   Denise Folwell, interview with the author, 16 June 2018.

10 Jess Bacon, Katie Turner, Freddy Folwell and Katie Francis, interviews with the author, 16 June 2018.

11 Malcolm Sage, interview with the author, 3 October 2018.

12 Smith, M., GMB.Net – *Building GMB in the 21st century world of work*, GMB, London, 2016, pp6-9. See also: Smith, M., 'The 21st century Tolpuddle tree', *Agenda. The Quarterly Newsletter from Unions 21*, Issue 1, Autumn 2016, pp7-8.

13 Dowler, E., Turner, S., and Dobson, B., *Poverty bites: Food, health and poor families*, CPAG, London, 2001, pp12, 80-81, 85-87, 126-127.

14 Larry Whitty, interview with the author, 7 January 2019.

15 Anon., 'Food for thought – GMB pushes for healthy free school meals', *GMB – Candid*, Winter 2013, p7.

16 Lansley, S., and Mack, J., *Breadline Britain*, Oneworld, London, 2015, pp38-41.

17 GMB, *Congress 2017*, Day Two, ff28-29.

18 GMB, *Congress 2017*, Day One, f34.

19 *Ibid.*, f30.

20 GMB, *Congress 2017*, Day Three, ff91, 97, 98, 104.

21 GMB, *Congress 2017*, Day One, f.36.

22 *Ibid.*, f32.

23 *Ibid.*, f35.

24 *Ibid.*, ff31, 35-36.

25 GMB, *Congress 2017*, Day Three, ff211-212.

26 GMB, *Congress 2017*, Day One, f73.

27 GMB, *Congress 2017*, Day Three, f219.

28 *Ibid.*, ff212, 219.

29 Lesley Stansfield, interview with the author, 23 November 2018.

30 Lesley Stansfield, interview, 23 November 2018.

31 GMB Press Release, *GMB union announces the sad passing of President Mary Turner*, GMB, London, 19 July 2017, f1.

32 Denise Folwell, interview with the author, 16 June 2018.

33 Fr. T. Murphy, *Funeral Mass in memory of Mary Josephine Turner*, London, Co-operative Funeralcare, 9 August 2017.

34 Sands, B., 'The rhythm of time', typed folio sheet among Mary's own papers. There is a slightly different version published in: Sands, B., *Writings from Prison*, Mercier Press, Dublin, 1998, p177. ■

Bibliography

Andalo, D., 'Rock in the Park: Welcome to the Republic of Brixton', *South London Press*, 5 June 1981, pp38-39.

Anon., 'People's March for Jobs a huge success', *GMW Journal*, June 1981, pp18-19.

Anon., 'Here's bread for the jobless', *Wembley Observer*, 4 December 1981, p5.

Anon., 'Express success... but Thatcher persists with her cruel policy', *GMW Journal*, Christmas 1981, pp.8-9.

Anon., 'The cook who came into the cold ...', *GMW Journal*, Jan-Feb 1982, p5.

Anon., 'People's March for Jobs', *GMB Journal*, April-May 1983, p4.

Anon., 'True to form, Mary plays Mum to the marchers', *GMB Journal*, June 1986, p19.

Anon., 'John Cope – London as eel pie', *GMB Journal*, June 1986, p19.

Anon., 'Our new directions', *GMB Journal*, October 1987, pp10-11.

Anon., 'Golden Girl: Mary Turner honoured at TUC Congress', *Candid*, Winter 2012, p12.

Anon., 'Mary Turner: Union activist who began by defending the interests of dinner ladies in Brent and rose to become President of the GMB', *The Times*, 21 July 2017, p56.

Anon., *Service of Thanksgiving for the life of Mary Turner, CBE*, St. Paul's Cathedral, London, 27 February 2018.

Beech, M., and Lee, S., (eds), *Ten years of New Labour*, Palgrave Macmillan, Houndmills, Basingstoke, 2008.

Benn, T., *The end of an era: Diaries*, 1980-90, ed. Winstone, R., Arrow Books, London, 1992.

Berresford Ellis, P., *A history of the Irish working class*, George Braziller, New York, 1972, rpt. 1973.

Blunkett, D., and Jackson, K., *Democracy in crisis: The town halls respond*, The Hogarth Press, London, 1987.

Boston, S., *Women workers and trade unions*, Lawrence & Wishart, London, revised edition, 2015.

Bower, T., *Gordon Brown: Prime Minister*, Harper Perennial, London, revised edition, 2007.

Boyd, A., *Jim Connell: Author of the Red Flag*, Donaldson Archives and the Socialist History Society, 2001.

Boyd, A., Devine, F., and Grimes, T., 'Norah Walshe and the rescue of Jim Connell', *Saothar*, No.24, 1999, pp91-94.

Brent Trades Council, *Stop the destruction of Brent. Report and programme*, 1982, Brent Trades Council, London, 1982.

Brent Trades Council, *Unemployment in Brent*, Brent Trades Council, London, May 1982.

Brent Trades Council, *Marchers – We won't let you down*, Brent Trades Council, London, 1983.

Brent Trades Council, *Brent Trades Council. Fighting for jobs, peoples' needs and union rights*. Annual Report, 1985, Brent Trades Council, London, 1986.

Brown, G., *Beyond the Crash: Overcoming the first crisis of globalisation*, Simon & Schuster, London, 2010.

Bryson, A., Nowak, P., Roper, C., and Smith, M., *Resilient unions: Strategies for growth*, Unions 21, London, 2010.

Callow, J., *GMB@Work: The story behind the union*, 1889-2012, Evans Mitchell Books, London, 2012.

Callow, J., *Freedom's Banner: GMB banners, emblems and symbols of struggle, 1889-2017*, TU ink, London, 2017.

Colgan, F., and Ledwith, S. (eds), *Gender, diversity and trade unions: International perspectives*, Routledge, London, 2002.

Coogan, T. P., *Wherever Green is Worn: The story of the Irish Diaspora*, Arrow Books, London, 2000.

Cope, J., 'Lay activists swamp London conference', *GMW Journal*, January-February 1982, p15.

Cope, J., 'Fight against privatisation', *GMB Journal*, December 1983-January 1984, pp6-7.

Cope, J., 'Our Mary gets MBE', *GMB Candid*, Spring 2010, p8.

Corbett, W., and Nolan, W. (eds), *Thurles: The cathedral town*, Geography Publications, Dublin, 1989.

Daniels, G., and McIlroy, J. (eds), *Trade unions in a neoliberal world*, Routledge, Abingdon, 2009.

Davies, R., 'Public – Private partners: End of the road for PFI contracts after collapse of Carillion', *The Guardian*, Budget Supplement, 30 October 2018, p2.

Dibb, S., 'Food for thought', *GMB Direct*, Issue 1, February 1992, pp18-19.

Doolan, G. (ed), *Mary Turner, GMB National President: Words of condolence*, GMB London Region, London, 2017.

Dowler. E., Turner, S., and Dobson, B., *Poverty bites: Food, health and poor families*, Child Poverty Action Group, London, 2001.

Dromey, J., and Taylor, G., *Grunwick: The workers' story*, Lawrence & Wishart, London, 2nd edition 2015.

Dunne, C., *An unconsidered people: The Irish in London*, New Island, Dublin, 2003.

Edmonds, J., 'Dick Pickering, 1942-1996', *GMB Direct*, Issue 29, November-December 1996, p2.

Evans, E. J., *Thatcher and Thatcherism*, Routledge, London, 1997.

Ezard, J., '100,000 join jobs march finale', *The Guardian*, 1 June 1981, p1.

Firmin, P. and Rickman, B. (eds), *Grunwick: Bravery and betrayal*, Brent Trades Council, London, 2006.

Fraser, K. M., *Same or different: Gender politics in the workplace*, Ashgate, Brookfield, USA, 1999.

Garcia, M., *Rebuilding London: Irish migrants in post-war Britain*, The History Press, Dublin, 2015.

Gibb, F., 'Marchers demand jobs not bombs', *The Times*, 30 November 1981, p1.

GMB, *Report of the First Congress. Spa Grand Hall, Scarborough, Sunday and Monday, 5-6 June 1983*, GMB, London, 1983.

GMB, *Report of the Second Congress. Princess Theatre, Torquay, Sunday to Friday, 3-8 June 1984*, GMB, London, 1984.

GMB, *Report of the Fifth Congress, London, 22-25 June 1987*, GMB, London, 1987.

GMB, *Financial options: Discussion paper for Central Executive Council, 8 September 1996*, GMB, London, September 1996.

GMB, *Culture change in the GMB, CEC special report to Congress 1999*, GMB, London, 1999.

GMB London Region, *London Region organising plan, 2001-2005*, GMB London Region, London, 2001.

GMB, *Organisation and recruitment guide: GMB best practice*, GMB, London, 2002.

GMB, *Report of Congress 2003, Winter Gardens, Blackpool, 8-12 June 2003*, GMB, London, 2003.

GMB, *Report of Congress, 2005*, GMB, London, 2005.

GMB, *Report for the CEC of the GMB of the internal investigation into the 2003 election of the General Secretary and 2004 election of the Deputy General Secretary*, GMB, London, 10 February 2006.

GMB, *CEC special report 2006: GMB@Work workplace organisation*, GMB, London, June 2006.

GMB, *A framework for the future of the GMB: Moving forward*, GMB, London, 2006.

GMB, *GMB Congress 2006: Winter Gardens, Blackpool*, GMB, London, 2006.

GMB, *Private equity's broken pension promises*, GMB, London, 2007.

GMB, *GMB – Britain's general union: Proceedings of the Annual Congress, The Brighton Centre, Brighton, 4-7 June 2007*, GMB, London, 2007.

GMB, *GMB Annual Congress 2008, held on 8-12 June 2008 at the Plymouth Pavilions, Plymouth*, GMB, London, 2008.

GMB, *GMB: Becoming an organising union*, GMB, London, 2009.

GMB, *GMB Annual Congress held on 6-9 June 2010 at the Floral Hall, Southport*, GMB, London, 2010.

GMB, *GMB Congress 2011, The Brighton Centre, Brighton, 5-10 June 2011*, GMB, London, 2011.

GMB, *GMB Congress 2012, The Brighton Centre, Brighton, 10-14 June 2012*, GMB, London, 2012.

GMB, *GMB Congress 2013, Held in Plymouth Pavilions, Plymouth, 2-6 June 2013*, GMB, London, 2013.

GMB, *GMB Annual Congress 2014, Held in Capital FM Arena, Nottingham, 8-12 June 2014*, GMB, London, 2014.

GMB, *Mary Turner: Biography*, GMB, London, 2014.

GMB, *GMB Congress 2015, Held in City West Hotel, Conference and Event Centre, Dublin, 7-11 June 2015*, GMB, London, 2015.

GMB, *GMB Congress 2016, Bournemouth International Centre, 5-9 June 2016*, GMB, London, 2016.

GMB, *GMB Congress 2017, held in Plymouth Pavilions, Plymouth, 4-6 June 2017*, GMB, London, 2017.

GMB, *GMB announces the sad passing of President Mary Turner*, Press Release, GMB, London, 19 July 2017.

GMB, *Mary Turner, 1938-2017: Memories of an amazing and inspirational lady*, GMB, London, 2017.

GMB, *GMB Congress 2018: The Brighton Centre, Brighton, 4-6 June 2018*, GMB, London, 2018. ▶

▶ GMB/CPAG, *CEC special report: Raising the kids: Stop in-work poverty*, GMB/CPAG, London, 2009.

GMWU, *Report of the Sixty-Fifth Congress. Pavilion Theatre, Bournemouth, 18-22 May*, 1980, GMWU, London, 1980.

GMWU, *Report of the Sixty-Seventh Congress, Congress Theatre, Eastbourne, 23-27 May 1982*, GMWU, London, 1982.

Grimes, T. (intro.), *Jim Connell, Author of 'The Red Flag'. Memorial unveiling, Crossakiel, 26 April 1998*, Jim Connell Society, Slane, 1998.

Gulliver, J., 'Gary Doolan: Requiem for a Fallen Hero', *Camden New Journal*, 20 September 2018.

Hall, S., and Jacques, M. (eds), *The Politics of Thatcherism*, Lawrence & Wishart, London, 1983.

Harman, H., *The century gap: 20th century man – 21st century woman*, Vermilion, London, 1993.

Harman, H., *A woman's work*, Allen Lane/Penguin, London, 2017.

Haylett, J., 'Roast dinner welcome – The London Borough of Brent welcomes the jobs marchers today', *Morning Star*, 2 June 1983, p2.

Hayman, K., 'Dinner lady joins Labour top brass', *Times Chronicle Series*, 12 October 1995, p5.

Holmes, K., 'Eat your greens', *GMB Direct*, Issue 24, January-February 1996, pp6-7.

Hughes, C. (ed.), *What went wrong, Gordon Brown? How the dream job turned sour*, Guardian Books, London, 2010.

Hurley, C., and Riley, S. (eds), *Recipe for change: A good practice guide to school meals*, Child Poverty Action Group. London, 2004.

Jones, A., 'The truth about Cammell Laird', *GMB Candid*, Spring 2012, pp16-17.

Kampfner, J., *Blair's wars*, Free Press, London, 2003.

Kenny, P., foreword, *GMB organising migrant workers*, GMB, London, 2014.

Kenny, W., 'Our Mary – Mary Turner', *Members First – GMB London News Update*, Summer 2017, p10.

Kent, B., *Undiscovered ends*, HarperCollins, London, 1992.

Klein, N., *The shock doctrine: The rise of disaster capitalism*, Penguin Books, London, 2007.

Kosman, J., *The buyout of America: How private equity is destroying jobs and killing the American economy*, Portfolio/Penguin, London, 2009.

Lansley, S., and Mack, J., *Breadline Britain: The rise of mass poverty*, Oneworld, London, 2015.

Ledwith, S., and Colgan, F. (eds), *Women in organisations: Challenging gender politics*, Macmillan Business, Houndmills, Basingstoke, 1996.

Ledwith, S., and Hansen, L. L. (eds), *Gendering and diversifying trade union leadership*, Routledge, London, 2013.

Lezard, T., and Costley, N. (eds), *My Tolpuddle: What Tolpuddle means to you*, intros. Benn, T., and Bragg, B., South West TUC, Gloucester, 2008.

Livingstone, K., *You can't say that: Memoirs*, Faber and Faber, London, 2011.

McIlroy, J., 'The enduring alliance? The trade unions and the making of New Labour, 1994-1997', *British Journal of Industrial Relations*, Vol. 36 no. 4, 1998, pp537-564.

McMahon, W., and Marsh, T., *Filling the gap: Free school meals, nutrition and poverty*, Child Poverty Action Group, London, 1999.

McSmith, A., *Faces of Labour: The inside story*, Verso, London, 1996.

Maguire, K., 'GMB's First Lady', *GMB Candid*, Spring 2010, pp12-13.

Massey, C. (ed.), *The man at the back: The life and journals of Lord Tom Sawyer*, Teesside University, Middlesex, 2017.

Matthews, D., *The London Gasworks: A technical, commercial and labour history to 1914*, unpublished DPhil thesis, University of Hull, 1981.

Minkin, L., *The Blair supremacy: A study in the politics of Labour's party management*, Manchester University Press, Manchester and New York, 2014.

Morning Star Reporter, 'Rousing start to great train journey for jobs', *Morning Star*, 24 November 1981, p1.

Morning Star Reporter, 'Jobs train: It's all change for demo', *Morning Star*, 28 November 1981, p1.

Mullin, C., *Decline and fall: Diaries 2005-2010*, Profile Books, London, 2010.

Murray, A., *A New Labour nightmare: The return of the awkward squad*, Verso, London, 2003.

No Sweat, *Solidarity with migrant workers: Facts, experiences, debate*, No Sweat, London, 2005.

O' Farrell, J., *Things can only get better: Eighteen miserable years in the life of a Labour supporter, 1979-1997*, Doubleday, London, 1998.

Orrey, J., *The dinner lady: Change the way your children eat, for life*, foreword Oliver, J., Transworld Publishers, London, 2005.

Pike, J., *The moral geographies of children: Young people and food: Beyond Jamie's school dinners*, Palgrave Macmillan, Houndmills, Basingstoke, 2016.

Postgate, O., *Thinking it through: The plain man's guide to the Bomb*, The Menard Press, London, 1982.

Raffray, N., 'Tributes as "trailblazing" union leader who led free school meals drive dies', *Brent & Kilburn Times*, 27 July 2017, p8.

Rawnsley, A., *Servants of the people: The inside story of New Labour*, Hamish Hamilton, London, 2000.

Rawnsley, A., *The end of the party: The rise and fall of New Labour*, Viking/Penguin, London, 2010.

Riley, B. (ed.), *People's March for Jobs in MK 1983: A souvenir*, Media Centre, Milton Keynes, 1983.

Robinson, T., *No cunning plan: My story*, Sidgwick & Jackson, London, 2016.

Rogaly, J., *Grunwick*, Penguin Books, Harmondsworth, 1977.

Routledge, P., *Gordon Brown: The biography*, Pocket Books, London, 1998.

Routledge, P., *Mandy: The unauthorised biography of Peter Mandelson*, Pocket Books, London, 1999.

Sands, B., *Writings from prison*, Mercier Press, Dublin, 1998.

Seldon, A., (ed.), *Blair's Britain*, 1997-2007, Cambridge University Press, Cambridge, 2007.

Seldon, A., and Lodge, G., *Brown at 10*, Biteback Publishing, London, 2010.

Seldon, A., Snowdon, P., and Collings, D., *Blair unbound*, Simon & Schuster, London, 2007.

Singh, S., and Purtill, T., *Diary of a People's Marcher*, intro. Corbyn, J., Southwark Unemployed Action, London, 1983.

Smith, D., and Chamberlain, P., *Blacklisted: The secret war between big business and union activists*, New Internationalist Publications, Oxford, 2015.

Smith, M., *GMB@Work: Growth, accountability and democracy in GMB*, GMB, London, 2011.

Smith, M., and Roache, T., *How unions make work pay*, GMB/Class, London, 2014.

Stanley, J., 'Thunderous reception for jobs protests', *Morning Star*, 29 May 1981, pp1, 3.

Toner, G., The future of the GMB, unpublished consultation document, Aspire HBSD, London, 2004.

TUC, *People's March for Jobs, May '81: Official Souvenir*, TUC, London, 1981.

TUC, *Report of the 121st annual Trade Union Congress, 4-8 September 1989, Blackpool*, TUC, London, 1989.

TUC, *Report of the 122nd annual Trade Union Congress, 3-7 September 1990, Blackpool*, TUC, London, 1990.

TUC, *Report of the 123rd annual Trade Union Congress, 2-6 September 1991, Glasgow*, TUC, London, 1991.

TUC, *Report of the 124th annual Trade Union Congress, 7-11 September 1992, Blackpool*, TUC, London, 1992.

TUC, 'Mary Turner: Winner Women's Gold Badge', *Congress Events*, TUC, London, 2012, pp42-43.

Turner, M., 'Fighting to keep school meals on the menu', *Morning Star*, 20 July 1982, p4.

Turner, M., 'For Maundy Money, now read dole', *GMB Journal*, October-November 1985, p9.

Undy, R., *Trade union merger strategies: Purpose, process and performance*, Oxford University Press, Oxford, 2008.

Walsh, J., 'The dinner lady who succeeded in a male-dominated movement', *Times Chronicle Series*, 6 February, 1992, p11.

Walter, B., *Outsiders inside: Whiteness, place and Irish women*, Routledge, London, 2001.

Warman, C., Routledge, P., and Evans, R., 'Tories not to blame, Prior tells marchers', *The Times*, 2 June 1981, p2.

Webster, P., 'London plans big welcome as climax of trek from north', *Morning Star*, 27 May 1981, p3.

Whooley, F., *Irish Londoners: Photographs from the Paddy Fahey Collection*, Grange Museum/Sutton Publishing, Stroud, Gloucestershire, 1997.

Wheen, F., *The battle for London*, Pluto Press, London, 1985.

Willman, P., Morris, T., and Aston, B., *Union business: Trade union organisation and financial reform in the Thatcher years*, Cambridge University Press, Cambridge, 1993.

Wintour, P., 'Respectability goes on the march', *The Guardian*, 23 May 1983, p2.

Wynne-Jones, R., 'RIP Mary', *Daily Mirror*, 21 July 2017, p27. ■

Index

Mary Turner